# Cheers for
# More Than a Manicure

Rarely do we read a book with such raw emotion, yet humor! *More Than a Manicure* is a genuine reflection of the beautiful soul of the author. As you read her story, you begin to see the wise and insightful person the author is through her conversations and interactions with her clients and their story. Carly Bennett Stenmark is a treasure, as is this book. It is a beautiful read!

~ *Susan Tolliver Richer*

A walk through Park City's salon history, names and places that once existed may be long gone, but still Carly works to keep her dream alive. *More Than a Manicure* is a story to which we all can relate regarding life's important lessons.

~ *Diane Cashel, high school counselor and long-time Park City local*

Those of us who knew and loved Carly most never guessed that she was an observant and excruciatingly accurate recorder of life in and around our crazy salon world! CHEERS to Carly, who is oh so much "more than a manicure!"

~ *Ann MacQuoid, former co-owner of Vie Retreat Salon, Park City*

Passion through words and deeds! Professional insights offering mentoring wisdom. Over twelve years of doing business we have never met face-to-face, and after reading this book I quickly realize just how special Carly is! Thank you for sharing!

~ *Richard Houts, President of Revere Cosmetics, 30 years of beauty industry manufacturing, education and distribution experience*

Carly's warmth and kindness radiate throughout this book. Not to mention her tremendous sense of humor. For close to twenty five years I have looked forward to my appointments with Carly. We share an affection that has grown and her wisdom is boundless. She cares so for each person who sits across from her, as is evident in these stories. Carly is a true heroine and I admire her immensely.

~ *Alix Railton*

# More Than a Manicure

## The Nail Files

Hi Terri,

please enjoy my story
in and out of the
nail room! :)

Carly Bennett Stenmark
Feb 2018

# More Than a Manicure

## The Nail Files

Carly Bennett Stenmark

## Surrogate Press

Published in the United States by

Surrogate Press

SurrogatePress.com

ISBN: 978-0-9860997-5-5

Library of Congress Control Number: 2017902686

Book cover art by: Gary Gautney

Book cover design by Katie Mullaly, Surrogate Press

Interior design by: Katie Mullaly, Surrogate Press

Photo credit: Debra Macfarlane

Dedicated to my loyal, dependable and supportive clientele who all contributed in making this book possible with their stories. Thank you all for not only your patronage, but for trusting me enough to confide in me the past thirty plus years.

If not for you, there would be no "Nail Files."

# Disclaimer

The stories in this book are based on true experiences. Some of the names have been changed to protect the innocent, not so innocent, the extremely guilty, and the sometimes clueless.

# Table of Contents

# I'm Not Really a Waitress

My first nail experience happened in Salt Lake City during the summer of 1980. A friend and I — with a night out thanks to husbands who agreed to stay home with the kids — decided to skip aerobics and go to the mall. We wandered in and out of various stores, looking at clothing, and of course, my personal favorite, purses!

Amidst all of the retail stores, I spotted a nail salon. I had never seen one before and was intrigued as we approached the door. We walked into the very small, one room to be exact, nail salon. The owner and technician Joni, was a beautiful French woman with a strong accent. She warmly greeted us with a big smile. I briefly thought about how I've always loved everything *français*, and asked the price of a full set of acrylic nails. I had, at the time, only read about acrylic nails. Even though I had my own nice natural nails, I always seemed to break one or two, causing me to trim the others and start the process of growing them all out again to a respectable length. Joni had a special during the month of June for a set of acrylic nails…$15.95. A lot of money in 1980!

I sat down at the nail table for the first time in my life. I watched closely as Joni pulled out files, plastic nail tips, and glue. She took my hands in hers, looked them over and asked, "Are you ready?"

I replied, "*Je suis prête.*" Joni smiled at my attempt to speak her language.

It took two hours to give me "showgirl length" nails. Red, of course. I broke one the next evening opening the car door. Annoyed, my husband, Rick, asked if the salon gave me a guarantee. I sighed and made an appointment for the repair the next day. As Joni repaired my broken thumbnail free of charge she instructed me to "treat my nails like jewels, not tools."

I smiled at her beautiful accent, which made me think of my longing to at least *visit* Paris one day. I thanked her and promised to be more careful.

At the time I managed a family restaurant. I initially started as a waitress during the night shift. Within months my boss promoted me to Head Waitress, then to Service Manager, and eventually to Night Manager. In less than a year, I made my way up to Franchise Representative. When management opened a new restaurant, I was among those chosen to train new personnel. Since my experience was with the night shift, I was in charge of those waitresses and waiters.

Each training job lasted about six to eight weeks, or until upper management deemed the new staff ready, then back to our restaurants we all went. I actually enjoyed this part of the restaurant business much more than dealing with employees, including family members that I had hired. One of the hardest parts was coping with employees who called in sick or worse still, didn't even bother to show up. My job description included filling in for "no-shows," whether it was a cook, busboy, dishwasher, or hostess.

My youngest brother, Jeff worked for a few months, until one night he didn't come in for his shift. My own brother was a no-show. And he had been doing such a good job! Then my youngest sister, Rebecka, after dining with a couple of her friends, did the infamous "D & D" (dine and dash)! Management began to wonder about my family, and with good reason.

I was so busy that I could not keep up on my regular nail appointments, so I invested in the products needed to fill and repair my acrylic nails myself. After four months, when I finally found the time to go in for a "real" nail fill, Joni asked who had been doing my nails. Hiding my hands in my lap, I confessed.

She asked me if I wanted a job!

My restaurant duties required much of my time. I changed to the day shift, six a.m. to three p.m., after which I went to the salon for training. I sat beside Joni and watched her work on clients steadily for one month, taking in everything I could about the art of doing nails. I trained like mad and focused intently.

Finally the day arrived. I did my first set of nails all by myself *on somebody else*. It took me four and a half hours and the nails lasted less than a week! Fortunately, the guinea pig was my mother. She was a good sport.

Needless to say, I did not quit my day job yet. I continued to work the day shift at the restaurant, and after my shift ended, I continued to train at the salon.

In a very short time, I started to get the hang of doing nails and this truly excited me. The more I worked at it, the more I found that I loved it. I waited anxiously for a client to call or walk-in, so I could begin to do what I enjoyed and looked forward to doing the most. Along with making their nails and hands look beautiful, the service I provided made them feel good about themselves. I loved chatting with them and making them feel special, which they were. I could tell the creativity was feeding my hungry soul, something that my waitress job lacked. This was just what I longed for.

Eventually, I decided to do what my heart told me to do. Yes, I followed my passion and began doing what I loved…nails! Everyone thought I had lost my mind. The amount of flack I received from my bosses at the restaurant was huge. They couldn't believe that I was actually leaving my good-paying job with benefits to do fingernails! Honestly, I found it hard to believe myself. Although it was hard work, I loved being a waitress. I consider it an honorable way to make a living, and I loved my customers. I just loved doing nails more.

Even though I took management's advice into consideration, I nevertheless gave my notice, and focused solely on my newfound career. I went to work at the nail salon. I was committed and eager to learn all I could about the nail business. And learn I did. I learned, for example, not to use super glue on the nails, as I watched it run into the cuticle. I tried to remove the glue with acetone polish remover, only to catch the client's cuticle on fire; again my mother. What a trooper she was!

I always tried to find ways to make the job of doing nails easier. Back then, the plastic nail tips came in little, individually purchased bags. I saved time by sorting them into an ice cube tray. I also made my own little "buffer blocks "from soft sponges that I cut into small squares and wrapped in extra fine sandpaper, which I also cut myself. These I used to buff out imperfections on the acrylic nail surface. Too bad I didn't think of marketing those at the time. Big hit!

I found in a short amount of time, I now looked forward to going to work. I used to drag myself to the restaurant thinking about how long my shift was and how tired I would be following that shift. I worried about the amount of tip money I would or would not make, as my hourly wage was quite low, I depended on those tips. Even though I was in the beginning stages of being a booked nail technician, that didn't enter my mind. I didn't focus solely on the money aspect of it. I knew I could build a clientele as long as I did my work exceptionally well, to the best of my ability. I was also able to talk with clients enough and make them comfortable with me. I made them laugh and I made them smile. Congeniality was my focus.

# Not Just a Pretty Face

Since I was building a nail clientele, I had quite a cut in pay following my heart's desire, so I began to supplement my income. I did several modeling stints (which was way more fun than waitressing) and began working for a company, located in the Salt Lake Valley, called Arc Entertainment. We were doing a television show called *Thaddeus Resents*, a thoroughly campy spoof on horror films. We filmed all over the Salt Lake City area, but I spent most of my time on these shoots running through graveyards in a skimpy, purple swimsuit, and very high heeled shoes, both of which came from Fredericks of Hollywood.

I kept my love of music in the loop by working weekends at a popular nightclub that featured various local bands; all while I continued to practice the art of perfecting nails.

One day, when I was working in the nail salon, my boss of these film shoots (and owner of the company), Marc, popped in with my new modeling/acting contract. He called it his *Dirty Dozen* and asked me to read it over and sign it. He said he'd be back to pick it up in a couple of days.

Marc resembled Jackie Gleason, the comedian, only shorter and wider. He was present at every job we did, supervising. I have to admit, he did know the business, but he gave me the creeps.

My mother always taught me to trust my instincts and more often than once, it had paid off.

Marc hired twelve girls for this particular job, and he gave us all stage names from James Bond movies. Mine was Rachel. After any and all filming, or the dreaded MM's (model meetings), the other eleven girls kissed him goodbye on the lips (no less) as we left, except for me. I would either turn my cheek to him or kiss his cheek. Looking back, I should have been brave enough to say, "Forget it!" but I was young and naïve.

I took Marc's contract home to read it, and the first eleven items of the Dirty Dozen list, were just the usual rules, for lack of a better word. But, the twelfth rule, simply stated; "I agree to accept all jobs offered to me." Period. One of my neighbors at the time, Sam, was an attorney. I called and asked if I could walk over for some advice. When I arrived he opened the front door and invited me inside. He put on his glasses and read my contract. After a few minutes, we discussed the document and Sam revised that twelfth rule, quickly typing away on his typewriter. It now stated that I would accept the jobs, as long as my morality was not compromised. I could refuse jobs based on nudity, or due to subject matter that I deemed inappropriate or in poor taste.

I left Sam's home relieved.

The following week, Marc came into the salon to pick up my signed contract. As he looked it over, his brow furrowed. I nervously watched and I assumed he got to rule number twelve. I could tell he was not pleased with my revisions. In fact, he was furious.

Marc said, "You are the only one who has not signed the contract as is."

I sat there quietly.

He added, "I haven't changed it for any of the other girls and I am not changing it for you!" His voice grew louder as he demanded, "You either sign it the way it was or else you are out!"

I knew what I had to do.

My hands shook as I stood up and my voice quivered as I said quietly, "Well, then I'm out."

Marc was furious! None of his girls ever stood up to him, either literally or figuratively. He started to leave, but then stopped, turned back, looked me right in the eye and added, with strong expletives, "One more thing. If God would have wanted my cheeks kissed, he would have put my lips on them!"

Marc shook his head in disgust and stormed out, his *Dirty Dozen* contract in hand.

My hands were still trembling as I thought about what just happened. I felt a bit nauseous. I started to worry about the loss of income. I struggled with the fact that I was out. My mind began to imagine all kinds of things. I started to question my decision, but only for a split second. Then I came to my senses. I composed myself, took a deep breath and realized I had done the right thing. Marc's reaction to my decision was just another affirmation. It felt good to stick up for myself. I was the mother of four young and impressionable children. It was important to me that I had their respect, and that started with respecting myself.

The week passed slowly until my Sunday-Monday weekend rolled around. And, of course, it was raining. My husband, Rick, and I decided to take the kids to lunch and a movie. As we watched the Muppets on the big screen, my mind wandered. I was still nervous about giving Marc the boot, but in my heart, I knew I made the correct choice. How could I live with myself, or even look my children and family in the eye, if I went against my better judgment.

Tuesday came fast and I hurried to the salon. As I began my day, Marc walked in. He handed me my revised contract. I read over that last page. It was exactly as Sam had re-typed it, except Marc added a number thirteen to his *Dirty Dozen* list. In so many words it stated that if I told any of the other girls about this revision, I would be fired on the spot and he'd bring legal action against me. As I read it over very carefully, Marc looked at me sternly, and asked, "Will you sign it now?'

I tried to add some levity as I signed the contract and said with a nervous smile, "I can keep a secret."

Marc wasn't amused as he turned and left the salon.

I put my head down on my nail table, and exhaled a huge sigh of relief.

# Room Service

My husband, Rick, lost his job due to his recurring bout with agoraphobia, the fear of open spaces. One day, he came home unexpectedly from work in the middle of the day, and out of the blue told me he felt "weird" again. "Weird" translated to his agoraphobia.

He had experienced this phobia off and on since he was seventeen years old. He actually quit school because of it and told me all he did after that was sit in his room and play his bass guitar. This was why he did not over indulge in any type of drugs or drink alcohol. He had in the past, but realized it triggered those weird feelings. (Ironically, and sadly, Rick ended up dying from alcoholism, about twenty years after we were divorced.)

But now his condition was back, ten years later. Rick did not leave our house for eight months; he did not leave our bedroom for close to four months. The kids and I watched television, listened to music and even ate our meals in the bedroom with him, thinking it would pass on its own, waiting patiently for some small sign of improvement. Rick had seen an advertisement on late night television about agoraphobia. There was a well renowned female physician from Australia, Dr. Claire Weekes, who was truly a pioneer in mental health care. She was one of the first to separate anxiety and stress from mental illness. One of her greatest achievements was to help those suffering from phobias and anxiety as they seem to go hand in hand. Such was the case with Rick.

Dr. Weekes wrote a book about dealing with and possibly overcoming agoraphobia, which was also available in audio as a vinyl record. Rick ordered the album.

It arrived two weeks later and he was thrilled. He played it over and over on the turntable in our bedroom, listening intently, taking notes. I desperately hoped this would relieve Rick of his fears. To this day, I can close my eyes and still hear her accent.

However, months passed and there was no sign of improvement in Rick. Finally, in desperation, I called the mental health facility he had visited when he was seventeen. I inquired about the counselor who helped him back then. Mr. Samuels was still there! I was thrilled and after I explained our situation, we set up a time for him to meet with Rick. Mr. Samuels agreed to come to the house, as Rick was unable to leave the safety of our home. He arrived promptly at ten o'clock the next morning and began to counsel him.

This first session was close to three hours long. After a couple of months of weekly sessions, Rick was finally able to walk out the front door to the mailbox on the street and pick up our mail. Oddly enough, the first few times, Rick had to walk to the mailbox backwards, with his eye on the front door, so he could run back inside in case he got scared and was unable to complete his trip.

Agoraphobia is such a strange phobia. As I studied and learned more about it with the help of Mr. Samuels, I realized that this would be a life long struggle for Rick, and my heart ached for him. Rick was perfectly fine as long as he was inside. In the beginning, it worked out great with the children. He stayed home and watched them, sent them off to school with a kiss and a hug at the front door, while I worked my three jobs. But as they got older the kids wanted to do more activities outside of our backyard and he just couldn't do it.

However, after close to a year of working with Mr. Samuels, Rick slowly resumed his life outside of the house. He was able to do some things to a certain degree, even though he was now unemployed. Which didn't matter, because by this time Rick had become disinterested in looking for work. He just wanted to sit and play his bass guitar, all day, every day. True, his health issue was not completely resolved, but it was somewhat under control, although he was never completely comfortable when he went outside.

Time passed and eventually we found ourselves in financial trouble. My three jobs were not enough to pays the bills. I worked hard to build a nail clientele, but for some reason my modeling jobs were few and far between. I felt Marc purposely left me out of job opportunities because I spoke up and wouldn't accept jobs that made me uncomfortable.

And I was right.

The other girls told me they got the jobs that Marc thought I'd refuse. It became quite clear that I was finished working for Arc Entertainment and Marc was finished with me. The saving grace in my mind was I no longer had to kiss Marc, even if it was only his cheek.

I still maintained my job at the nightclub, saving my tips each evening for my weekly trip to the grocery store.

The bill collectors started calling our house, and things got tough. My grandmother used to say, "When poverty comes through the door, love goes out the window," and she was right. I was so stressed out and tired of working so much. I began to resent the fact that I had to be the sole breadwinner. Life was hard back then, four little kids, in debt, and bill collectors blowing up the phone constantly. I was gone all of the time, exhausted when I was home, stressing about the bills and trying to make ends meet.

Rick and I began to argue, which created more stress on all of us. I began to lose respect for him, and he grew tired of me being a nag. I was fed up, simply just tired of all of it. Rick continued to play his bass guitar, and not work. He was perfectly content with the life we were living.

I, however, thought in my own young and naïve way, it would be easier on my own…wouldn't it?

I wasn't sure, but I was about to find out.

# 4
## Secret Keeper

I was sure about one thing. I absolutely loved doing nails, and I was doing them well. Early on, I adapted my own motto: *Clients pay me good money to do the best job I can possibly do.* And so that is exactly what I strived to do.

In addition to the reward I felt for doing a good job, I particularly loved the interaction with clients. I truly enjoyed learning all about their lives; personal and professional, and loved getting to know them on so many different levels. I confided in them and they in me. We shared our most personal feelings and never gave it a second thought.

One day I was preparing for my next client to arrive. Her name was Shannon, and she was a pretty blonde. She came in every two weeks for an acrylic nail fill, and we quickly became friends. She grew up in Idaho, was married with five beautiful daughters. They moved to Salt Lake City after graduating from BYU. She and her husband were both very involved in their faith.

Shannon came in for her nail appointment this particular day and confided in me about a "reunion" with an old high school boyfriend. During that hour, I heard all the details. When she realized what she had admitted, Shannon looked at me, with tears in her eyes and asked me to please keep this a secret.

"Of course," I replied. "I would never tell a soul."

But I think, after the fact, Shannon was so embarrassed about the confession; she cancelled her next appointment and never rebooked. I guess maybe she felt like a line had been crossed, in a couple of ways. I often thought of Shannon over the years, and wondered how things turned out for her.

I do know that they moved from Salt Lake City, back up to Idaho, hopefully to work things through. I really liked her. When a client leaves that you really like, it always leaves a hole in your heart, particularly when the ones that leave are the ones you look forward to seeing every week or two. That is the hard part of the job. You look forward to seeing them regularly, and then suddenly the friends you make are gone. You can't help but question yourself, asking why? Was it the quality of your work? Was it your conversation? Was it the cost? Whatever the reason, it is hard and that never feels good.

Believe it or not, doing nails is without a doubt, very rewarding. Many have asked me over the years how I can just sit there for hours on end, hunched over doing manicures and pedicures? *"Isn't it tedious?"* is usually the first question, followed by *"How boring!"*

Not for me. I loved it all…except for one issue that wouldn't come to haunt me until years later. That being my poor posture! I'm rather tall, and I've had a problem with good posture, even before I did nails. I slouch because I always wanted to be short, like my best friend, Janice.

She was, and still is, so petite and cute!

Janice and I met in fifth grade at Edison Elementary School, and to this day, we are still close friends. She is my longest known friend, and I just love and adore her. During our school days, it seemed like all of the girls in high school were so petite, except for me. I was so tall. I towered over all the "cute" boys. I was very insecure about my height, among other things, when I was a teenager.

I think about it now, and I am very happy I have my height. I just wish I had paid more attention to my slouching back then, especially when I started doing nails.

One thing is certain. I love making people happy. And when people saw their nails after spending about an hour or so in my chair I did just that! I soon realized what kind of business I really was in. I was in the "feel good" business. I made people laugh, and I made them smile. They were happy with their nails when our time was up, but sad they had to leave. They told me how much they enjoyed our conversations and looked forward to our visits.

Millie, another client in the Salt Lake Valley, said to me, as we hugged and I thanked her, "This is the highlight of my life, it really builds me up." I smiled as I realized I was not only their nail lady, but also their counselor (with no formal training), trusted confidant, their friend, and they mine.

It quickly became more than a manicure.

# Wife Goes On

**R**ick and I divorced. But to get there, Rick made a bid on KRCL, his favorite radio station, during a fundraiser for a non-contested divorce, donated by a local attorney in the area. The divorce cost us seventy-five dollars, which we split. Yes, my divorce was as a result of a radio call-in contest. How weird, and lucky, is that?

Rick moved in with Don, another musician friend of his, and they played as a duet around Salt Lake City. His phobia and fears were under control somewhat, but he was still dealing with the uncomfortableness of it all on a regular basis. I couldn't help it; I still felt sorry for him.

He was still unemployed, which meant no child support. I was now a divorced mother of four children trying to support my family on my own. I still worked at the nightclub on weekends. One Friday night, a band from the San Francisco Bay Area played, and I met the bass player, Ryan, who had previously been a member of the bands Quicksilver Messenger Service, Country Joe and the Fish, and one of Marty Balin's groups, prior to Jefferson Airplane, called Bodacious DF. When the band returned home to San Francisco, Ryan stayed in Salt Lake City. I later learned this was not his choice. I also learned and experienced first hand the reasons why, and there were many.

But before I figured all that out, things progressed, as they do in the early stages of romance, and we moved in together in an apartment in South Salt Lake. From the beginning our life was turbulent and unpleasant at best. Ryan would drink and be mean. We would argue, but then when he sobered up, he cried and proclaimed how sorry he was. He always said he didn't mean it when he said and did horrible things while drunk. And I believed him. As long as he did not drink, life was good. I enjoyed being with him and I loved his sense of humor. Alcohol free, we got along great. Unfortunately, Ryan never stayed that way for long. It was just the same old song on repeat, "John Barleycorn Must Die!"

(I feel the need to explain my last statement for those who are unfamiliar with somewhat older music. It is a song by the band, Traffic. The song came from a poem by Robert Burns written in 1792. John Barleycorn is not a real man's name. It is actually a metaphor for alcohol. The saying, 'John Barleycorn must die' is a reference to alcohol and a hope that the drunks will kill John Barleycorn by ceasing to drink alcohol and become sober.)

In the spring of 1982 after a weekend of hell, I decided I needed a break from Ryan. I made the decision to leave him, yet again, but this time I was serious! I devised a plan. Since he had no car of his own, I moved far enough away, out of walking distance, so Ryan would not be able to come and see me or try to persuade me to take him back, as he had been able to do in the past.

I jumped on the I-80 freeway, headed east, took the Park City exit and found myself truly in heaven. What an absolutely beautiful place and another plus – it was the sister city to Courchevel, France! How lucky is that? Even though Park City was only 25 miles from Salt Lake City, it was like another world away to me, *kind of like moving to Paris,* I told myself. I made my way to the nearest newspaper stand, bought the Park Record, and found the Mt. Air Cafe. I went in with my paper, sat down, ordered a cup of coffee, and then turned to the want ads.

As I sat there staring at places for rent, my eyes kept straying to the scenery out the window, which was breathtaking. Growing up in Salt Lake City, amazingly, I had never been to Park City. I came from a modest family and was the oldest of six children. My father was a hard working, long distance truck driver, and my mother, an equally hard working homemaker. Of course we never skied – just couldn't afford it.

I went back to the paper, and eventually found a four bedroom "condo" (duplex or apartment if you are in Salt Lake City) to rent in Old Town. The owners met me there and laughed when I inquired about air conditioning, saying it wasn't needed. They informed me everyone couldn't wait for summer to come along. I didn't know what that statement meant then, as I had no idea how hard the winters were.

I drove back to the city and told my parents, "I'm moving to the mountains."

# Polish My Art

**M**y Salt Lake City clientele was small, but steady. The salon I started with had long since closed and I was now working for a well-established nail salon in Trolley Square called The Nailsmith. The owner was a man named Baxter. He invented an electric nailbrush, in which we were all trained and required to use. It figures. I just got the hang of my manual brush!

Baxter was a very good nail technician and he thought the electric brush made the job of doing nails a bit less time consuming and tedious. I disagreed, but my peacekeeping nature won out, mainly because he was my boss. I used the brush as instructed, and didn't make waves.

The Monday after my visit to my newly found mountain wonderland, Baxter called a mandatory salon meeting. I had a few other things to do on my day off, such as laundry, grocery shopping, and cleaning my house, but it was mandatory. Which was fine because we did get paid for those mandatory meetings, and my plan was to give my notice afterward, anyway.

Baxter began the meeting by informing us that he was opening a nail salon in Park City and needed nail technicians to rotate up there a couple of days a week. I was a bit surprised, but have always believed in things happening for a reason. He asked for volunteers, but they were scarce among this group. I kept quiet as I looked around the room. Nobody raised a hand, and a few murmured, "No way. Not me."

I remained silent.

Baxter continued on with his plan by sweetening the pot, because he thought he had to in order to get anyone from his staff to cooperate. Finally, I spit it out. I told him I already moved to Park City. I rented a place for my children and myself, and therefore did not need to rotate. I could be there full time.

Needless to say, Baxter was overjoyed.

You know things are meant to be when they easily happen, as they did in this case. I picture the whole process, as little men upstairs moving us around like the chess pieces. How perfect was this? I couldn't believe my good fortune. I was thrilled that I moved…and with a job!

However, Baxter's second nail salon location in Park City was short lived. He charged so much more than anywhere else, he eventually priced himself right back to Salt Lake City.

At this time, other than Baxter's place, there was only one true nail salon in Park City (in fact very few salons of any kind existed at all) so I applied at Lori's Nail Parlor. The owner, Lori, was a strong, kind, and confident woman who had been doing nails in the area for quite some time. She took a chance on me, but said I needed to lose the electric nailbrush that I had become so comfortable with, thanks to the Nailsmith, due to the many power outages that routinely occurred in Park City. I said, "No problem," and she hired me. I was to start the following week. I had only been taught by Joni to do acrylics using a plastic nail tip. Lori informed me that the nails were more secure if they were sculpted free hand. *Gulp!*

"You will need to practice sculpting a nail, no tips," Lori told me as she glued a nail on the end of an orangewood stick and cut it down.

"I can do that," I said trying to sound confident.

But the fact was I'd never done it before and I was nervous. *Fake it till you make it, Carly!*

And that was exactly what I did.

I practiced as if it were a real, natural nail, even adding a form against the end of the nail tip. I practiced over and over until I perfected a nice, evenly sculpted acrylic nail. Lori seemed pleased with my progress.

"You are ready to work on real clients now," Lori said with a smile.

"I only have another week left to finish up my notice with The Nailsmith," I told her hoping I could start then.

"No problem, I'll see you then," Lori said, then added, "Keep practicing."

She handed me a small bag with the supplies needed to continue perfecting my tip free acrylics.

I smiled, "Thank you, I will."

I showed up on my first day with my right arm and hand in a cast.

Lori looked at me wide - eyed as she said, "How are you going to do nails with a broken arm in a cast?"

I held up my arm and hand, waving my first two fingers and thumb.

"I asked the doctor to leave out my thumb, index and middle finger, so I could still use a nail file." Lori smiled but I detected a hint of concern, after all this was her business.

I hoped she realized that I had serious passion, a strong work ethic, and dedication to my job.

She pointed to my desk and I was thrilled.

# Who Needs a Prince?

*U*nfortunately, Ryan, the musician I moved away from found his way to Park City. He called my parents' house pretending to be the husband of a friend, telling my mom they misplaced my new phone number. My dear mom thinking she was doing a good thing told Ryan I recently moved to Park City. It wasn't hard with that information to find me. He bummed a ride from a friend and called me from a payphone. I listened to his words and he sounded so sincere. He wanted to get back together.

"I love you and I love the kids so much" he professed.

He expressed remorse and sorrow for his actions and wanted another chance.

"I promise it will never happen again." He tried to reassure me over and over again that he was sincere.

Oh how I wanted those words to be true, and I did love him. I finally agreed to meet him and talk.

Ryan continued making promises of sobriety, persuading me to let him back in my life. He closed in, using his nickname for me, "You can trust me, Carlyla," he said softly as he looked directly into my eyes. Tears streamed down both our cheeks and I succumbed to his persuasive ways. I let Ryan move back in with us.

He loved to fish and took the kids fishing two to three times a week. The kids were excited to have him back. They liked him and had fun with him. Looking back on it, I was sure they were unaware of the trouble between us, as they only saw the fun times. Ryan kept his promise of sobriety. I had not seen *John Barleycorn* for weeks.

Life moved along and it was good, until one night it wasn't. The kids were down in Salt Lake City for the weekend visiting my parents. One of my clients, Sarah invited me to an aerobics class after work. She picked me up in a Porsche, which I thought was pretty cool. After the class, which almost killed me, Sarah dropped me at my condo. I went inside only to find Ryan sipping on a bottle of rum. He was angry with me, thinking I saw another guy who drove a Porsche. I started to explain and he started to yell.

I yelled back, "It was my client, Sarah!" Of course, he did not believe me and yelled even louder telling me I was a whore. He slapped me across the face. *Hard.* I could see this was going nowhere fast. I headed for the door and once outside, I screamed for help, as I ran up the stairs to the street. He was right behind me as I reached the top. He reached out and grabbed my hair. I screamed as he threw me to the ground. I tumbled down the steps and Ryan ran down behind me.

I yelled, "Help me, please, somebody help me!"

Ryan ran back up the steps and disappeared into the night, just as the police arrived. The officer picked me up and I told him what happened. My right arm was killing me, so he called the doctor's office. It was after hours, but the doctor met us there, and cast my arm. The officer drove me home. He handed me his card, and I was to lock the doors (nobody did back then) and he specifically told me to call him immediately if Ryan showed up. I have no idea where Ryan spent the night, or the next day. My mom brought the kids home on Sunday and I told her I fell down the stairs. It was kind of true. Ryan came home early Tuesday morning. He was unshaven and looked rough. He played with the kids and helped them get ready for school, all the while I gave him the cold shoulder. I didn't want to upset the kids by starting something with him in front of them. Ryan walked them to the bus stop and when he returned, he began to explain, "I was only trying to keep you from running hysterically into the street!" He added, "You could have been hit by a car!"

I asked him, "Then why did you take off if you were trying to help me?"

Ryan answered, "I ran off because I knew the police would come and I was afraid of going to jail." I knew it was complete crap but I couldn't help myself. I wanted this to work and he was so convincing. *Maybe I had over reacted, maybe he was just trying to keep me safe from the traffic. I knew that nobody wanted to be in jail, maybe, just maybe, it will be all right this time.*

You guessed it, I believed him. Okay, I admit it, I was weak, broken arm and all. Like most women in abusive relationships, I thought it was my fault. If only I hadn't done this or that, said this or that, or looked at him that certain way. I always made excuses for his behavior. I put up with a lot of things during that short period of time. Looking back on it all, the truth was, I wanted this relationship to work, and I was in love. *Dang it!*

# 8

## That's "Berry" Daring

I t was now fall in the mountains, which has always been my favorite time of year, and things were a little bit better – or at least that's what I told myself. Ryan got up every morning and rolled a pack of his own "special cigarettes" that would carry him through the day. This was his substitute for alcohol. I know. I *know*, but at least he wasn't mean and abusive when he was high.

The holidays were coming, and we had been getting along very well. In fact, we had already survived half of them, Halloween and Thanksgiving, and now the winter season was definitely upon us.

One day, I decided to go down to the Salt Lake Valley to do a little Christmas shopping. I got the kids off to school, and Ryan was in bed sound asleep. He had been playing in a three-piece band a couple of nights a week and arrived home late the night before. I knew I had until three o'clock to get back. I got in the car and headed down the hill to Salt Lake City.

I bought some gifts, and as I loaded them into the back seat of my car, yes *my car*, I looked down on the floorboard. I noticed there were a few *items* that did not belong to me. Among them, a woman's wallet, a tube of bright, berry colored lipstick, and a discarded *used* tampon.

Interesting.

By the time I got home, Ryan had left the house. I knew he had another gig that night, and I wouldn't see him until late in the evening. The soup I put on in the crockpot before I left was almost finished and it smelled so good in the house. The kids arrived home from school, and as usual we did homework and ate dinner together. After the bath rituals, a little TV, and the bedtime rituals, I waited up for Ryan. He returned home late… and hungry. The gig had gone well, so he was pleased and in a very good mood. I fixed him a big bowl of soup, and watched as he scarfed it down.

Suddenly he stopped eating and looked at me in disbelief. I guessed that's when he found the tampon in the bottom of his bowl. If looks could kill…

"You are a sick bitch!" he yelled.

I calmly asked, "What's the matter? You liked it last night!"

He stomped out the door. I didn't see him again until the next afternoon, but in the meantime I had a very calm night of peaceful sleep.

Sadly, it did not end there.

I admit when it comes to my matters of the heart, I have always been a slow learner. When I fall in love, I usually fall hard. I always want to believe the best in people. They can change for the better, if they want to. Clearly, Ryan did not. He returned after his gig the next night. There was no mention of it again, although I did notice him inspecting his food extra carefully.

I just wanted to get through the holidays. But, really, is there ever a good time to make a break? During those next couple of months, my altercations with Ryan resulted in a dislocated shoulder, various bumps, bruises and stiches. He put me through hell, and I called it love.

But a person can only take so much.

One evening, Ryan and I had an argument that once again turned physical. He slapped my face and it did not stop there. I cried and begged him to stop. Of course, he didn't. It finally became unbearable. The kids were in bed asleep when I escaped to a neighbor's house. I knocked on the door and my friend's husband, Kirk, answered. He looked at me, upset and bloody, and immediately pulled me inside. I quickly glanced at the wooden cabinet as he led me into the kitchen. His wife, Sally, wet a washcloth, and held it out for me. I grabbed it, thanking her as I sat down on the chair Kirk offered me. I wiped my wounds and my tears while continuing to weep. They were worried and asked me where the children were. I sobbed as I told them they were in their beds asleep. I was confident Ryan wouldn't hurt them. It was me that made him angry, not the kids.

Sally and Kirk wanted to call the police, but I convinced them that I was okay; that it looked worse than it actually was. My friends glanced at each other in disbelief, and the looks between them told me they disapproved, as they should.

In that moment, I realized that once again I was making excuses for Ryan's behavior. In my heart I knew I needed to get out. I made some comment about moving out with the kids, as I composed myself. I murmured quietly, "I need to go home."

Kirk wanted to walk me back to make sure I was safe. "Please do not confront Ryan," I begged. I convinced him that Ryan was probably passed out from the alcohol, so there was nothing to worry about. Kirk agreed to leave Ryan alone.

"But, I *am* going to walk you home," he said sternly.

When Kirk slipped into the bedroom to put on his shoes, Sally followed behind. I was alone in the living room and I knew Kirk kept a pistol in that wooden cabinet by the front door. I quickly opened the drawer and took the gun without them knowing. It was heavy, but I paid no mind as I slipped it under my Night Ranger T-shirt, and left the house by myself.

*I had snapped.*

I was only a few feet out their front door, when Kirk came running after me.

He stopped me, held out his hand, and said, "Give me the gun right now!"

I was in tears, sobbing uncontrollably, when I handed it over.

"What are you thinking?" he asked with a concerned look in his eyes.

I had no answer; I had no idea what I was thinking. I didn't even know if it was loaded or what I had intended to do once I walked into the house. I hadn't really even thought beyond taking it. Thanks to Kirk, I never got to find out.

Kirk instructed me to go home, and sit on the steps. Unbeknownst to me, Sally had already called the police, and they were on their way. Kirk told me not to mention my momentary lack of judgment. I didn't, and the police arrived quickly, in response to a domestic dispute. Ryan tried to talk his way out of it, but there I stood beaten, bruised, and still bleeding. My "sleeping" children came running out of their rooms, begging the police to take him away.

"We hate him, Mom!" they cried.

That was a huge turning point for me, and finally, I did learn.

Ryan went to jail and I went to counseling. The house we were renting in Deer Valley was in Ryan's name, which I never fully understood, since he had no viable job. The owner, Marilyn, was an attorney and had been for many years. At that time, she was the youngest woman in the state of Utah to pass the bar, and she was no dummy. I think she saw the writing on the wall that evening we met with her at her home located in the Avenues, a very hip part of Salt Lake City, to sign the lease.

Ryan's fifteen-year-old daughter, Sunny, was also living with us. I was thankful she was not home that horrible evening. She and her dad had a strained relationship as it was, and Sunny and I became very close quickly, she even called me Mom pretty much right off the bat. She had been living in a home for young girls in Watsonville, California, since the age of six. Sunny's mother had taken her own life when Sunny was only three years old. Ryan had taken her out on the road with him while performing with Quicksilver Messenger Service. But of course, it was a difficult life for a child. Ryan had found this home and it was working out well until Sunny became a teenager and started to act out. The school called us one day and told us she had to leave. We were told she was no longer obeying the rules, and it was time for her to leave. Sunny was a bright, beautiful and highly spirited young lady, whom I had grown to love. She called her father by his first name instead of Dad. I remember picking her up from the airport that first day.

While Ryan was putting gas into the car, she asked, "So, how is Ryan doing?"

"You mean your dad?" I asked somewhat parental.

Sunny answered, "Yes, Ryan."

I told her, "He is doing well." I remember thinking, *No point involving her in our troubles.*

I cared deeply about her, and I felt sorry for her, but I knew I could not take her with us. That would be a permanent tie to her dad, and I had my hands full with my own kids as it was.

I called Ryan's sister, Patti and explained the situation. I heard her sigh as I filled her in with all of the details. She informed me that this was not the first time she had heard a similar version of this story. Patti paid for Sunny's bus ticket and I drove her to the station the next morning. Before she got on the bus, we looked at each other and started to cry. I held her close as I promised to keep in touch. I assured Sunny that everything would be fine, and then I put her on a bus to Oregon. I watched the Greyhound pull away, and wondered if I would ever see her again. I closed my eyes and said a little prayer.

At this time, I came to understand why Ryan's wife had committed suicide. My life with him was so much fun in the beginning. He hid his alcoholism from me and with good reason. Slowly but surely he began to drink more and more. You see that's what alcoholics do. They think they can have a beer, a drink, or a glass of wine, and they are confident they can handle it. But Ryan couldn't just have one drink, because one would always lead to another and another and another. One drink was too many and a hundred wasn't enough. We were together for about a year and a half, and that was way too long. It is hard to admit, but I even had thoughts of taking my own life at times. Ryan made me that crazy. Fortunately, those thoughts were fleeting, as I knew deep down in my heart and soul, I could never do that to my children. I loved them far too much to add that to their lives.

So, the realization of Ryan's wife leaving her precious three-year-old daughter to get away from him was so hard for me to come to grips with. Life with Ryan had to have become unbearable, hopeless and despairing. Sadly, I understood. I called Marilyn the next morning, explaining the situation. She was going to be in Park City at her cabin in White Pine Canyon.

"Why don't you come by the house around noon? We can have coffee and discuss your next step," she asked.

I agreed. By the time I arrived on her doorstep, she had already called the jail in Coalville, Utah, and found out all the details. *She was good!*

"I spoke to the arresting officer," she said, and then added, "I knew there was something about that guy I didn't like!"

We both agreed I needed to move out and find a place of my own, one that Ryan did not know about. Marilyn helped me obtain a restraining order in the next two days and also started the process of eviction on Ryan.

"I want that son of a bitch out of there," she said angrily, but added in a soft tone, you and your children are welcome to stay until you find a place."

I smiled and thanked her.

Marilyn added, "I wouldn't wait too long if I were you, he could be released after three days."

I smiled, thanked her and said, "Okay."

I had some serious house hunting to do. I searched desperately to find a place for my four children and myself. I was so afraid Ryan would be released before I could get everything out of the house *he* had leased. I think it would have been easier having four dogs, coupled with the fact it was ski season!

I finally found a place to rent, and it was one that I could afford. The owner, Scott, lived in Hawaii and we communicated by telephone. Yes, a landline! It was only two bedrooms, so I told him I only had two children. I hated lying to him, but I was so desperate, and the clock was ticking. Time was not on my side.

Scott asked if I could send him a photo of us, so he could see who was renting his place. I took a picture of my two youngest children, Ricky and Megan, and myself and sent it via snail mail. For some strange reason, I thought it would be better if they were little. Since Scott lived in Hawaii, I remember thinking I would probably never see him, after all Hawaii was a world away as far as I knew.

We moved over a weekend and I began putting our new home together. The two bedrooms and one bath were located upstairs, so I started putting our life back together room by room. I gave one of the bedrooms to the boys, and the other bedroom to the girls, and I slept on the couch. The coat closet and bathroom in the hall downstairs became mine. The place was small, but I truly never gave it a second thought. I was so grateful to be in our own space, without Ryan. I was in survival mode and we all do what we have to do to survive, especially when children are involved. I knew our life would be so much better without him in it, no matter the sacrifice. It was a small price to pay for safety and peace of mind.

In the spring, Scott the owner of the house, showed up out of the blue at my work. I almost fainted. No warning, he was in town, and wanted to meet us in person. Scott was a nice looking, well-dressed man with an unassuming smile. *It's going to be all right,* I thought to myself. I told him I was walking back and forth to work, catching the bus if it happened to come by, since I had no car. Scott graciously offered to pick me up after I finished work. My car had lived its life, which is what you would expect from a hundred-dollar car.

"What time are you finished?" he asked.

I smiled and told him, "Six o'clock."

Then I panicked! I called the kids and screamed, "Clean up the house! *Now*!"

I demanded the two oldest disappear somewhere! But as the end of the day approached, I came to my senses. It was time to fess up and face the music.

Scott arrived promptly at six o'clock and as we drove to the house, I confessed and sincerely apologized as I explained my situation. His main concern was where we were all sleeping. When I told him about the sleeping arrangements, he took it well, smiled and thanked me for always being prompt with my rent and keeping the place neat and tidy. He then commented on my adaptability and resiliency. However, he admitted that his brother, who had fixed the leak in the roof, and did some other minor repairs on the house, thought there were more than two children living there. I guess I really wasn't fooling anyone, but thankfully, Scott let us stay.

# On the Same Paige

*H*is name was Bob, he was the director for the Prevention Center in Park City and he literally saved my life. I was so nervous my first visit. I had never been to a counselor before. My mom told me that a counselor would just blame everything on her and my father. Little did I know, my counseling sessions soon became my way of life.

I worked in a salon called Park Avenue Stylists and was just beginning to build my clientele again. I told Bob, the counselor, that I did not make very much money, had four children to support, numerous bills to pay, plus living expenses. I wondered if he thought those were just excuses to get out of going to counseling. However, I assured Bob that I was legitimately worried about the cost. At the same time, I also expressed my true desire to get better emotionally.

Bob informed me how the center operated on a sliding pay scale and they would base my payment on my income. I listened, and sat there with fingers crossed, hoping I would qualify. I needed this and I knew it, but I was embarrassed by my current situation and I felt like a huge loser. Silence.

I thanked Bob, as I stood up prepared to leave.

"Carly, wait a minute." He looked me in the eye and asked, "Can you afford a dollar a week?"

I must have looked surprised, and when I did not answer, Bob came back with, "How about fifty cents?"

I was so embarrassed at this point; I kept my head down and said I could afford the dollar, biting my upper lip.

So, every Monday from then on I was in his office at noon. He soon figured out once a week was not enough, so for the first three months I saw him three times a week. I grew to love these sessions and began to look forward to them with excitement instead of dread. It is hard to tell someone your deepest, darkest, and most humiliating stories, but I had to. I needed this, not only for myself, but also for my kids. I had to start setting a better example of a healthy relationship. After all, this would be the road map for their relationships later on in life. As difficult as it was, I was figuring myself out for the first time in my life.

Ryan spent only a few days in jail. Another musician friend of his bailed him out. His court date arrived, and at his hearing a judge ordered him to stay away from me and attend AA meetings. As part of his punishment, he had his choice of either six months in jail or six months of counseling for spousal abuse. Of course, he chose the counseling. Ryan began with a female counselor named, Paige, at the same place I was seeing Bob. At that time, there were very few places in Park City that were not private practices, either of us could afford.

Unbeknownst to me, at the time, Paige happened to be Bob's significant other. I don't think Ryan knew they were significant others either. Now, you have to understand that Ryan was a very handsome and extremely charming man. He had a way with words and I am sure it usually worked on most women... but not this time.

I think both counselors had him figured out.

Paige and Bob compared notes every Monday evening, and as expected Ryan's and my stories did not add up. Fortunately Paige and Bob could see through Ryan's attempts to be the victim, and as a result, they did not help Ryan reunite with me (which is what he wanted). Paige and Bob could plainly see what was going on.

Now for the hard part; Bob had to convince me not to go back to Ryan.

It was difficult for me not to be fooled, because Ryan did as he was told; he was in counseling, and faithfully attended AA meetings. He faithfully stayed away from me, until he showed up on my doorstep late one evening, with the AA manual in hand, professing the many changes he had made and was going to make. Ryan begged and cried to have me back.

"I will do anything for us to be a family again, I love you and the kids so much. I need all of you in my life. I've learned how to control my anger."

I stared blankly at him as he continued.

"I've missed all of you so much. Counseling has worked wonders for me. I am in the AA program and I have no desire to ever touch alcohol again"

Ryan bowed his head and began to full-on cry, acknowledging how sorry he was that he had hurt me.

I continued to listen quietly, arms folded across my chest. I thought about all of the broken promises. I thought about his weakness with alcohol. I went over all of it in my mind. I remembered in a couple of minutes how far I'd come, as Ryan begged me to let him come inside. "Just to talk, it's freezing out here," he said shivering.

I wouldn't even let him in the door.

Instead I calmly threatened to call the police if he didn't leave. This time, I did not fall for his lines, excuses, or promises. I knew the truth, thanks to Bob.

My strength infuriated Ryan. He said counseling had turned me into a "cold bitch."

As I closed the door, I realized he really hadn't changed at all. I felt so strong and empowered, for the first time in a very long time, and that was a good feeling.

I smiled thinking about how far I had come.

## Awakening

Ryan's six months of required counseling ended, and of course he stopped his sessions. He returned to court and was ordered to leave Park City for good. The same police officer, Robb, who was called to our house that horrible evening, escorted him to the freeway entrance. He told Ryan if he returned, he would go to jail. Those were the days back then, a police escort to the freeway!

I continued with my therapy sessions and with my life. I loved my job, my kids were doing exceptionally well in school, and they were all happy and healthy and had adjusted quite well to our new way of living. Life was finally coming together.

Three months passed and a three-bedroom condo came on the market for rent. No secrets this time around. I met the owners with all four of my children and he and his wife said yes to all of us. I was thrilled. We moved in the following weekend. I had my own bedroom and closet again!

The following Monday, the kids were in school and I was catching up on my household duties. There was a knock on my door. I looked through the peephole and there was Ryan. He resurfaced again. I opened the door and promptly told him if he didn't leave, I would call the police.

Ryan looked at me, somewhat surprised.

"I drove straight through from California," he exclaimed. "Can we please talk?" Before I could answer, he added, "It has been months since I have had a drink!"

I flatly said, "I don't care, I *really* don't care and you need to leave now."

He shook his head as he walked down the stairs to his car. I watched him drive away.

That was the last time I heard from Ryan.

Given his reckless lifestyle, my guess is he is either dead by now or in jail. Perhaps he makes someone else's life miserable, or hopefully, now thinks positively and productively. Maybe he finally got it together. One thing I was certain of as far as I was concerned, John Barleycorn *had* died. Finally.

Many years later, Ryan's daughter, Sunny, found me. It's not hard to find someone in a small town like Park City, as it was back then, particularly when you know their occupation. She called the handful of salons there were back in the day, until she found me. We had a very nice conversation. She had been through beauty school and was employed at a salon in Medford, Oregon, and she loved it. Sunny told me how much I had inspired her to be in the beauty business and although she missed our talks, they had made a huge impact on her and gave her the desire to make her life better, unlike Ryan. She had always expressed an interest in doing hair and nails. I was flattered and happy she found her place. Sunny was on a good path. She told me how much she missed us; but had fond memories of being together as a family back then.

"Have you heard from your dad?" I inquired.

I wasn't afraid or nervous when I asked about Ryan. I had grown and evolved so much in the last seven years; I was no longer that scared, timid little girl he once knew and controlled.

I was a confident, strong and secure woman now and there was no going back.

"I have no idea, he has been MIA for years," she replied.

Sunny told me neither she nor her Aunt Patti had heard from Ryan, and they didn't care if they ever did. It turned out; he was a missing person who nobody really missed at all.

# Wildfire

I began working at a salon where the owner, Camille, was saving her tips for breast augmentation and she made no bones about it. She wanted to put a jar on her station, which read *Tips for Tits*, but we all vetoed that.

Camille loved the soundtrack from the movie, *Yentl*. She played the cassette repeatedly until one day it mysteriously disappeared. *Hmmm*. From that moment on any other tapes that wore out their welcome, quickly went to "*Yentl-vile.*"

That was the space between the wall and the hot water heater. One of the hairdressers, Dan, found that spot and it was perfect, protecting us from listening to something eight hours a day, five days a week. I know it wasn't very nice, but sometimes we just couldn't take it. When questioned about the missing tapes, we all pretended we didn't know anything about them.

Camille accepted the missing music in the beginning, but then started to seriously wonder who was stealing her cassette tapes. She especially missed Yentl, and told us if it didn't reappear, we were all going to have to take a lie detector test!

Dan asked, "Seriously?"

"Yes!" she confirmed.

Dan offered to buy her a new *Yentl* cassette, so we all decided to help him by chipping in on the cost. It was so much less expensive than getting someone to move that hot water heater, and much easier than telling her about our secret hiding place! That needed to remain our little secret! We all found it interesting that after all of that, she never played *Yentl* in the salon again.

I borrowed her Audi one day to run to the Salt Lake Valley and pick up product for the salon. As soon as I started the car, the music began belting out. Yes you guessed it… *Yentl!*

I quickly switched to the radio.

Park City was a very small town back then, so everyone in the business knew everyone else in the business. I think back then we were one of three salons. We had no receptionist and took turns taking calls for appointments. They eventually moved my desk next to the phone, as it was usually for me, one of my kids calling after school.

Being a single Mom was not easy, juggling work and kids. My mom would come and pick them up on Fridays after school and return them on Sunday afternoons a couple of times a month and that was a big help. It gave me a well-needed break and her longing to see her grandchildren was taken care of.

One day at work, the phone rang when I was right in the middle of doing a set of silk nail wraps. I later learned (the hard way) that silk nails do not hold up in our dry climate. Anyway, when I answered the phone, I heard a scream "Chantele is beating up Sean!" Ricky and Megan were afraid they might be next. I tried for several minutes to calm everyone down and by the time I had semi-succeeded, I tried to hang up the headset only to find I was stuck! I had glued my hand to the phone. It took several orange wood sticks soaked in acetone to pry it loose, not to mention, how the acetone took its toll on my skin. And the poor handset was beyond repair.

Fortunately, Radio Shack was across the hall. The sweet geeks in Radio Shack took pity on me and gave me a deal. But most importantly, all the children survived. However to this day, I think on some level, they are all still afraid of Chantele, just a little.

All in all I have to say, I am blessed with wonderful children. They have been through the ringer with me, yet we hung in there together through good times and bad. I know they still loved me even during all of those times when I just couldn't love them more. We came through it all and stayed intact. I realize now it was probably hard for them, they had a lot of responsibility at young ages and I'm sure they were frustrated more than once…hence the smack-downs from Chantele.

I continued with counseling. Ryan was finally out of the picture, and I loved my life again, especially going to work! I was building a Park City clientele and I loved every second of it. We had a great team at Park Avenue Stylists and we enjoyed working together. It was our own little family. We began to know one another's customers and that was fun.

I noticed this customer of Kelly's, one of our hairdressers, come in for a haircut; he was handsome and personable. He seemed genuine, was friendly and I liked his smile. He was a ski instructor, and his name was Clark.

Clark was quite the character. He did things like played his harmonica, danced and moonwalked whenever he came into in the salon. I liked his personality and his seemingly fun-loving ways, even though I never actually talked to him. This was just an observation on my part, but he had good energy. I could tell he was a kind soul. He made me smile and I wanted to get to know him better.

One day, as I was doing an acrylic nail fill, my client invited me to her home for dinner the upcoming Saturday night. "I have a plan," she said. "I also invited a ski instructor friend of mine to dinner to meet you. I hope that's okay."

I thought, *Why not?* So I accepted. "Sure. What's his name?"

"Greg."

*Oh.* I must admit, I was disappointed. I was hoping for Clark, but I went anyway. *That's okay.* I thought. *I have to get out and meet new people.*

We had a wonderful dinner, prepared by her chef, and served by her waiter. This kind of in-home service was all new to me, and I was impressed. The conversation was interesting and I enjoyed the evening so much, I didn't want it to end.

I had borrowed a car for the evening, and at the end of the night Greg asked me for a ride home. Upon arrival, he invited me in to listen to him play guitar. I think he may have heard about my love for musicians. He played a couple of songs, and I listened with interest, as I do love music, but my interest began to wane when he played the Michael Murphy song, "Wildfire."

That has always been one of my least favorite songs, but that's just me!

However, there was no chemistry for either of us. I felt it and I believe the feeling was mutual. I told him I needed to return my friend's car, even though I had really borrowed it until the next day, so I left. However, the night was still young and my mom had the kids! So I went to Main Street to have a little fun.

I carefully parked the car, walked into a private club (which is what we Utahans call a bar), and there was Clark! I didn't know he worked there. I thought he only did ski instructing. But I later learned to do that you have to have other jobs to make ends meet.

I smiled at Clark and waved. He saw me and happily walked over to greet me.

"Hi," I said, "I'm Carly from the salon."

"I know who you are," he replied with a big smile.

But being that he was working, thirsty patrons cut our conversation short.

I ordered a glass of wine as I watched him hug every woman who walked in. Clark was so popular! There was something about him. Close to closing time, he asked me to wait and come up to his place a few doors down and have a drink. I accepted.

Once there he lit a fire, we talked, and Clark played his guitar for me. He said he'd written a song and wanted me to hear it, so he began to play this absolutely beautiful melody. He finished the six-minute song and asked my opinion.

I told him the truth. "It's beautiful," I said, because it *was* beautiful. "What's the name of it?"

"The Duck Song," Clark replied with a straight face.

Okay, that seemed a little weird, but he was cute, so I went with it.

"Do you want to hear it with lyrics?" he asked.

"Sure! Okay," I replied enthusiastically. I've always been a lyrics girl.

Clark started to play it again, and after a *very* long intro, he started to sing. *"Quack, quack. Quack. Quack. Quack"* to the beautiful melody.

I totally cracked up.

As the night went on, we laughed, drank wine, and talked for hours, and…I ended up spending the night.

Morning came quickly and I was mortified when I woke up. *Oh, no!* I thought. *I just had my very first one-night stand!* I was freaking out! I do not do this. I am Mormon girl – a Mormon girl, that is, with a horrible hangover. I quickly started gathering up my things. Where were my clothes? My shoes? My purse? I wanted to slip away fast!

Clark rolled over as I was dressing. "Where are you going?" he asked.

Without looking at him, I answered quickly, "I have to go home. At noon I have to help decorate for a fundraiser at the hotel."

Clark looked at the clock. "It's only six a.m.," he said groggily.

I kept throwing clothes on, not speaking.

"Did you sleep well?" he asked. I grimaced. Sleep? "Did you like the bed? Was it comfortable? It's my grandfather's."

*Oh, my God, shut up!* I thought. I mumbled a quick, "Yes," and then raced out the door.

As I left, I heard him say something about going to breakfast, which I ignored. That was the last thing on my mind. I was so embarrassed. The thought of sitting across from him was just too much, although I was starving. I was scared to see his face again in the light of day!

Of course, it had snowed overnight; it's Park City in winter, why wouldn't it? There sat my friend's car on Main Street, completely covered as a result of the plows clearing the roads. I was in a sexy red dress, and very high heel pumps, trying to walk down a steep, snow-covered path, on a Sunday morning, looking like the Whore of Babylon.

When I got to the car, I cleaned the snow off the windshield with my arm. Unfortunately, the town was up, and all the people going for coffee at the Main Street Deli watched me through the window. I kept my pounding head down, hoping no one recognized me. I am not wild like this! What the hell was I thinking?

*Good Lord, I wonder if Counselor Bob makes house calls.*

# Oh, What a Knight

s I drove home, my thoughts turned to a cheeseburger, fries, and a diet coke. I drove straight to Burger King. Of course it was CLOSED! I went home and decided sleep was just as good. I woke to the alarm on my clock radio. George Thorougood belted out, "I drink alone."

I thought, *Maybe I should have.*

A quick shower, then off I went to help decorate the local hotel with my co-workers. I wasn't lying when I told Clark I had to be somewhere at noon.

I relayed my "adventure" the night before to my hairdresser friend, Dan. He just smiled and said, "good."

No big deal to him.

Embarrassed, I kept busy with the decorating. I hung paper streamers, trying my best not to think about the previous night, or my aching head. Hoping Clark would dump Kelly and find another hairdresser was paramount in my thoughts. I was nervous about seeing Clark in the salon. What was I going to do? Staying buzzed with alcohol was not an option. I had kids!

I went to see my counselor, Bob, on Monday, and he thought my adventure was good. It was a small town then and he knew and liked Clark.

"Time to move on," he advised. "Forget Ryan, and focus your energy on this."

"This *what*?" I asked. "I had a one-night stand!" I put my face in my hands as Bob laughed. Plus, I was still hung over.

However, I woke up refreshed the next day. I was younger then and the pain from being over-served lasted only a day. As I dressed for work, my mind was spinning. *How would it be now when I see Clark in the salon? Will he act as if it didn't happen? Maybe he will ignore me? I had heard that could happen.* My stomach churned as I walked to work in the "moon boots" I had saved up to buy. If I didn't do nails, I would have been chewing on mine.

I entered the salon to find a dozen red roses sitting on my desk. I breathed a sigh of relief, and I smiled.

My first client, Liz (who was also a friend), came in for her acrylic nail fill. "Where did the flowers come from, she asked then commented, they're so beautiful!"

I quickly told her a somewhat edited version of my weekend events.

"Be careful," she warned, "I know him from The Club and I, too, know how comfortable his grandfather's bed was."

I detected a hint of jealousy in her tone, as she stared at the roses.

It didn't matter. Roses and all, I decided I would probably only see him when he came in for his haircuts. He had not called and I went back to feeling bad about myself. *This is just my payback for being promiscuous*, I thought. *That's what you get, Carly.* I was embarrassed and I vowed, *never again!*

The following day I arrived at work an hour early (due to riding the bus) and there was a woman walking down the hall in front of me. She smiled as we both stopped at the door. I knew this face, but couldn't put a name with it.

I opened the door for her, and she asked if she could get a pedicure, even though she didn't have an appointment.

"Sure," I replied. "Give me a few minutes to set up for you."

She sat down, put her feet in the warm pedicure water as I made coffee.

"I'm a runner and my feet are pretty bad," she confessed.

As I took her feet out of the pedicure bath, I introduced myself and she did the same.

"I'm Belinda," she said.

That's it! I suddenly recognized her. *She's Belinda Carlisle, lead vocalist of the Go-Go's, one of the most successful female bands of all time! How cool was this?*

I thought about if the bus had not come by, I would still be walking to work. I wouldn't be sitting here with a famous music person! I felt as if it was my lucky day and it was only eight in the morning.

I continued with her pedicure and did finally tell her how much my daughter and I loved her music. She was gracious as she thanked me.

I was still sanding away on her callouses when hairdresser Dan arrived at nine. He recognized her immediately as he poured himself a cup of coffee. Flipping a couple of pages in the book at the front desk, he asked if he could speak with me in his most professional voice.

"Excuse me," I said to Belinda and walked up to the front desk.

"You have to ask for her autograph!" Dan quietly but sternly whispered while still looking down at the book.

"I can't," I replied just as quietly. "I'm too embarrassed to ask!"

He picked up a pencil and in big letters across the top of our appointment book, he wrote the words, *You HAVE to, Carly!*

Pretending to be discussing something else, I quietly declined again and went back to my client, just as the phone rang.

After a couple of minutes, Dan brought over a piece of folded paper and told me I had a message. (No cell phones back then, kids.) I opened it; worried it might be a message from the school my children attended. I read the words, *ASK HER!*

I knew how persistent Dan could be, so finally I did ask. "I am going to be one of those people who probably drive you nuts," I said.

Puzzled, she asked as her brow furrowed, "What do you mean?"

I was shaking as I mumbled the words, "Can I please ask you for your autograph?"

She answered happily, "Of course!" She couldn't have been more gracious. I motioned to Dan and asked him to bring over the paper tablet. With a slight smile on his face, he walked over and handed it to me.

"How many would you like?" Belinda asked.

"I would love to have three, if that's not too much to ask." I answered shyly.

Absolutely!" she said, and then added, "Whom should I make them out to?"

I answered politely, "One for my daughter, Chantele, one to Dan, the hairdresser over there behind the desk, and also one for myself."

Belinda began to scribble away and handed the finished autographs to me with a perky, "There you go, Carly!"

She smiled as I thanked her. I was so excited for Chantele. The Go-Go's were one of her all-time favorite girl bands. I was earning big points this time. *Coolest mom ever, I thought!*

# 13

## Rebel with a Cause

The rest of the day was uneventful until about five o'clock when the phone rang. I answered it, and on the line was Clark. "Do you want to go for a glass of wine after work?"

"I would love to," I said truthfully, "but my kids have been home from school since three and I should go home and get dinner for them."

"What time do you get home?" he inquired. "Can I stop by and meet them?"

"Okay…" I replied slowly. I was surprised that he wanted to meet my kids! I told him six o'clock and gave him my address.

I hung up the phone elated secretly hoping it wasn't just a one-night stand!

I cleaned up my desk for the day and rushed out the door. I had a little less than an hour to get home. I started to walk across the parking lot when I spotted the free bus again! I ran towards it and hopped on. In fifteen minutes I was home, straightening up the house.

Clark pulled up on his motorcycle and came to the door; the kids sat quietly at the table doing homework when he knocked. I answered the door, invited him in, and introduced him as *my friend* to my kids. Clark shook each kid's hand one by one as he said hello. I liked that. Then he asked, "Who wants to go for pizza?"

They all cheered and my son Ricky asked if he could ride Clark's motorcycle.

"Not this time, buddy," he replied, as he rubbed his blonde hair.

We walked over to Pizza Hut. I watched him as he talked to the kids about school and asked if they knew how to ski.

"No!" they all replied in unison. "But we want to go skiing!"

"Well, I'm a ski instructor. So next winter we'll all go together. And I'll teach you how to ski."

I couldn't believe my ears. Clark made plans to ski with my children next winter, which was close to a year away!

After we walked home, he took each kid for a short ride, one by one, on his motorcycle, and that was it.

It really was my lucky day.

Clark was so handsome and physically fit. He worked out all the time and he seemed to be emotionally together as well, unlike Ryan. Clark read constantly, he particularly enjoyed the Carlos Castaneda books. Clark had one quote he had memorized from the author Carlos Castaneda and used it almost daily.

*"The trick is in what one emphasizes. We either make ourselves miserable, or we make ourselves happy. The amount of work is the same."*

Then he would add, "Maintain total smoothness." I liked that.

Clark came into my life exactly when I needed a genuinely nice person. He treated me like a queen, and he made me laugh...a lot! There was a bit of a rebel inside his free spirit, but I liked that as well! What girl doesn't love a bit of a bad boy?

Clark was a ski instructor, a car detailer, a real entrepreneur, and a free spirit. He was very musical, played several instruments including the piano, trumpet, guitar, and a mean harmonica (primarily on the chair lifts). That worked for me! I could listen to him for hours and I did just that.

My life was good again.

We were having a great time just hanging out and being with the kids. We did everything together as a family for a couple of months.

However, as springtime emerged, so did his free spirit.

Clark came over one evening and casually told me, "I'm moving to Hawaii for the spring and summer, just for a few months."

He acted like it was no big deal, and that he'd be back before we knew he was gone.

I told myself it was okay and tried to hide my disappointment.

He told the kids the next evening when he came to say goodbye. "I'm going to Hawaii for work, but I'll be back in a few months," he said with a smile.

Then he hugged us all and off he went to Hawaii.

I tried to go about my life. After all, we weren't in love or anything like that. I must admit, however, I was sad and brokenhearted when he left. I knew I had to get through it and after a good month of counseling with Bob, I began to heal slowly.

I couldn't deny I was in pain from his absence, but I said to myself every morning and every night these four little words; *"This too shall pass."*

# "A Good Man-Darin is Hard to Find"

**W**e were now in the full swing of summer, the kids were out of school and enjoying the warm weather. It was Friday and my mother was on her way to pick up the kids for a few days, which provided a much-needed break for me.

Liz invited me to the bar where she worked as a cocktail waitress. She was tired of me moaning over Clark and she reminded me of how much of a jerk he could be. After all, she *had* warned me to be careful with him. When we were out together, she kept telling me, "Look around."

As I looked out at the dance floor, I saw a longhaired blonde guy with a red-blinking, light-up red earring. I liked that guy! His name was Robb. He was in Park City just for a couple of months, younger than me, and was a trust fund baby. He resembled David Lee Roth, the one-time lead singer in the rock group Van Halen. Close enough to a musician for me!

By the end of the night, I was sitting on his lap, drinking beer with a lime in it, and a friendship was formed. He lived in a little house in Old Town, which had a sign in the front of the yard, which read, "The Happy Hut."

In addition to building my nail clientele, I began apprenticing with Kelly to do hair, all the while working steadily to increase my nail business. I spent time at the *Happy Hut* practicing on Robb and his four roommates, trying to perfect my haircutting skills. However, no matter how much I tried, being a hairdresser was not working out as I had expected. I was not confident about it, particularly hair color. I once had an instructor tell me that doing hair color was 10% skill and 90% guesswork, either you have it or you don't.

I quickly decided to stick to what I knew and loved…nails. Besides that, if my clients didn't love the nails I applied, I could take them off! Hair color? Not so easy to remove.

One evening as summer was rapidly coming to a close, and the crispness of fall began to set in, Kelly and I decided to go to The Club and wait for Robb to join us, have a drink, and get something to eat. Those were the days, when I could drink and eat "bar food" and not gain an ounce. As we were talking and waiting, someone came up behind me and put his hands over my eyes. "Guess who?" the mystery voice said.

"Robb!" I guessed.

"Nope," was the answer.

I spouted out a few other names, only to be told over and over again I was wrong.

I heard a little giggle from Kelly.

After I ran out of guesses, I spun around on the bar stool, and suddenly I was looking straight into the face of Clark, back from Hawaii. He had been gone since the ski resorts had closed in early April, over five months!

He cupped his hands around my face, and said, "The entire time I was gone, all I thought about was you. Can we go somewhere and talk?" He also asked how the kids were. "I'd love to see them," he admitted.

I stood up, said goodbye to Kelly and actually passed Robb on the way out the door, mumbling something about needing to leave, and never looked back. After all, our relationship was strictly friendly and fun. It was nothing serious. I was just his friend who became his hairdresser!

I hopped on the back of Clark's motorcycle and we drove to my place. He took out a ten-dollar bill, paid the sitter, and offered to take her home. I called her parents to make sure it was okay, and of course, they decided to come pick her up. They didn't want their daughter on the back of some dude's motorcycle, which I understood.

The kids were fast asleep in bed, so I opened a box of wine.

As we sat, Clark confessed, "I went to Hawaii with a wealthy woman…just taking care of things for her. I lived at her house."

I didn't ask any questions or details. I didn't really want or need to know the particulars. Clark was back and that was all I cared about.

Although I was puzzled by his admission, I kept quiet and just listened.

"I left because I was scared of the possibility of falling in love with you." He had never been married or had any children, so I imagine this freaked him out. "I'm so sorry," he said, his eyes welling up with tears, "I thought I could run away, and that my feelings would lessen if I was away from you for a few months. But that didn't happen. In fact, my feelings for you deepened." Clark paused as if he really had to get up the courage for what he was about to say next. "I love you…not just you, but also your children. I want to be in your lives."

I was both touched and shocked. "Are you sure?"

Clark cupped his hands around my face and kissed me slowly, deeply, and passionately. I had my answer. That kiss told me he was absolutely sure.

We spent the next few months with my children, learning about each other and enjoying life. From that time on, the six of us were really inseparable. We really were a family. Even though he'd never married or had children, he was willing to take all five of us on. That truly impressed me.

Life was good.

Then one evening, when we were at my condo, the phone rang. I picked it up. "Hello?"

"It's Liz. Is Clark there?" I handed the phone to him.

Clark listened and then I heard him say, "No, that's a job for a single guy and I no longer consider myself single."

After he hung up, I asked him "What was that about?"

He said, "She wanted me to dance at a birthday party for a co-worker."

Puzzled I asked, "Dance? Why would she ask you to dance at a party?"

It was at that moment I learned of his previous occupation. Yes…I was dating a male stripper…a stripper who went by the stage name of *J.C Sparkles.* Apparently I was the only one in town who didn't know. I flashed back on Clark's g-string underwear. They were way cooler than any of the ones I owned! *Ohhh…I get it now,* I thought to myself. I began to laugh hysterically and finally managed to sputter, "You're a stripper? That is so embarrassing!"

"Male exotic dancer," he corrected with all seriousness.

I laughed even harder. "Are there any other secrets I should know about?"

"No. That's it. I promise," he replied sheepishly.

And that *was* it.

We married in May of 1985. I guess it really wasn't a one night stand after all!

And we all learned to ski!

## Sweet Escape

People in this business have a tendency to jump around and I was no different. I left Park Avenue Stylists and started working in a new salon, located at the Resort Center of Park City Ski Area (as it was called then). It was an après ski place, owned by a woman named Joanne. She always took her lunch break at home, and then came back from lunch very tired and sleepy, to the point that she literally fell asleep in her chair, waiting for walk-in clients. The salon was just getting started and not that busy, so we depended highly on walk-ins.

One day after she returned from lunch, she took her usual place in her chair, tilted it back, and prepared for her usual nap. I asked her if she had been to the doctor lately. "Maybe you have narcolepsy," I concluded with a worried tone.

"Oh, no. It's not that. I go home for lunch every day and watch porn with my male customers," she said casually, as if it was something *everybody* does.

*What?* I was flabbergasted. How do you respond to that?

"Yeah, it's a lot of fun," she continued, as she settled into her chair.

Naïvely, I asked, "Are you…a prostitute?"

Joanne laughed, "They don't pay me to watch porn with them! It's just fun."

I gave my notice the following morning; a twenty-four-hour notice. I knew I had to leave. Shortly after I left, the salon closed and I heard she and her husband divorced.

After that I became *The Mobile Manicurist*. Yes, I went from house to house, condo to condo, with my suitcase packed full of everything I needed to do hands and feet. My clients loved it. They didn't have to go anywhere or even get dressed. They could watch their favorite television programs while I worked on them. But most of all, they could sit in the comfort of their own home, waiting for their nails to completely dry. After all, a woman is really only helpless when her nail polish is wet!

During the one year I was a traveling manicurist, two of my closest friends from Park Avenue Stylists, hairdressers Dan and his wife, Nancy Dexter, decided to open a new salon in town called Dexter and Co. They needed a nail technician and I made myself available. I enjoyed my mobile manicure business but realized I needed to build more of a clientele, and it was difficult to do so while being mobile. Kelly had also left Park Avenue Stylists and was working with them. It simply made sense for me to join them, as well. We were all close friends and knew we worked well together.

We had some fun and interesting times. Starting out it always takes time to build a successful business, and we all knew that, with the exception of Kelly. He was booked constantly. The rest of us were slammed in the winter, but business would die down when the tourists returned home. After all, we were living and working in a ski resort, but not Kelly, he was always busy!

During the off season, when customers were scarce, often times Dan would put a note on the door that stated we would be back later. No time mentioned, just *later*. Then we would walk up Main Street to a well-known bar and restaurant, where we would stay two or three hours, eating and drinking. No mobile phones back then, thankfully. We were really enjoying our slow season.

However, we soon realized we didn't want to stay slow — not if we wanted to survive. Fortunately, we snapped out of this phase quickly and focused on building our businesses. I enjoyed that time with Dan and Nancy, as they were (and still are) two of the coolest people I have ever known.

It was easy to stay engaged in the salon, because there was never a dull moment. We had a lot of crazy-character patrons back then.

One winter, a woman came into our salon and wanted her hair cut and colored. But she refused to take her fur coat off because the coat hanger was too close to the front door. Dan proceeded to color her hair while she wore her fur. After she left, he confessed that he had actually got a couple of small drops of color on the coat.

Horrified, we asked, "What did you do?"

Dan was very soft spoken and he quietly told us. "I just waited until I started the haircut, spun her around and quickly snipped the color out. You couldn't even tell," he said.

Personally, I built a fairly decent clientele at Dexter and Co. and was happy there. We were busy enough to stay afloat, especially since we had Kelly, who at the time was really the best hairdresser in town. Everyone went to Kelly and everyone loved him. He was so busy, we used to joke he had one client in his chair, one in the shampoo bowl, one processing under the dryer, one standing at the desk, one walking through the door, and one on the phone…and it was true.

With that said, he would also disappear on a regular basis now and then. No call. No nothing. Just no Kelly for two or three days. Then all of a sudden, he would come in to work as if he had been there all along. No explanation, no excuse, no reason why. The clients that had been stood up were angry with him (and us). However, they'd rebook with him as if nothing was wrong. He was *that good*.

One day, Kelly did his usual disappearing act, and once again we called his home, his mother, his sister, desperately trying to find him. A week went by and we never heard back from him. We soon realized his clients weren't popping in for their appointments either. We thought maybe this time he'd done the right thing and called his clients to let them know he was ill. Only time would tell. We knew Kelly would rise from the ashes eventually, because he always did.

Except this time, it was in a very unexpected way.

Dan sat down with a cup of coffee and opened up the local paper, The Park Record. There was a full-page ad for a new, hip full service salon and spa in town called Vie Retreat. The ad was complete with pictures of their new employees...including Kelly.

He had resurfaced.

Vie Retreat definitely was up-and-coming. In short order it became known as *the* place to be as a stylist and as a customer. The few local salons (three or so back then) were all a bit nervous about Vie Retreat, even though no one would admit it. We all knew we had some serious competition.

# Capacity to See Beyond

*A*few months later, I started receiving calls from, Debra, one of the owners of Vie Retreat.

"Carly, are you *married* to the salon you work for?" she inquired straight to the point.

"Yes, I'm very happy here," I replied. And that was the honest truth.

"You come highly recommended and we only want the very best working here," Debra offered.

I was flattered and I have to admit, I was always pretty handy with a nail file, but my answer remained the same – no.

The calls continued every couple of weeks, asking if I was sure. Debra was persistent and she was determined, I could tell. I gave it considerable thought, but I loved Dan and Nancy! There it was. Clark and I hung out with them on a regular basis and I didn't want that friendship to end. I couldn't bear to hurt my friends. I was struggling between the friendship I had and what I thought I needed to move forward in my career. I weighed it back and forth. The Dexters were reasonable people. Surely, they would understand a business move. The friendship could continue. It may take some time, but I felt it was strong enough to survive. However, the struggle continued and it was real. It was going to take me quite some time to figure out the best possible decision for me, coupled with seemingly endless nights of sleep deprivation, I had to see beyond the friendship.

I was still working at Dexter and Co. in the winter of 1985, when Clark had a serious ski accident while teaching skiing at Park West Ski Resort. He had to have major surgery and was in the hospital for two weeks and in bed for five months. I think he was most upset about the doctors having to cut off his brand new teal colored ski suit!

I went back to work after the first week of caring for him. He called me several times a day in extreme pain. I kept track of the calls, and on call number fifteen, I couldn't take it anymore. By the time I got home he was hallucinating.

I loaded him into the Saab, and drove him straight back to LDS Hospital. I pulled up to the emergency room entrance, jumped out and grabbed a wheelchair.

I ran in, pushed him through the door, where I was met by two male aides, as I shouted, "You have got to take him back, because he is not better yet."

He was there another two days, while they discovered he was allergic to the pain medication, hence the hallucinations. The doctors released him from the hospital and from that time on it was Tylenol only for his pain, which really didn't cut it, but he had no choice. He had to live with the pain for a while longer and let the healing process run its course.

During all this I was still getting calls from Vie Retreat asking if I was ready to make the move. Debra was very persistent! Clark recuperated at home, so money was tight, particularly when I found out that he actually was free skiing on his own time when the accident occurred. I should have figured out they would not have let him teach skiing in the teal colored ski suit. I was beyond angry and most of all, I was worried. I was self-employed, with no health insurance; the bills began to flow in. Since he was free skiing, it was goodbye Workman's Compensation, hello medical bankruptcy.

We filed Chapter 13 and the next seven years were really tough. In spite of being content working at Dexter and Co., I thought the salon could not match Vie Retreat's offer and they confirmed my thoughts. It was time to move on and grow my business even more.

I gave the usual two-week notice, which seemed like the longest two weeks of my life. If you've ever had to work through a two-week notice, you know it seems like an eternity. It was a very long and stressful two weeks. It is especially hard when the feelings of friends are involved. I remember Clark asking Dan if he was going to "do something for me" before I left.

"Do what?" Dan asked in his calm, low and soft spoken tone.

"Well, like a party or something." Clark answered in his own well-meaning tone.

I was embarrassed as I stared down at the wood floor.

The look on Dan's face was priceless, as if he'd just been asked for his first-born.

Dan answered flatly, "No."

It wasn't until I owned my own salon years later that I realized just how difficult it is when people leave. When you throw friendship in the mix, it becomes very personal.

# 17

## Happy Disasters

Off I went to the new, hip, full service salon and spa, Vie Retreat, owned by two strong, competent and somewhat intimidating women, Ann and Debra. It was quite the change. The owners were happy to have me, and I was happy to be there. These ladies had thought of everything in this place, but I secretly wished they had installed a tanning bed. Yes, in those days I used the fake and bake freely, giving no thought to the damage I was doing to my skin. I pay the price these days.

Many of my clients from Dexter and Co., did not care for the new place. But they soon adapted, or pretended they did. Change is tough on all of us. We were just going into the busy season of winter, and I was one of three nail technicians working there. The competition was fierce! It was an adjustment for me, as I am not competitive at all. I tend to shy away from all of that.

One of the manicurists named Sue was the hardest one for me to be around. She did not like the fact that I had not been to school to learn the "proper" way to do nails, even though I had feverishly attended nail classes and seminars on a regular basis. The fact that I had not been to a nail school was unacceptable to her. She not only talked to the owners about it, but also to our clients.

Competition really is a weed in the garden of love. In order to please everyone, I started to sign up for any or all nail classes and competitions with local supply companies. I was also hoping Sue would get off my back, but my efforts didn't make her any happier. So to keep peace, I asked for her help in some training. That worked, but I couldn't stand sitting at her desk training with her while she smoked cigarettes. It seems so strange now, but back then, it was allowed. The law had not yet passed in Utah against smoking indoors in public places, and no one seemed to mind. It was the "norm" back then.

We had quite a few celebrities come into Vie Retreat during the ski season, and that was fun. I remember actress Louise Fletcher (Nurse Ratched from the movie, *One Flew Over the Cuckoo's Nest*) was in town for a film. I happened to get her for a pedicure and acrylic nail fill. She asked if I minded if she smoked. I thanked her for asking, but said I would appreciate it if she did not smoke because I didn't smoke, and the liquid I used for the acrylic nails was very flammable. She may not have liked it, but she went along with it. I worked on her every two weeks for a couple of months and I stayed strong on my policy of not smoking.

One of her appointments happened to be when I was going to be out of town, so we scheduled her with Sue. When I returned and she came in for her next regular appointment with me, I asked her how her service was while I was gone. She looked at me, and said, "It wasn't your work, but she did let me smoke."

We had some very interesting hairdressers working at Vie Retreat. One of them was a guy named Giovanni. He was good at what he did, and he knew it. Giovanni had tons of confidence, and he loved to pound his chest, but sometimes his boyish enthusiasm got the best of him. He was a married man and he loved his female clientele, often bragging, "I can bring you to orgasm just by shampooing your hair!" *Really?*

I never witnessed any evidence of this actually happening but that didn't stop Giovanni from continually boasting about it. One day as he was at the shampoo bowl trying to work his magic on his two o'clock appointment, in walked the husband of his ten o'clock appointment. The next thing we knew, water was going everywhere as the hose from the shampoo bowl flopped around and around and Giovanni was on the floor. The angry husband walked out, as Giovanni pulled himself up and grabbed a towel for his bleeding lip. The salon was quiet as Debra and Ann guessed what had just happened; *jealous husband, no doubt.*

You would think that might help Giovanni to cool his jets, but no such luck. Ruth Westheimer, better known as Dr. Ruth the American sex therapist, media personality and author came walking in one winter day and he happened to get her. I don't know what happened back at the shampoo bowl, but we all heard her say, "Boy, have you got a lot to learn!" in that well-parodied accent of hers!

Yes, Giovanni thought he was all that and a bag of chips! He strutted around Vie like he was *God's gift to women!* In my eyes, he wasn't even a good looking man, being overweight and so full of himself made him even less attractive to me.

Although, looking back it was pretty funny when Giovanni accidentally used floor wax on a client's hair. The cleaners had poured it into an empty conditioner bottle but didn't label it. We all watched in horror as Giovanni tried to get his hands out of her hair, saturated with floor wax! They were completely stuck, not to mention the toll it took on her baby fine hair!

There were a lot of arousing, interesting and sometimes downright strange stories at Vie Retreat. I remember when a top city official's wife came in and asked for Debra's advice on the big, puffy, dark bags under her eyes.

"Would that expensive Rene Guinot eye cream you sell help my eyes?" she wondered.

Debra looked carefully at her eyes, touching the problem areas, testing for puffiness and without judgment, caution or disrespect, in all honesty asked, "Have you ever considered plastic surgery?"

The woman left without buying the eye cream. I still see her on occasion and she looks great so who knows! One thing about Debra, she didn't sugar coat anything and you could count on that. Plus, this was her expertise. She knew her skincare and makeup like no other!

She always had our backs, though. I remember a tough client who wanted her haircut into a "bob." After Paulina, the hairdresser, finished with her new look (which, by the way looked a thousand times better) she started screaming at her to the point she had her in tears. Then the client stormed up to the front desk where Debra sat and continued her rant.

Debra listened quietly for a moment. The angry client became louder and louder as she went on and on and on.

Finally, Debra stood up and said exasperated as she hit her hands on the counter, "My God! It's only hair!"

We never saw the ranting woman again, but Debra had a point. I loved how Debra knew what was important in life and what wasn't. Unfortunately, she learned it the hard way. She lost her only daughter at a young age about four months before I began working there and still she soldiered on. God bless her.

I worked late one evening, which was not unusual for me. I finished up with my client, said thanks and told her goodbye. I locked the door behind her and went back to my desk to clean up for the day. I sat at my desk, when all of the sudden I heard a small thumping noise coming from downstairs against the wall, followed by a quiet, "Hello?"

My nail table was at the top of the stairs against the back wall so I stood up and looked down. I saw a woman "feeling her way" up the stairs. Her eyes were closed as she struggled to carefully find the next step.

"Oh hi, I'm coming. Please stand still." I instructed her as I rushed down the stairs. I was scared she might lose her balance and fall backwards as she was close to the top. "Are you okay?" I asked with concern. *Who the hell is this and what is she doing here at seven-thirty at night!*

The helpless woman answered, "I was getting my lashes dyed and I fell asleep. I think Debra forgot about me."

I sighed and in the calmest voice I could muster up I asked, "What time was your lash dye appointment?" as I took her by the arm and began to lead her back downstairs.

"Five o'clock," the woman answered. Five o'clock? *Oh, shit!*

I guided her back to the room and helped her up on the bed. I retrieved the now cold bowl of water used to rinse her lashes and excused myself.

"I will be right back."

"NO! Please don't leave," she demanded.

"I am just going to the bathroom to warm up the water so I can remove the dye. I promise it will only take a second." I reassured her.

"Okay, but please hurry back!"

"I promise," I said as I walked out, leaving the door open.

I filled up the bowl as fast as I could and went back into the room. I removed the dye from her lashes and she asked, "How are they?"

"Well, they're still there, and they look great. Nice and dark," I said thinking she was lucky she was a very dark brunette.

We walked upstairs and I reached to unlock the front door.

"Wait! I need to pay. What do I owe you?"

"No charge," I told her with a smile. *Please keep your mouth shut though,* I thought "somewhat" jokingly!

We already had a bad experience with a man in town, whom Ann had talked into purchasing for his wife (as a Christmas present) a series of ten massages from our top massage therapist, Trent. Long story short, his wife left him and moved in with Trent shortly after. Debra and Ann were both mortified! We didn't need the eyelash story on top of that one!

I went home the night of the eyelash mishap and thought about not telling Debra. She had so much to deal with as it was, but also worried if I didn't tell her, I could be in big trouble. The next morning, I went in bright and early. Debra sat at the front desk preparing for the day. I didn't know what to do or what to expect. I hadn't worked there long enough to really know either of them very well.

Debra looked up as I walked in, "Good morning," she said cheerfully.

"Good morning, Debra, how are you today?"

"Just fine," she answered and I believed her. She was in a good mood.

"Um, Debra did you forget something last night?' I asked.

She looked up over the counter and said, "Like what?"

"The eyelash dye client downstairs," I answered a bit hesitantly.

"*OH. MY. GOD,*" she shouted. Then she paused and began to laugh hysterically! We both did.

I told her the whole story and she called the client immediately to apologize. The client accepted her apology and they had a good laugh together. It was a source of amusement in the salon for quite a while and the client remained a client. A sincere apology goes a long way!

I decided I needed to make money all year long, not just during ski season. I made the unprecedented conscious decision to book with locals first, then tourists. It was tough in the beginning. I definitely had my time of sitting around, but I hung in there. I began walking up and down Main Street, going to local businesses, introducing myself and handing out my business cards. I never ate at a restaurant without leaving one or two on the table. I rewarded extra good service by writing "good for one manicure" on the back of the card. I handed them out to my children's teachers, their friends' mothers, my neighbors and anyone else I could think of. I gave away quite a few manicures, pedicures, and full sets of acrylic nails, but eventually it paid off. I had a clientele and I was busy. My clientele continued to grow; especially when they figured out they could get in to see me all year long, even in the winter. They liked my work and they liked me. They said they found it therapeutic.

Over the years, I would run into clients who had taken off their acrylic nails for whatever reason and they would ask if they could just come in and sit and talk with me for an hour. "I don't even need the nails," they would say. They trusted and confided in me and I was proud of that accomplishment. Once when one of my clients and I had just finished a long and serious conversation about her marital woes, she looked at me and in all seriousness said, "Just you and my priest, Carly."

During year four of our marriage, Clark and I decided to buy a house, which was under construction. In fact, it was merely a hole in the ground. Everyone asked us if we were sure we wanted to build a house together, as that was deemed one of the hardest things on a relationship. They all wanted to know just how strong our marriage was.

My answer was always the same. "I can handle it, I've been through knee surgery!"

# 18
## Pink Glove Service

We had superior hairdressers and workers at Vie Retreat. Debra and Ann made sure of that as they molded us into an exceptional, stylish and hip team. This was the winning combination the owners were searching for. Giovanni had been let go for an indiscretion with a female client in the bathroom downstairs. Sue had moved to Texas. Kelly had done one of his disappearing acts once again, but the owners didn't just let him show up and take up where he left off. They fired him. The Dexter's had closed their salon and Nancy was now working with us. My sister, Rebecka, was also there. She was eighteen and had just finished beauty school. It was her first real job in a real salon.

We had very talented estheticians, massage therapists, and of course, manicurists. Ann and Debra now professed that they had the cream of the crop; the best of the best and their expectations were high. We had to look and act professional at all times, wearing only black and white, separate or in combinations. My closet to this day is filled with black clothing! I learned so much from these two women. They both were the epitome of style and grace. Looking back on it, they really molded and shaped all of us.

The owners really were two sides of the same coin, when it came to running a business and managing people, clients and workers. They backed each other up on all decisions big and small. If they disagreed, they did it in private, I am sure of that. They had each other's backs and were a united front. Kind of like a great parenting team!

Debra thought it important to find out everyone's astrological sign, while Ann rolled her eyes about it, but always with a smile. Debra gave us all makeovers, strongly suggesting we lose the foundation, makeup and lip-gloss. "If you need to cover something up, you only need to use lipstick and powder."

Debra also focused on good skin care, sunscreen and a natural look. (No wonder there was no tanning bed!) But let's face it, she knew her stuff. She was a natural beauty, a model and an actress. I quickly learned she was all of those things on the inside, as well.

Ann focused on making the customers feel at home, as she basically knew everyone in town. She brought them coffee and pastries from Mrs. Fields Bakery across the street as she chatted warmly with them. Ann had the ability to calm everyone. She had an unassuming smile and a welcoming "Texas" way about her, not to mention she was extremely intelligent.

Ann and Debra both had an innate sense of style and taste, a huge work ethic, but above it all was the way they treated everyone that was beyond impressive.

Our customer's happiness and satisfaction was number one, and if for some reason it wasn't…well…it meant dismissal. Even the top moneymakers were not beyond getting fired and we all witnessed that beginning with Kelly. We also had a top esthetician, Shilo, grossing about five hundred dollars a day. She became a bit of a diva, professing she was too valuable to be dismissed. Not so! We were called in for a meeting early one morning and were informed Shilo was no longer working there.

We all sat there in complete shock as Debra told us, "If anyone else thinks they are irreplaceable…think again." In essence, we all walked the line. That was one of the many things that made the salon so successful. They handled Shilo's dismissal just like pros, telling her clients *Shilo decided to move on.* Then they put them with someone else in the salon whom, in the owners' own words, was equally as brilliant.

I remember one of Shilo's clients coming in one afternoon after Shilo was gone. This client had become good friends with Debra and Ann. When she asked what had really happened, Debra promptly replied, "I fired her ass," and then added, "I've been dying to tell someone that!"

Debra also reminded us that we didn't just "get" these clients, meaning they didn't just magically appear at the door, and suddenly decide on us. She sat on the phone telling people how great we all were. Then it became up to us to prove her right and keep them coming back. I found it interesting how well Debra put us together. She relied on her ability to match clients with the perfect person. Personality along with talent and ability was key in her matchmaking effort. Not to mention, the astrological pull.

When you find yourself in a perfect situation like that you consistently do your best, because people *pay* you good money to do a great job, and you're appreciated for it.

So you just do it! It's a self-fulfilling cycle.

Well…good things don't always work out to last forever. If they did we would all still be working at Vie Retreat. We all know for whatever reasons things can change. One day I was asked to basically be on my own as an independent contractor instead of an employee. Collecting my own money and paying my salon expenses, seemed like a better move at the time. Little did I know, it was much harder figuring out the expenses and such on my own. I soon came to realize after a few months, I really was better off running the show by myself, and for myself.

Feelings once again were hurt and both of the owners were angry. That part was very difficult for me and although I gave the dreaded two-week notice, my things were packed for me the next day and my final check was issued. Debra did not mess around. In fact, I was actually charged for the three plastic bags they put my belongings in. Yes, and the fifty-four cents per bag deducted from that final check. Debra was a good business woman and she was good at making a point! I got it loud and clear.

When I left, my sister Rebecka stayed and continued to work at Vie Retreat. Back then, Rebecka and I were much closer than we are today, so working apart was difficult. We both missed being together so much that she would visit me often at my new place. We would go to lunch and discuss how to figure out a way to work together again.

One day I heard about a salon closing because the owner moved out in the night and skipped town. It was actually Park Avenue Stylists, where I had worked before. My sister and I had talked about opening our own salon, so I called the landlord of Park Avenue Stylists and we met him the next day to take a look at the salon. We walked in expecting a turnkey business, only to find a large empty room. The previous owner didn't leave anything behind; she even took the plate covers for the lights and outlets! With a $5,000 loan (with interest) from our parents, we became business owners and our salon, Sisters, was born!

# 19

## Watch Your Step...Sister!

O wning a salon is an interesting business and definitely a challenge. I learned that it is rare to find someone who cares about your business as much as you do. I also learned that a person who feels appreciated will always do more than what is expected. I think Rebecka and I both fell short in this area, never being business owners prior to this venture. We had some great workers and some not-so-great workers. I learned to truly appreciate the latter and soon understood Debra and Ann's concerns as owners of Vie Retreat. Being a working owner is very hard, plus there are so many ongoing expenses. But we both tried our best to make the salon warm and welcoming.

One Sunday, I went in to do some inventory and paperwork. Of course, we had a landline phone and I noticed the message light was blinking. I pressed play and heard one of my clients, Corrine's, voice. A new, hip and very large salon had opened up recently and Corrine felt the need to tell me she no longer would be coming to Sisters for her nail care services. "Please cancel my standing nail appointments. I'm going to the new salon from here on out. Your salon just isn't nice enough, Carly."

I was crushed. I stared at the phone for what seemed like an hour. I cried for what seemed like longer than an hour. Finally, I took a deep breath and pulled myself together. I walked over to the desk drawer and pulled out my thank you cards. I composed myself as I put pen to paper.

*Dear Corrine,*

*I received your voice message today. I want to thank you for your past patronage, I truly appreciate it. If I can be of service to you in the future, please don't hesitate to call and best of luck to you. Thanks again,*
*Carly.*

I stuffed it in the envelope with my business card. I addressed it, stamped it and mailed it first thing the next morning. Taking the high road is not always easy, but I felt I did do exactly that. Months later, I ran into her at a fundraiser. I smiled and said hello. I could tell she was embarrassed as she stammered out these words: "Hi Carly, I've uh, uh been uh meaning to call you. I got your uh, uh nice note, um…thank you," Corrine said looking down.

I watched her silently as she stuttered out her apology.

"I, uh, was going to call you, I was, uh, wondering if I could uh get a pedicure from you, uh sometime soon?"

Wow, she was acting so nervous! This surprised me, as I always thought of her as being so tough, strong and resilient!

I answered her with a smile, "Oh, I am so sorry, I am completely booked, but thanks for thinking of me, Corrine."

I turned and walked away with my head held high and that is sort of like the high road, right?

One interesting and funny thing is, by and large, most people stop tipping you when you own the salon, because they have the strange notion that you are making more money! I always marveled at that. Ann and Debra were so right when they warned me. "When you become a salon owner, your expenses are more than doubled." I didn't realize that until I became one. Fortunately, Rebecka and I were working owners. We didn't have to rely solely on our workers to make money for the salon. However, we did count heavily on them to do their jobs in order to help us cover the ever mounting salon expenses.

Working in a resort town in the service industry can be challenging and rewarding all at the same time. We had our share of walk-in traffic at Sisters, and we tried to accommodate those impromptu customers, as well as our beloved locals.

Once, just after my sister returned from her 6-week maternity leave, this difficult tourist came strolling in (without an appointment) first thing that morning. We were able to fit her in for a cut and color. I was busy at my desk doing nails, when Rebecka went in the back room to mix up the color. I asked the lady, in hopes to soften her a bit, if I could get her some coffee.

"Yes, cream and sugar," she replied coldly.

"Is the powdered white stuff okay?" I asked, referring to Coffee Mate.

The look on her face told me it was not.

Rebecka piped up from the back room, "I brought some real creamer in with me. I'll be right out with the coffee."

I sat down and began working on my client. Rebecka emerged with the color in one hand and coffee in the other. The client contently sipped her precious coffee with cream quietly as

Rebecka applied her hair color. I didn't realize it at the time, but Rebecka did confess later that day, she came to work that morning armed with a breast pump! The difficult tourist did not seem to mind, she even asked Rebecka for a second cup.

Learning to work with family was definitely a challenge. I love my sister, but it turned out not as a business partner. She felt the same way about me. Both of us had very different ideas about running a business. I was always very responsible and careful with money, while Rebecka was carefree when it came to finances, both personal and professional. In fact, our parents knew this when they loaned us the money to start the salon. I remember my mother telling me not to put anything in Rebecka's name due to her lack of financial responsibility and I agreed.

We had an accountant, Shelley, who helped us with the books, payroll and taxes. One day she came in after she received the fourth garnishment on Rebecka. Shelley handed me the paperwork. I looked it over and gave Rebecka an irritated glance as she worked her magic on a difficult head of hair.

I looked back at Shelley as she said," Rebecka has an interesting way of dealing with her bills, ignore them until they go to judgment, and then she gets her wages garnished and takes care of the debt that way." Shelley shook her head in amazement.

It wasn't until years later that Rebecka no longer had to worry about her finances. She married a wealthy man who took care of her and her children very well. In fact, she had a couple of marriages like that! I once visited her at her new residence, a palatial 6,000-square-foot home. Her new husband had surprised her with a brand new Lexus before he left on yet another business trip. I looked around at her new digs and shook my head. "How do you always manage to do this?" I asked curiously.

"Do what?" Rebecka answered coyly.

"You find these wealthy men, move into their nice homes where you have no living expenses, they buy you expensive cars, and then they are never home!" I observed as Rebecka laughed. "I'm serious, sister, you've got skills. You should teach a class!"

We both laughed, but I have to say this last marriage is probably the one for her. My sister is happier than I've ever known her to be. She is married to a wonderful man, and our relationship as sisters is stronger than ever and that makes me happy. We have come back around and are in each other's lives because after all, we are family.

Now let's get back to us working together at Sisters Salon.

We had a good business going. We were busy and clients seemed to enjoy coming into the salon. I was there six days a week and sometimes even on Sundays. It was harder for Rebecka to be there as often because she had small children. I had teenagers still at home, which can be much harder to control their comings and goings. They don't take teenagers at a day care facility! Even though I knew it was difficult for my sister to be there as often as I was, I still resented the fact that I was there all the time. I was exhausted when I was home coupled with the fact I received a huge amount of grief from Clark.

He wanted me home more often and understandably so. This led to arguments both at work and at home. The stress was mounting and I didn't know how to handle it. What was the solution? Unfortunately, it felt like there was no good solution. Life at home was getting harder and harder. Clark was doing his thing, being a ski instructor and detailing cars, which was good for him. But he felt like all I did was work at the salon. He was right, and I had to deal with coming home to an angry husband on a regular basis. The stress was mounting.

In an effort to see each other more often, I asked Clark if he wanted to clean the salon every morning before he started his day. He was in between seasons and needed the work anyway. Clark agreed. We needed a good cleaner who was trustworthy and Clark was definitely that! My folks affectionately called him "Mr. Clean."

We only had one vehicle at the time, so we rode into town together, he cleaned the salon spotless and went about his day. We paid him an hourly wage and he received a paycheck every two weeks, even giving him a W-2 at the end of the year.

Clark really was the best cleaner in town, but eventually being my janitor got to him. We continued to argue and he complained constantly about me spending too much time at the salon. It became an unbearable cycle and ultimately he filed for a divorce. It was hard on all of us and there was a time when we didn't even speak to one another, but I am very happy to say we found our way back to being close friends. Clark is a really good man, full of integrity kindness and love. My children, early on, became his children, as he was the only father they ever really knew. We were all extremely lucky to have those years with him. He gave up a lot when he embraced all of us with open arms.

I used to remind my children of that fact as often as I could, particularly when they were upset with him, as kids get from time to time. When Clark and I married, life, as Clark knew it, ceased to exist; he gave up his freedom, time and his money! Raising four children is expensive, but he never once complained about it. In fact, a couple of years after we were divorced, I ran into John, a Delta pilot we both knew at a local restaurant. He asked me, "How is Clark doing?"

I replied, "I think he is doing fine. We are divorced now."

"You're kidding! he exclaimed. "You're divorced?"

Before I could answer, John said with a puzzled look on his face, "But you guys were so nice!"

"We're still nice, John, we're just no longer married," I answered with a smile.

# Tinted Love

**M**eanwhile at Sisters, Rebecka and I continued to work like mad, not only on our precious clientele, but also on our relationship as sisters. Funny thing, a few clients asked us where the salon name came from and who were the sisters? I realized, while working at Vie Retreat, when clients asked for a recommendation for a hairdresser I would recommend Rebecka without saying she was my sister. I didn't want people to think that I was recommending her because of that. She was just a very talented hairdresser (she still is), especially with hair color, but we had our struggles personally and professionally.

Never being salon owners was just one of those struggles. I felt like owning a salon was like running a daycare. The hairdressers call in sick when they aren't feeling inspired or particularly creative that day, because they consider themselves *artists*, which they really are. We had good and bad hairdressers who became friends, and good and bad hairdressers who became enemies. I learned early on to treat employees like they make a difference and they will. I tried very hard to keep that in the forefront. I do remember one of our hairdressers saying to me at the end of a particularly busy day, "Carly, thank you for always saying thank you to me, that's so nice to hear." Even so, when the time comes, they make the decision to move on and it's always hard.

But as a salon owner you *do* take it personally.

I quickly came to understand firsthand the anger, hurt and disappointment from the other salon owners. Nevertheless, you just have to keep going and respect their choice, as hard as it may be.

The infamous *front desk person* was equally as challenging. We couldn't impress upon that person (there were many) the importance of the job. We often ended up not having anyone, because that was better than having someone awful, or even mediocre, at the job. People either lacked the emotional maturity to be the front desk person, or couldn't keep the appointment book straight.

I was very picky about that book. Good, legible handwriting was a must. We had a front desk training manual that was required reading, but instead I would often find them pouring over the Victoria Secret catalog. I guess good lingerie won out over customer service. It was very frustrating. The seven years we were open, I think we only had two women who actually worked out well as front desk people. I had the fun job of dismissing the ones that didn't work out. In fact, that was part of my job description, as my sister was too scared to do it. I wore a deep purple jacket (a power color, I was told) on the days I had to fire someone. I would do the deed, and then call the town locksmith to change the locks. My sister would cut his hair in exchange for his services.

I remember one particular day I called him to change a lock.

"Who is it this time?" he asked.

"You're going to have to find a new hairdresser, I replied solemnly, and I will cut you a check."

Yes, it was Rebecka. My sister and I had run our course, so to speak. We met and discussed our situation and it was a mutual agreement that we part ways. Although we both decided this was the best thing to do, that period was tough. Forget about the family barbeques! I tried for about a year to make it alone, but with the loss of income, not only my sister's, but also other key people who had left prior to her, it just wasn't possible. Truth be told, I was really tired of managing people, and running a salon was all consuming. I just wanted to manage myself and do what I loved. I didn't want to worry about hairdressers not showing up, or product orders, or paying the light bill. An opportunity arose and I sold the salon to one of my new hairdressers.

Sisters was gone. R.I.P

# Vegas Night Life

$O$ ne of the things I love about my job is that most of my clients become friends. It is a forced social life, coupled with the fact that I love being at home, and I enjoy being alone. I've often wondered if the reason for that enjoyment stems from the fact that I am with people all day long. But I am smart enough to realize that being alone is all very glamorous until someone needs a kidney! I once had a client who said to me, "If Mr. Right comes and knocks at your door, one thing is for certain, you will be home."

And she was right.

This particular close friend started out as a client. Her name is Riley and she is a beautiful blonde with three equally beautiful teenage girls. One day she invited me to join her in Las Vegas for the weekend. She was going on a business trip for a few days and wanted some company. I agreed, as I was excited to get out of the cold for the weekend.

We arrived in sunny Vegas, went to our hotel, and checked in. Ask we rode the elevator up to our room, she pleasantly made conversation with everyone that got on and off the elevator, smiling and being ever so friendly.

I envied that.

We walked into our room, changed quickly, and headed for the pool. While we relaxed and chatted, she told me I needed to get out more, be friendlier to people when they approached me, particularly the male species.

I am very shy when it comes to that.

"No one is going to knock at your door and say, 'Hi Carly, I heard you were single, do you want to go out?' Not even Mr. Right."

I laughed and thought to myself. *Is this going around?*

"I'm serious!" she reinforced, slightly irritated that I wasn't taking her advice to heart.

I told her I'd think about it.

The rest of our time at the pool she did some paper work while we took in the warm rays from the sun. After a couple of hours, we had enough sun bathing, so we went back to our room to get ready for the evening.

Riley showered while I applied my makeup in the other room.

Suddenly she popped out of the bathroom and said, "It's okay if you put your make-up on in here. I grew up with four sisters and one bathroom!"

I laughed. "Thanks, I said appreciatively, but I already have my makeup spread out on the bed along with my clothes."

We arrived at the restaurant on time and each ordered a glass of wine, as we sat down at our table. The waiter came back, wine in hand. I ordered a Caesar salad with chicken and Riley ordered a fruit plate. Following dinner, we went to a magic show in the hotel that started about 10:00 p.m. We were both dressed in stylish, hip tops, and mini skirts, along with sassy high heels.

Riley was a friend of the magician so we were invited backstage after the show for food and drink. We spent quite a few hours with the magician and the cast, talking, laughing, eating, and drinking. It was a wonderful night.

Afterward, as we walked through the lobby at about 3:00 a.m. heading back to our room, people were everywhere! It was like the middle of the day. Yes, we were definitely in Vegas! We made our way towards the elevator and I stopped short. Riley was behind me talking to four attractive, nicely built young men, one of whom was in a wheelchair. She crouched down, beside the wheelchair, holding on to the side of it, talking to him intently and smiling, being her usual confident, friendly self.

I really envied that.

Suddenly she got up, abruptly, smiled and waved goodbye, and walked towards me at a very fast pace. She grabbed my arm, and whispered, "Let's get out of here."

We rushed to the elevator, got on and watched as the door shut tightly. She leaned the back of her head against the wall and she closed her eyes, obviously stressed.

"What's the matter?" I asked, totally confused.

"Those guys wanted to know if we were working," she exclaimed.

"Working?" I asked naïvely.

"Working *the hotel*," she replied wide-eyed.

In shock, I thought to myself, *that's what you get for being so friendly*!

Then I looked at Riley and said,"Wait! Who was going to take the guy in the wheelchair?"

She gave me a look, as only Riley could and shook her head. She wasn't amused.

Then I added, "I don't know if that's a compliment or not!"

Riley said, "I'm going to take it as one, but please don't tell my girls."

I promised I wouldn't and I kept that promise.

# Like it Loud

*S*hortly after the demise of Sisters, I went to work in a relatively new place in town called Seasons Body Retreat. I talked to several salons and decided this shop would be a nice fit for me. There were no hairdressers, as this was primarily a body treatment place, specializing in massage, facials, manicures, and pedicures.

I did mostly acrylic nails then, and 95% of my clientele wore them. The owners were reluctant at first about the acrylic nail odor, but quickly came around when they realized that I brought two-hundred-plus clients into their business. They put me in a small room, no window, no music, just me and my air purifier.

The front desk couldn't book my appointments due to the volume, so I had to get my own phone and do it in between clients. Didn't matter, I just wanted to do what I loved. Plus, I actually made more money than when I owned Sisters, and without the headache and stress of it all.

Once again my clientele followed me, and by and large, most were happy. It was a beautiful, serene setting, but it had one big drawback. It was so quiet…and they wanted it to stay that way. The door to my room was to be closed at all times. It was normal to have the receptionist pop her head in and "shush" us.

If I wasn't told to be quiet, I was told to turn down the music (I had brought in my own CD player), or to turn up the air purifier!

One morning I came in, closed the door to my room and began going over my day. I looked up at the door and something was different. It took a minute, but I soon realized what it was; a brass plated sign on the back of my door, inside of my room that read "Quiet Please."

Not a handwritten sign, but an engraved plaque, bolted into the door! I had two very loud clients who were convinced it was put up specifically for them. It was hard to say, as it was pretty much a toss up between Dixie, Beth and me! We all had a good laugh about it. I could only take being "shushed" for about six months. It was time to start looking for another place to work.

I had a good reputation in Park City, and a large clientele, so I interviewed with salons and decided on a place called L & Company. There were a lot of things that factored into making my decision, but right at the top of my list was the front desk person. They had the best one I had ever come across. Her name was Terri and she was smart, funny, friendly, and incredibly efficient. I loved her and so did my clientele. She knew her job and she did it well. She made my clients feel so at home, but later confessed that she was worried when I came to work there. I was surprised at what she said next.

"I told the owner we needed to clean up the place before your clients starting coming in." I smiled as I looked around the place. It was not Vie Retreat, but it was a nice, clean and comfortable salon.

"At least until we can dumb them down," she said with a smile.

One day as I was waiting for my client, a winter tourist walked in and asked Terri if she could get a manicure. I was the only manicurist there, so she brought her back to me.

"Can you give this lady a manicure sometime soon?" asked Terri.

I looked at my watch.

"I have someone coming in twenty minutes but I could give you a quick one until she comes," I told the lady.

"Anything you can do would be great, I really need it. It's so dry here."

"Well, let's get started." I pointed to my client chair. "I'm Carly. What's your name?"

'I'm Cynthia, thanks for taking me. I hope it's not your lunch hour."

I shook my head no as I smiled and thought about how I never took a lunch hour. No time.

As I began to work I noticed on her right thumb she had a huge cut.

"What happened here?" I asked with concern.

"I guess it's from the dryness here. It split open about a week ago and I can't get it to heal," she answered.

I looked closely at her thumb.

"That's really a bad one. Would you like me to fix it up for you when we do the manicure?" I asked. She looked puzzled.

"How would you fix it up?" Cynthia inquired.

I began to explain.

"Well, after you soak in the anti-bacterial water, I will dry your thumb and then try to trim up some of that dead skin around the slit. I will see if I can file it flush before I moisturize with an oil infused with tea tree oil among other healing properties. Then I will glue it for you."

"Glue it?" she asked with a look of surprise.

"Yes, I answered, putting the glue on it will help encourage those layers to grow back together more quickly."

"No, thanks. My husband said he would take me to the doctor if it wasn't better by tomorrow."

"Okay," I said and finished her manicure.

Cynthia went up to the front to thank Terri as she left.

Two days later, Cynthia returned and asked Terri if she could speak with me.

Terri brought her back, "You remember Cynthia."

"Of course, I said looking up from my pedicure client, how are you?"

"I'm fine, Carly. I won't keep you, but I went to the doctor about my thumb yesterday."

I worried she was there to tell me I shouldn't be using the glue or playing doctor for that matter, *but au contraire!*

Cynthia continued, "The doctor cleaned it up, trimmed the skin and then he *glued* it and charged me $155.00! I could have had it done with the price of my manicure."

She seemed annoyed.

I smiled and said, "Well, next time, Cynthia."

The hairdressers employed at L and Company were very talented. They were young and energetic and it was a fun place to work. We all got along well and the energy was good. I finally felt as if I had found my employment home. I had landed.

But no matter where you land, there is always going to be a few people who don't like the change. I get that. I acknowledged their feelings and sympathized with them, as it was hard for me as well. Change takes time. Soon we all adjusted and accepted the change and they were seemingly content. It didn't take as long as my other moves, but I believe this was largely in part due to the welcoming staff. They spoke to every client as they walked in, offering them coffee, tea or sparkling water. It was like being back with Ann and Debra. I missed that with the other places I tried. Clients would come in and begin to tell me how much they enjoyed this place. A happy clientele is a must in this business.

## 23
## Funny Bunny

There is always at least one client that makes you want to scream. This was Bunny, and she always dressed in white. I truly did enjoy her personally, however, her checks would never clear. My accountant suggested that I give up depositing them, as it made her bookwork much harder. I started calling the automated service at the bank to see if her checks would clear. Then I made a special trip to the one location of her bank in Salt Lake City. The teller actually started laughing when I asked if Bunny's check would clear. He apologized as he tried to compose himself. I had no choice but to switch her to a cash-only basis.

Then it began.

All of the excuses and all the promises of *next time*. I'm a nice person who doesn't like confrontation, so I would just go along. More often than not, she would come in with a twenty-dollar bill towards her ever mounting balance. Often, she wouldn't even have a twenty. She would simply tell me her husband would bring it in later, and I always believed her. That was not very smart of me, as it was never the case.

Bunny was the only client I ever had to fire and it was hard. It took me years of her promises and her occasional payments of twenty dollars here and there before I cut her loose. Before that, she continued coming in every Friday at three, for her weekly services and payment excuses. Finally, I got tough with her. I took a big, deep breath as I told her that I shouldn't have to chase money around that I had already earned. I informed her that she owed me over six hundred dollars. (Of course, this was in a message that I left on her home and cell phones, since she never answered any of her calls.) I told her until she caught up, I had to take her off of my books.

I didn't hear back from her all week.

Then on Friday at three, she walked in for her standing appointment. I almost fainted. I made sure I had someone in her spot that day just in case. I had a feeling this would happen. I asked her if she had received my messages.

"No, where did you leave the message?" she asked with a scowl on her face.

My voice was shaking as I told her, "Your home phone and your cell phone."

With that, she walked into the waiting area, pulled out her cell phone and sat down to find my messages. *As if!*

She stormed back into my room and angrily said, "I've been in the hospital with swine flu!"

This was a small town then, and I knew better. The truth was, actually, she was at a birthday party that exact weekend. She had been spotted!

She slammed down an envelope on my desk and said, "There's your money!"

Then she stormed out, slamming the door so hard I was surprised the glass window in it didn't break.

My hands shook, as I absolutely hate confrontations. I avoid them at all costs, obviously!

The client in the chair was worried, "Are you okay, Carly?"

I managed to answer, "Yes."

Clearly, I wasn't, but I pretended to be and got through her acrylic nail fill. I was embarrassed. I apologized and thanked her when she left.

I continued with my day, and that evening began my deposit. I opened the envelope Bunny left me to find my money inside. Yes of course, another twenty-dollar bill. I subtracted it off her total and closed the IOU book.

*Oh, Bunny*, I thought to myself, as I shook my head.

Although, many years later, I have to admit, as much as she drove me crazy, I couldn't help but feel for her when I heard the news of her husband's passing. I sent a card expressing my condolences to her in Colorado. I didn't hear back from her, but that was okay. A few months later, I heard from a mutual friend that she had passed away, as well. The friend emailed me a copy of her obituary from the newspaper in Colorado Springs. Very few people had heard this news in Park City. I called our local paper and explained that she was a long-term resident who was deceased. I inquired about the cost to put the obituary in the local paper. I told them I was not related to her, but that she had no children or living relatives, and she was an only child. I just wanted to let her old friends know. They gave me a deal at half price. It would be in the next edition.

When I returned home that evening, my husband and I sat down with a glass of wine and began to discuss the day.

I told him I paid for Bunny's obituary, he stared at me in disbelief.

"Did you really?" he asked.

I answered, "Yes."

He looked at me with some confusion.

Before he could say anything else I said, "I'll just add it to her bill."

And with that I closed Bunny's IOU book for the last time.

# 24
## Recessionista

I have an array of clients who, unlike Bunny, regularly pay, but still can be challenging, especially when they leave you. This is thirty-plus years later, and it's still emotionally hard for me that they left. I've spent years sitting across from these clients, who became friends, holding their hands, rubbing their feet, confiding in them about my life, learning about their lives, and listening all about their children, husbands and pets. It is really hard when they go.

I had one long-time client named Stephanie, and for many years she told me that if her husband made plans the same time as her every-other-week nail appointment, all hell would break loose.

"Nothing comes between me and my nail appointment, and Randy knows that," she exclaimed proudly.

Nothing except the downturn of the economy in 2008.

Stephanie sat teary-eyed as she told me, "This will have to be my last visit to the salon. I am so sorry, Carly, but I can no longer afford to come in. Randy's work has come to a standstill."

"That's okay," I told her.

But deep down inside I couldn't let go of my disappointment. Stephanie was a good friend, a very close friend and confidante, not to mention a long-term client. I was beyond sad. I was devastated.

It was so much more than giving up the income Stephanie provided me. I was truly going to miss her. I decided to give her a couple of gift certificates. Stephanie was appreciative, even bringing me a plant or a bottle of wine.

*Once the economy improved, she would be back,* I thought.

A few years passed and the economy did improve. I ran into her at an outdoor concert. She had a nice pedicure and her nails were done. We hugged and talked about our kids, and even took a picture together. I saw her on several other occasions, pedicure and nails done, but she never did come back to me.

Times like these do make me question *what did I do wrong?* I was always told it was either price or personality. I knew my prices were right in line with the other salons. But I couldn't figure out for the life of me what happened. I started to feel badly about myself and question my work. Finally, for my own emotional health and well-being, I just had to let it go. I still see Stephanie on occasion, and still consider her a friend, even though she is no longer a client.

I have another client, Lilly, who comes in sporadically who is one of those ladies who seems tough until you get to know her. I must admit she intimidated me the first few times she came in. Then we became friends and I actually grew to love her. Lilly was so appreciative of my work.

After our appointment was over, she held up her hands and said, "Life is good. I have ten perfect nails. I can't stop staring, it's like having little Monet's on my fingers!"

That's when you smile and stop doubting yourself and your work. Those clients really make it all worthwhile.

I did have several acrylic nail clients over the years that decided to take them off and it is quite the process. You have to be very careful, trying to preserve what is left of the natural nail.

One client in particular named Kate came in to have her acrylic nails removed, but was curious about the process.

As I started to explain that there were a couple of ways to do it, she waved her hand and stopped me mid sentence.

"Just go ahead and take them off. I don't need to know how."

Once I began, she pulled her hand back and said with a concerned look, "But I'm not looking for pain, either!"

I laughed and assured her, "Don't worry, I will be extra careful."

I remember when I put the next big thing on her nails…Shellac! After a couple of months, Kate came in for her final time.

She confessed she felt "trapped."

She just wanted the Shellac nails off and to get her own nails in some sort of resemblance to healthy. To this day, Kate is no longer a regular client, but when she needs her toes and fingers done, she calls me and I appreciate it.

# Up Front and Personal

I am sure there are a myriad of reasons why clients leave. Some we know and some we are not privy to, but one thing I can say with conviction, it doesn't feel good when they do leave. I've learned to try not to stress about it and just be grateful for the ones that happily stay. I found out early on that people have to do what works for them. You can't make clients stay with you if they really don't want to. All we can do is try our hardest to keep them happy by being reliable, on time, and doing the best job we can.

But sometimes, even that isn't enough.

I had a long time Park City resident who made an appointment with me while I was working at Vie Retreat. Apparently, Ellie called and spoke to Debra about being unhappy with her current nail technician. She wanted to make a change and of course, Debra sang my praises. Ellie arrived promptly and sat down at my desk. As she put her hands in front of me, I took a look. The nails were perfect. I mean absolutely flawless. I began to remove the nail polish off of the beautifully done acrylic nails.

"Who has been doing your nails?" I asked somewhat confused.

Ellie answered with an unfamiliar name.

"They look great. Why did you want to leave her?"

Again, I was young. Now that I am older, I would never ask that question!

Her answer was plain, simple and to the point.

"I don't like her personality."

That was over twenty-five years ago, and to this day Ellie is not only a loyal client, but also a close friend. We meet for lunches, dinners and an occasional glass of wine.

I guess sometimes personality goes a long way, but I really don't want it to seem like I haven't lost clients to other nail technicians. I certainly have. I know I am not a perfect person and I also know there have been times when my personal life has, in fact, affected my work, often without me even realizing it. We are all prone to letting life get in the way. I have to work hard to try and separate the two and it isn't always an easy task. Sometimes clients can be unforgiving for a bad nail job, especially if you haven't shared the reason behind the distraction.

Speaking of distractions, I once had a client come in who was prepping for a colonoscopy the day of her acrylic nail fill, but came in anyway because she wanted her nails to look good for the procedure. I'm here to tell you, more women than you think worry about how their hands look no matter what the occasion.

Jackie came in a half an hour early for her five o'clock appointment.

(By the way, this always makes me laugh and think of my sister Rebecka. When a client would walk in that early her response was always the same. "If she wanted the four-thirty why didn't she ask for it?")

Anyway, Jackie sat down with a look of drean on her face and announced this fun fact, "I am having a colonoscopy in the morning."

At first I thought she was kidding. Turns out, she was not.

"I hope you don't mind," Jackie said, "I will have to use the bathroom more than usual while I'm here."

"No problem," I told her, "but this is definitely going in the book!"

We got through it, but Jackie did have to excuse herself quite a few times and her acrylic fill turned into an hour and a half appointment. Thankfully, she was the last client of the day.

Then we have the clients who are so sick, they practically cough up a lung, yet still drag themselves in to have their nails done. So far, I've been lucky. I usually don't get sick, in fact, in my whole nail career, I have never once called in sick. I've come in to work when I really haven't felt good and powered through the day when I know I'm not contagious, but I have good reason. Where do I put all of those clients? It's not like I can tell them I need to move them to the next week or two! I've also had to do some rearranging for trips and planned surgeries, but I have never called to cancel appointments due to illness. Knock on wood.

However, I have had clients who called in and canceled because *they* were sick and didn't want to make me sick, and I appreciate that. But not everyone wants to try and reschedule, so they usually come in anyway, Bird Flu or not.

I have a client who refers to my nail appointment book as, "My sacred schedule."

I remember once, a long-time client, Tamara, came in for her standing appointment, an acrylic nail fill. She actually *was* sick with the flu. "I'm sorry, she said, I woke up sick, but I am already a week overdue and my nails are a mess."

I would have suggested she go home, but she lives about forty miles away, and had braved the elements that snowy winter day. I didn't have the heart to turn her away. I reached in my drawer and pulled out one of those white medical masks.

Tamara exclaimed, "Oh good you have a mask to wear!"

I handed it to her and said, with a smile. "This is for *you* to wear. I'm not the sick one." Then I stood up, walked into the bathroom and immediately washed my hands. I returned to my nail table. "Your turn," I said with another smile.

It was a quiet hour and a half, as those masks make it hard to carry on a conversation, but at least I was playing it safe and it worked. I didn't get sick!

For obvious reasons, we didn't give each other the usual hug goodbye, but her nails looked great and she was a happy client when she left.

In the end, we are not only in the beauty business, we are really in the *feel good* business. I always felt it was my job to make my clients feel better than when they came in. I tell them my stories and listen to their stories. We laugh together and we cry together. One day after a seriously long and tear-filled conversation, my client, Diane, looked over at my business card and read it out loud. "More than a Manicure," and then sincerely added, "Isn't that the damn truth!"

# Runaway Reality

In life, we all go through happy and not-so-happy times, and obviously my life has been no exception. Sometimes I console myself by saying that an easy life would have been a boring life, and mine was anything but. That really doesn't help, but quite honestly, doing nails was (and still is) often an escape from my own reality, and it's better than running away! I share my sorrows with my trusted clients and they share theirs with me. It's like an eight-hour counseling session every workday.

Although, you figure out early whom you can trust with your confessions. There are definitely the ones who you must keep at arm's length. You learn quickly who the gossip girls are, and who can be trusted, especially in a small town like Park City.

Interesting story: I once had three different girls come in on the same day, no less, and tell me about the wonderful guy they were dating. I was elated for Girl Number One, as she had searched for quite some time for her Mr. Right. She thought this was the one.

Enter my one o'clock, and she had found her Mr. Right, too. They were both so happy and excited! The green-eyed monster began to creep out and I felt a twinge of jealousy, just a little. *Is this how my day is going to be?*

Then, in walks my five o'clock, telling me a very familiar story about her newfound love. What a coincidence, he was also in the real estate business, and sounded very much like the Mr. Right of Girl Number One and Girl Number Two.

It wasn't hard to put two and two together. Or in this case, one plus one plus one.

But I never said a word. I knew I would have some extra handholding to do soon when it all fell apart. And I did when it did.

Being trustworthy is a huge part of my business, as well. I have developed such a closeness with so many of my clients, I would never dream of betraying them. For example, I have a client who is married to a wealthy man and has been for over twenty years. They travel out of the country to incredible places about six to eight times a year. Before she travels, she writes me a check for the balance in their joint checking account, made out to her one and only grandchild. It is in a sealed security envelope. I am to call the granddaughter if they don't return as planned and give her the envelope. I have never opened this envelope and fortunately, they have always returned. It's that kind of trust I am talking about.

For years, manicurists were often thought of as big mouths, like the television manicurist character, Madge, *You're soaking in it,* in the old Palmolive dishwashing liquid commercials. We were stereotyped and thought of as unreliable, gossipy, and flakey. I worked hard to dispel that notion, but have to admit, it came relatively easy. Once you realize where you can go in this business, you instinctively know how to handle confidences.

For example, I have a client, who before she starts to confide in me, will say, "Please don't put this in your book." When our hour is up, she says how much better she feels and I love hearing that. Her husband refers to me as her therapist. I really don't give her or anyone else advice. I mostly just listen and when needed, I empathize or sympathize, whatever the situation calls for. By and large, sometimes clients don't really want *any* advice. They just want and need a compassionate soul to listen.

This brings me to my long-time friend and client, Patti. I was busy working when she called from Carlsbad, California, where she and her husband had recently moved.

I glanced at the phone but was in the middle of a manicure, so decided to let it go to my voicemail. After saying goodbye to my manicure client, I went to my phone to hear her message. It was short and sweet, as they say.

*"Carly, it's Patti. When you are finished with work today and have a few minutes to talk can you please give me a call."*

I thought she must be planning to visit Park City! I smiled at the thought of it and finished up my day. I was meeting three other clients/ friends for dinner that night, so I decided I would drive to our meeting spot early and then call Patti. I drove there and parked realizing I had 30 minutes. Perfect!

I dialed her number and she answered.

"Hi Patti," I said excitedly.

"Carly, I have ovarian cancer."

My heart sank as I gasped and covered my mouth.

I managed to say softly, "Patti, no."

Patti told me her story and I listened carefully.

"You are going to beat this, Patti, I said confidently, I know how strong you are."

Patti thanked me and then added, "Please keep this between us, Carly. I've told my family, but I just don't want anyone else in Park City to know just yet."

"Of course, I promise," I said holding back tears.

"I've always considered you more like a sister than a friend, Carly."

I managed to say, "Me, too, Patti."

I went to dinner that night and feigned exhaustion from work.

My mind was preoccupied and two words kept crossing it — *Ovarian Cancer.*

I drove home in silence vowing to keep my promise. I thought about the surgery she was going to have and I said an extra-long prayer for Patti, still convinced she would survive. I've always believed in the power of positive thinking.

# Glow with the Lava Flow

The following evening as I sat home alone contemplating dinner, I had an epiphany. I had come to the realization that it was time to start the fun process of dating. Friends wanted to line me up and I had always said no, but I began to rethink it. It was past time to get back out into the world of relationships.

I started by telling clients if they had any one in mind to let me know. I was ready or as they say in France, *"Je suis prête!"* As long as he wasn't a real estate agent, I joked.

Actually, in the beginning, I kind of threw down the gauntlet on any Park City guys. It seemed the ratio of women to men was considerably higher back then. Everybody dated everybody. There was a comment I heard that stuck with me one day while I was at the gym. I overheard a guy I knew say to his weight lifting partner, "You don't lose your girlfriend here in Park City, you just lose your turn." *I don't like the sound of that!*

I began a heated romance with a Mormon guy from Salt Lake City. My friend Karen worked with him and she was definitely in his corner.

"His name is Devin and he is a really nice guy, a business man who lives in American Towers." *Well, at least he lives in style!* I was familiar with the condos located in downtown Salt Lake City.

They were beautiful and had spectacular views particularly from the rooftop pool!

"What's his story?" I asked Karen.

"Well, he owns his own software company and he is very successful, good looking and I think you will love his humor, and he travels quite a bit, in fact, he just got back from ten days in Hawaii. You could go on some fabulous trips."

*I've never been to Hawaii and maybe I will get to Paris after all! Sounds good so far.*

"He just broke up with his secretary a few months ago and he is ready to date now," Karen announced and happily added, "You will *really* like him Carly."

I smiled, but I was curious so I asked, "Is she still his secretary?"

"Yes," Karen answered, "but it was a mutual break-up so don't worry about that."

*Is that his version or the secretary's version?*

I wondered, but decided to give it a shot. I trusted my friend and her judgment, plus she knew me well.

"Okay, why not," I told Karen.

"Good, I will give him your number."

The next morning he did call and we made plans for dinner.

"How is seven o'clock on Friday night?"

"Sounds great," I told him.

"Do you know a good restaurant in Park City?" Devin asked.

I thought about it. This was a hard choice because there were so many good restaurants in Park City, so I decided to pick my personal favorite, *Chez Betty*. This was an American eclectic French restaurant off the beaten path with very good, fresh and seasonal food, and the chef there was known to be excellent.

"Yes, I love Chez Betty."

"I'll make the reservation," Devin said.

"I will be coming from work, so I will meet you there," I told him. It was the truth, but I wanted to have my own car. Just in case.

Devin answered, "Oh, okay, are you really coming from work or do you always have a get-away car?" Then he laughed and so did I. *This was sounding better all the time!*

I found myself looking forward to Friday.

The week passed quickly and Friday arrived. I got up extra early to prepare for my date. I took a change of clothes. I couldn't show up in my acrylic dust covered black work clothes. The day was busy and it was time for me to freshen up for my date. I did just that and as I drove to the restaurant my heart was beating fast. It was ten minutes before seven. *Can't arrive too early. I will drive around the block for one song. The last thing I want to do is sit at a table by myself in Chez Betty, looking like I have no life when this man walks in. Can't appear too anxious either!* So I walked in promptly at seven.

The host was gracious as I entered the restaurant.

"Good evening, may I help you?"

"Yes, I am meeting someone," I told him looking around a bit. I had a description from Karen, but that was it.

"Right this way, Miss Bennett," the host guided me to a small table next to the fireplace. *Devin must have told him my name*, I thought, as the host walked away.

A very tall, good-looking dark haired man stood up and smiled. I extended my hand. "Hi, I'm Carly Bennett," I said with a smile.

Devin looked up and said, "Thank you, God."

I laughed as I sat down. Devin ordered a bottle of red wine.

We spent the next two hours talking. I found out Devin had been on a mission to Spain, and years later he still wore the LDS garments to prove it. Although he drank alcohol, he was what the Mormons call a *Jack Mormon*, which is a Mormon who is not strict in his behavior particularly when it comes to obeying the Word of Wisdom. The Word of Wisdom are important rules, for lack of a better description, that are believed to be revealed from God to help us care for our physical and spiritual health while we are here on earth. These rules aren't really commandments, they are more like suggestions to help Mormons care for their bodies. Caffeine is also included in this along with other suggestions to help us along our way. They are probably the most disobeyed rules in my opinion, but back to my date.

This guy was successful, good-looking, and intelligent and had a terrific sense of humor. I have always enjoyed someone I can mentally spar with, and he seemed perfect for me. He wore a three-piece suit to work, and I liked that. He wasn't a musician and honestly he wasn't really even into music. He only really liked and listened to REO Speed Wagon.

Our conversation continued, "Do you have children?" Devin asked.

I answered honestly, "Yes, I have four children who are grown. I also have seven grandchildren."

'Wow," Devin said somewhat surprised, "you look really good."

I smiled and thanked him. I am always amazed at that response. I know a lot of women my age who are grandmothers and they look great!

"What about you, do you have children?" I asked.

"Yes, I have five daughters," Devin said with a smile, "they are the light of my life."

*Holy shit! Five daughters! Karen left that part out. Why am I so surprised? He is a Mormon!*

"Oh, wow, that's cool. How old are they?" I asked trying to remain calm.

"They are 14, 12, 10, 8 and the youngest just turned 6."

*GULP!!!! He has five YOUNG daughters! I see now why Karen left that up to Devin to inform me!* My head was spinning a bit and I was definitely surprised, but I still didn't see it as a deal breaker. *It's not like we are getting married tonight!*

The wine arrived and the waiter filled our glasses. I took a huge sip. I needed to have some of that liquid courage for my next question.

"So, what happened to your marriage?" *There I said it. Those girls are still pretty young.*

Devin told me his story about how he and his wife had been separated for close to a year, but were not quite divorced yet.

"What's the hold up?" I asked.

"It's complicated when you have been married in the Temple," Devin told me. Although I was raised Mormon, I was never married in the Temple so this was something I knew nothing about. Devin continued on and I listened intently. "But we are working on it and it shouldn't be that much longer," he added.

*Okay, but that didn't answer my question.* "So what went wrong?" I tried a different approach.

"Oh, there were so many things," he replied.

"I'm listening," I said. *He wasn't getting out of this tonight.*

# Essentially Single

*D*evin took a deep breath and told his tale in great lengths starting with an inner struggle he had, essentially feeling like he was abandoning his girls. He continued on telling me about his family life. His father was murdered in New Orleans. His mother had abandoned the six of them. *What the hell?*

Devin continued to tell me about his wife and how she was so LDS that it effected their relationship tremendously. I heard how all five of his daughters were born in the month of September because she only believed in having sex to celebrate the birth of Christ on Christmas day.

"Any counseling for the two of you?" I asked.

"Yes, on and off for several years," Devin said, "but it didn't help." He continued his story, "The final straw was one evening when I told her I felt like she didn't like anything about me."

"How did she respond?" I asked curiously.

"She told me she prayed every night to God to help her see some good in me, with no luck. I asked her if I was such a bad person, why did she stay with me?"

*What was her response to that?* I wondered.

Devin's eyes filled with tears. "The church and the kids."

My eyes widened. My sympathetic nature won out and I placed my hand on top of his. "That had to be a terrible realization," I said as I rubbed his hand.

*What a cold-hearted woman she must be.*

I looked around the restaurant and realized we were the only patrons. The staff was standing up at the front desk waiting patiently for us to leave. I checked the time. It was ten o'clock.

"Devin, it's getting late, I have to work early in the morning." I stood up and was light-headed and not from the wine. This was a lot to absorb. I have to admit, I liked Devin and I felt sorry for him.

"Can I see you again or have I scared you to death?" he asked with a smile.

I smiled back and said, "Yes, I would like that."

Devin held the door to Chez Betty open for me and then he walked me to my car. He picked up my hand and kissed the top of it.

*That was polite coming from a sex-starved man! Making love only on Christmas Day? What? That's so weird!*

"Goodbye, Carly, I will talk to you tomorrow," Devin said interrupting my thoughts.

"I will look forward to it. Drive safe, Devin."

I drove home listening to my new *Counting Crows* CD. I played the song "Round Here" which was one of my favorites and turned it up loud as I listened closely to the lyrics.

I knew in my head what I should do, but my heart had a different opinion. After all, Devin was getting divorced, he had been honest with me. He could have lied about it all and strung me along, but he didn't. *Hey, plus Devin had a girlfriend before me! What about his secretary?*

I told myself all the things I could to rationalize falling for a separated but not yet divorced man. Looking back on all of it the best thing would have been to tell Devin right from the start to throw away my number. *Call me in two years when it was all said and done and you have gone through all of the crap associated with a messy divorce.*

But I didn't. Instead I followed my heart, without realizing I was doing ninety miles an hour down a dead end street. For the first time in my life, I left all of the free-spirited, right-brain thinkers, and music men behind and headed in a completely different direction with my Missionary Man (as I playfully nicknamed him).

# 29
## New York State of Mind

The next year was spent together, going to movies, and instead of dining out at Denny's, Applebee's, or Pizza Hut (the only places my previous starving artist dates could afford), we went to high-end places I could never pay for myself, and I loved it!

We also traveled together to various cities (on his dime) including Los Angeles, Santa Fe, San Francisco, Boston, New York, Las Vegas, Seattle, and Austin, Texas. That may not seem like such a big deal, but to me it was. I really hadn't traveled much at all and I had never even been out of the United States. We discussed our plans for the future deciding on France as soon as he was divorced.

"It will be our celebration," he told me with a big grin.

That was at the top of his list because he knew how much I dreamed of visiting Paris. I was so excited. *What a nice man, always thinking of me.*

I remember one time when we were in New York City I stared out the window of our hotel room right at Times Square. I was in awe. The next morning, we walked down the street and I had the best bagel I had ever tasted. We had tickets to see *The David Letterman Show* that afternoon. At that time, *The David

*Letterman Show* had a reputation for being nearly impossible to get tickets to and also for being freezing cold in the theatre. As a joke, Devin sent a Christmas card to David Letterman in July due to the temperatures inside. The producer of the show replied with tickets to the show. So we went! The guests that afternoon, included Tim Roth, Claudia Schiffer, and Slash (lead guitarist of Guns and Roses). And of course, one of my all-time favorite musicians, Paul Schaffer, was on hand, as he and his band were regulars. The show was incredible.

Afterwards, we walked around taking in the sights. I enjoyed seeing the street artists and vendors. It was quite the experience for a girl from Utah, and I loved every minute of it.

The next evening we had tickets to see the play, *Miss Saigon*. The spectacular scene in which a helicopter actually lands and takes off onstage through the open roof was breathtaking and loud. That was my introduction to live theatre. We had an early dinner at Limoncello, an Italian restaurant, prior to the show, where I enjoyed one of the most incredible meals I've ever tasted. After the theatre we hit a couple of nightclubs on our way home and had a nice glow on.

When we arrived back at our hotel room, we had a nightcap from the mini bar and laid on the bed watching *Pulp Fiction*, Devin lit up a joint. You would have thought that was the funniest movie we had ever seen. I have to admit I was fairly seasoned with alcohol back then, but not so much with marijuana. I went into the bathroom and decided to strip off my clothes and slip into something more comfortable…Devin's garments. When I giddily traipsed back into the bedroom, dancing around in my new *pajamas*, Devin was not amused. In fact, he was extremely angry with me. I was only having fun, but my fun had come to a screeching halt. He yelled at me saying, "That is not funny! It is not only sacrilegious, but you are going to hell."

I think there was also some mention of me being the Antichrist.

Talk about a buzz kill.

I yelled back, stating the obvious, "You are in a hotel room with someone who is not your wife, drinking alcohol, smoking marijuana, and watching an R-rated movie, and *I'm* going to hell?"

I guess he wasn't really *that much* of a Jack Mormon after all.

Surprisingly, our courtship didn't end there. Once he chastised me, and I promised not to ever do it again, he took back his harsh words and apologized, as did I, blaming it on the alcohol and such. I really was sincere in my apology. Growing up as a Mormon, my conscience got the better of me and I felt ashamed and embarrassed for making fun of such a sacred part of the religion, once I sobered up. We forgave each other and continued on our merry way, drinking, traveling and having a grand old time while I waited patiently for his divorce to be finalized.

# 30

## OMG, Seriously for Real?

Devin had a business trip planned that happened to fall on his fortieth birthday that year. It was in Las Vegas. I began racking my brain to figure out how I could get away for five days. It was summertime and the Sun City tourists were in Park City to get away from their home hot spots, places like Arizona and Florida. I tried to come up with a plan, but the biggest problem was no income for five days. I still had to support myself. Finally, I had to break the news that I would be skipping this trip.

"It's no big deal," he assured me, "I have several meetings planned that will require a huge amount of my time and energy."

"I guess," I said with a pout. I wanted him to be a little more disappointed than that.

"It's only Las Vegas," he added reassuringly.

So I stayed home.

While he was gone, Devin called a few times a day and into the evenings. We would chat about how much we missed each other, and wished we were there together. The date of his birthday fell on a Saturday. I felt sad that we wouldn't be able to celebrate together, so I made a plan. I decided last minute to take an evening flight Friday and surprise him. I charged my ticket on my own credit card, and being last minute it wasn't cheap.

Six-hundred-fifty dollars and two hours later, I was headed to the Salt Lake City airport. I took an overnight bag and his birthday present with me. I had saved up to purchase an expensive suit, shirt, and tie for his fortieth birthday. I was so excited not only to see him, but also to surprise him with this suit I knew he had his eye on.

I arrived shortly after 9:00 p.m. and checked into my hotel room. To avoid spoiling the surprise, I registered as a non-registered guest. No name. I got all dolled up, wearing a very sexy dress and sassy heels. When I stood in the hallway in front his room, I placed my finger over the peephole before I knocked. I wanted it to be a complete surprise.

It was.

Devin opened the door just a tiny bit. I timidly said, "Happy Birthday."

Without opening the door any wider, he nervously asked, "What are you doing here?"

I became suspicious. "Can I come in?" I asked a bit more bravely.

"It's best you don't," Devin answered.

I pushed lightly against the door and he stepped aside.

"I thought it was room service," he shouted over his shoulder to a very buxom, half naked blonde on the bed.

"Are you here to join us?" she asked enthusiastically.

I turned and marched out the door.

Tears streamed down my face as I ran to the elevator.

"Carly, come back," Devin called from the partially closed door. "Let me explain!" But he didn't run after me. Of course, if people had seen him they probably would have taken a dim view of a half-naked man running down the hallway.

*BUT WHO CARES ABOUT HIM? Dammit, I do! Me, the patient woman who never bothered him about his divorce coming to fruition, never gave him grief about taking his sweet time. Me, the woman who had picture perfect hair at all times, her make up always on, including lipstick and powder! Me, the woman with the smooth perfectly clean-shaven legs. Me, the woman who was always smiling, happy and in a good mood. Me, the woman who believed him without question, loved him at all costs and never questioned him, dealing with it all in a positive, collected and supportive way. Now, I have to deal with this bullshit on top of everything else? What a fool I've been! Diana told me to run for cover, but I didn't listen to her! I thought I knew better. Devin talked, I listened and I believed. What the hell is wrong with me?*

I returned to my room a complete emotional mess. My return flight was not until Monday afternoon. I had to get out of there. I called the airline and booked the first early morning flight back to Salt Lake City. This was turning into a very expensive weekend, not to mention a heartbreaking one. I hardly slept that night, crying into my pillow until it was a sopping wet mess. My cell phone rang off the hook all night, so eventually I turned it off just to get some peace. I secretly hoped his evening, and his birthday, were ruined.

Fortunately, there was no way for him to find out where I was. I was an angry, hurt, and sad non-registered guest. I assumed, as I finally drifted in and out of sleep, given the blonde's comment, that she was a professional.

In the early morning I woke up groggy and tired (from lack of sleep), but ready to leave. I was still angry, but the hurt had been replaced with disgust. I turned on my cell phone, and had several missed calls and over twenty messages. Without listening, I deleted them all. I then called his work number and left him a very composed, brief, controlled voice message that went like this: "It's over. Don't you ever call me again and good luck with your divorce."

I was surprised at the calmness in my voice, but the fact was I was numb. I'd crashed and burned along with my self-esteem.

I thought I'd found the perfect man, a man I had dreams of marrying some day. Devin and I had made plans, so many plans after his divorce. *After his divorce… I feel so ashamed and so foolish. I* was embarrassed I fell for his lies. I'd been dating someone who was tangled up, someone with no intention to get untangled as he professed many times over. I believed he was telling me the truth, but the real truth was he had no intention of getting a divorce. I was "Jolene" and I hated myself.

I shook all my thoughts away as I jumped in the shower. I dressed quickly and brushed my teeth. No time for make-up this early morning. I just wanted to go home.

The hall was quiet as I walked to the elevator. The door opened and I stepped in. I wondered why I had such bad luck with men.

*I'm a nice person*, I thought. *Why can't I meet a nice man and hold onto him?* I began to feel sorry for myself. I have yet another failed relationship. I feel like a big, fat loser, once again. Three failed marriages and here I am with another failed relationship. *Why does this keep happening to me? I don't get it!* I thought hard about it. I was always so nice to Devin. He often told me how lucky he was to find me. "You know how to treat a man", he would say. I couldn't help but wonder what the hell happened? I had no earthly idea. I closed my eyes for a couple of seconds and asked God to help me figure it out. *Dear God, Please give me some useful insight. Help me to understand where I went wrong. I loved this man and he seemed to love me. My heart is breaking and I don't know which way to turn. I need your help and your loving guidance. Amen.*

I opened my eyes, still deeply hurt and confused. What was the answer? I thought hard about it and suddenly it came to me. *Thank you God. It wasn't me at all. I wasn't a loser. I was an idiot for believing him, I was sure of that, but it was all him.* Devin was a sexual deviant. Had to be. He was a Mormon guy who had been told his entire life he had to walk, when all he really wanted to do was run. Devin had pinned back his ears and took off at the starting line even before he heard the shot and never looked back.

The door opened a few floors later, breaking my train of thought. I suddenly realized I was in the main lobby. I stared at all the people sitting with their drinks and cigarettes in hand, playing the slot machines. They didn't seem to have a care in the world, yet my world had just unexpectedly crumbled to dust. My guess was that these people had been there all night. (After all, this was Las Vegas.) While I tossed and turned all night trying to grapple with the sting of a betrayed trust from a man I believed, a man I thought I loved, they were sitting at the slot machines, waiting to hit the jackpot. They were anxiously waiting for the bells and whistles to go off in hopes of the big win, a new beginning to a bigger and better life. Just as I thought I'd hit the jackpot with Devin. I thought I'd won a new life, too. I felt so lost and alone as I made my way past the hopeful souls. I realized I was surrounded by nothing more than a dull void, an emptiness that was all consuming.

I approached a sweet-faced woman at the front desk. She greeted me with a big smile, as she asked, "How can I help you?" I needed that kindness this morning. I smiled back as I told her, "Good morning, I am checking out early. Is there a bellman on duty this early?" I asked.

"Yes there is," she replied.

"Is he a *large* bellman?" I asked sincerely.

The look on her face was puzzlement, as she answered, "In fact he is quite a large, tall man."

"May I please speak with him?" I inquired.

Soon a very tall, well-built man stood before me. "How can I help you? he asked, genuinely intrigued.

I looked him up and down. "Turn around," I requested.

He smiled and obliged, and I studied him as he did so. He was a large bellman. *Perfect*, I thought.

Once he turned a full 360 degrees and faced me again, I handed him Devin's suit and said, "Enjoy."

Then I walked out to my cab and climbed inside.

I arrived at McCarran Airport with a good hour to spare. I grabbed a large cup of black coffee and a sesame seed bagel. I remember feeling sick to my stomach as I took that first bite. I couldn't shake the image of the night before. The man I loved with a hooker! I walked over to the trashcan and tossed in the bagel. *Another waste of money, I thought.*

As I took a big gulp of my coffee, I looked around at the rows of slot machines. What the heck! I sat down at a freestanding progressive slot machine, which my mother always told me was bad luck. I decided my luck couldn't get much worse, as I put a fifty-dollar bill in the slot machine. I pulled the handle instead of pushing the button, also considered bad luck by my superstitious mother. I pulled the handle another three or four times, with no luck. *It figures.* I sighed. I decided to bet three dollars at a time, and then pushed the forbidden button.

All of a sudden, bells and whistles started going off. People came and crowded around me. I was sleep deprived, so it took a moment to sink in that I had won.

"What have I won?" I asked one of the Asian men who kept trying to touch my hair and kiss my hand for good luck.

He pointed up to the top of the progressive slot machine. It was flashing the numbers $3,462.38.

Out of nowhere someone showed up with a camera and snapped my picture. They then handed me a box of chocolates and a small bottle of champagne. A man came over and counted out the money in my hand, in one hundred dollar bills. I think I was in shock when they called us to board the airplane. I quickly gathered my things and ran to the gate.

As I sat in my seat and stared at the picture of me taken at the slot machine with my chocolates and champagne, I thought, *what the heck just happened back there?* Shortly before take off, a male flight attendant, Bruce, I knew from Park City came up to me and called me, "Ms. Bennett," which was weird because we're friends. I thought he needed to be professional. "Please gather your things, Ms. Bennett, and come with me."

I did and he smiled as he seated me in First Class. Bruce brought me a mimosa, which I drank, even though it was only nine in the morning. Who cares! I ordered another.

I was starting to feel much better.

On the way home I stared out the window, Las Vegas was getting smaller and smaller in my own rear view mirror. I thought about how I had dodged a bullet with Devin, and ended the relationship. This could have continued on all the while I was getting in deeper and deeper and still he would be a married man. I was convinced he'd stalled out on his divorce on purpose. Yes, I was brokenhearted, but all things considered, I felt pretty lucky. I laughed as I shook my head in disbelief. My luck had definitely changed and I was going to follow suit. No matter what he says, no matter what he does, how many promises he makes, how much he begs and pleads, I will never forgive him and certainly never take him back. I leaned my head against the back of my seat, closed my eyes and said goodbye to Las Vegas and to Devin.

And now there was one very sharply dressed bellman in Las Vegas.

# "Teas-y" Does It

I went to work early on Tuesday morning. As I prepared the water for my first appointment of the day, a man's pedicure, my mind was still preoccupied with the weekend's events. They kept playing over and over in my mind. I realized then that my heart was definitely broken. This was going to take a minute. *What now, I thought?* The huge sense of relief I had felt by eliminating yet another toxic relationship with a man before it really even had started was being replaced by an overwhelming feeling of loss, sadness, and pain. I hated to admit it even to myself, but I loved Devin.

I was mad as hell at him, but there was no denying that I loved him. *How am I going to get through this?* My eyes filled with tears as I relived the memory of Friday night. I remembered my voice message to his work phone. *Did I really never want him to call me again?* It has to be this way. I have no choice. I can no longer trust him. I was so confused. I have to pull it together before 8:00 a.m.! *You've got thirty-five minutes, girl.* I reminded myself about Friday night, and THEN questioned what he did on other trips without me. I slowly realized…this was probably not the first time. I played out all the scenarios in my mind, as I waited for my first appointment.

I convinced myself that Devin wasn't just a sexual deviant, he must also be a sex addict, I told myself. I knew that was a real addiction some people struggled with. I read about it in *Cosmopolitan.* The article said there was help through counseling. I believed in therapy, it had helped me! But what if Devin had been doing this all along? He could have an STD and maybe I had one, too, for all I knew!

*Stop it, Carly before you drive yourself crazy!* Too late.

I was indeed making myself crazy and I had to stop. I closed my teary eyes and bowed my head. *Dear God! Please give me high altitude strength!*

Then my new client, Tony, walked in, and I had no choice but to shift gears. I took a deep breath as I tried to compose myself and managed a cheery hello. I pointed to the pedicure tub.

"Hi, Tony, how are you today?"

"I'm doing awesome. How are you?" Tony asked.

"I'm doing okay. Go ahead and put your feet in. Make sure the water temperature is good," I instructed.

Tony plunged in feet first and laughed as he said it was perfect.

Then he added, "I like it just on the border of tearing up and wanting more!"

*Okay then! This is going to be an entertaining appointment!*

"So Carly, how long have you been doing this?"

"A very long time, close to twenty years." I answered.

"What? Did you start when you were just a baby?" Tony laughed.

*There's nothing like a compliment about your age to perk you up right off the bat. I liked this guy.* "You are funny, but no, I am older than you think, but thank you," I said with a smile. I continued with, "I have very young looking parents. I am blessed with good genes."

"Are you married?" Tony asked.

"Not anymore," I answered, "I'm divorced."

Tony asked, "Any boyfriends?"

"I had a boyfriend, but I caught him with a hooker in Vegas on Friday night."

Tony spit out the sip of coffee he just took and said, "Seriously?"

I laughed and nodded my head. I don't know if he believed me or not.

"My wife warned me about your dark sense of humor!" Then we both laughed. I've always found it fun to keep them guessing.

I finished Tony's toes in record time and he was on his way home.

I have a fair number of male clients who in the beginning would balk at the idea of having a pedicure. Typically they come in at the insistence of their wives, and this was one of those times. It usually takes just one appointment before they are hooked.

Such was the case with Tony. He booked every four weeks and instructed me to charge it to his wife when she came in the next time. "I always let her handle these things," he said.

I smiled and answered, "No worries."

Tony left and I thought how lucky his wife was, even if he stuck her with the bill.

The day flew by rather quickly and I was thankful. I decided a trip to the gym was desperately needed, so off I went. I put on my headphones, jumped on the treadmill and started running. Aerosmith was playing their hit song "Crying" on my Walkman.

I turned up the volume as I ran faster listening to those piercing lyrics. I bumped up the speed even more as I ran, praying for those endorphins to kick in fast!

The next morning when I entered the salon my day began the same way it had started yesterday: with a man's pedicure. I flashed on the movie, *Groundhog Day*. I made a pot of coffee and turned on the salon music. K.D. Lang belted out her hit, *Big Boned Gal* as the coffee brewed. Thoughts of hitting the gym again flooded my mind.

My client, Ron, opened the door and walked in right on time. I poured each of us big cups of coffee, as we chatted about our weekends. I left out the hooker part. I told him about my luck at the slot machine and he was floored. "The most I have ever won is twenty-three dollars," he said. "What are you going to do with all of that money?"

"Pay off my credit card," I said with a big smile. "It all feels surreal," I told him as I shook my head. That was where my weekend tale started and ended. That was as far as I needed to go with that story.

I began the part in Ron's pedicure that everyone loves the most, the foot massage. Two songs and about six minutes later, I finished and patted Ron's feet as I mindlessly said, "Okay, now you have suckable toes."

*Oops! Did I just say that out loud? I was only teasing but that was not good!*

I was shocked, embarrassed, and mortified! This was a little joke between myself and a client, Jillian, who was a single, confident, and strong woman. Jillian would come in for her pedicures and tell me, "I don't need polish. Nobody ever sees my toes." I would polish them anyway, teasing her by saying, "You never know. You could meet someone wonderful today, and at least you will be ready with suckable toes!"

But honestly, I didn't mean to blurt my silly comment out to Ron that morning! I know I was blushing when I apologized to this eighty-two-year-old man. "Ron, I am so sorry, please excuse my inappropriate remark," I said, dying inside.

Ron smiled and said, "That's okay, Carly. That's my wife's idea of sixty-nine!"

*Whoa! Now, that's a visual!*

When I am not putting my foot in my mouth, I quite enjoy my male clients. Honestly, their feet are usually in better shape than those of my female clients. Most men wear shoes and socks, and they rarely go barefoot. Ron was definitely the winner in that category. His feet were so soft and not a callous on them!

Ron also frequented the salon for his haircuts with Nancy, the most successfully booked barber in Park City. Before he slipped into her room, he would always stop at my door, and most of the time, I would be doing a pedicure.

"Go ahead, Carly," he'd say, "tell her about my toes."

My reply would always be the same. "Best toes and feet ever, they are baby soft."

Ron always got a kick out of that. I missed him when he passed away a few years ago. I enjoyed our time together without a doubt. He told the best jokes in addition to having the best feet. Although Nancy, the barber, was a close second in the joke department! She could remember and tell a joke like no other. I was (and still am) so impressed with that skill.

I had another male client who came in later that same week. Barry was a big guy who played football in college. When I dipped his feet into the paraffin wax tub, I commented on how he was the first to dip, as I had just completely sanitized the tub and filled it with fresh wax the previous night.

"Good, I don't like sloppy seconds," he replied with a teasing laugh.

I smiled and thought about his comment, but didn't say a word. I bet that expensive suit I gave the bellman in Las Vegas would have fit Barry just fine.

My day ended with George, another one of my client's husbands. *This has been a day filled with male pedicures*, I thought as I filled the tub with tepid water. Most of my male clients like the water a bit on the cooler side. I thought about the first time George was in. He had a serious ingrown toenail that was hurting him, particularly in his ski boots. I was worried I hadn't been able to get it all out, as it seemed too soon for him to be back.

"Hi George, I said cheerfully as he walked in the door, go ahead and put your feet in, make sure your water is okay."

I watched his face as he stuck his feet in the lukewarm water. No grimace. Must be okay. I let him soak for just a couple of minutes before I sat down to begin his pedicure.

"Is the ingrown toenail bothering you again?" I asked with a worried tone.

"No, not at all," he answered ever so matter-of-factly.

"Oh, I thought that was why you were back for a pedicure so soon," I commented.

"No, you gave me the heroin and I liked it, so here I am back for more," George said.

Well, that was a first! I had not heard that comparison before. I actually laughed out loud.

# Hello and Goodbye

We do hear some funny stories in this business. I had an educator for Redken (a color and hair care line) who occasionally came to Sisters Salon to teach classes on hair color to our hairdressers. Her name was Haley and she owned a successful salon in Provo, Utah, for many years. She happened to be the cousin of Rick, my previous husband. Haley had a full clientele and a very successful salon. I had not seen her for quite some time, until I went to a family funeral. We struck up a conversation, she knew I had sold Sisters and wanted to know how I was doing.

"Things are going well. I am pretty stress-free these days. How about your salon?" I asked. "Are you still doing education for Redken?"

"I sold my salon five years ago and we are now in the convenience store business. My husband and I own three in the area."

I was surprised, as she had a thriving salon business and seemed to love it. *"Really?"* I asked.

"Carly, I am so much happier being out of the salon business," Haley confirmed.

"I thought you loved it," I exclaimed, "what happened?" I was so curious.

"One day I was working on one of my long time clients," explained Haley, "and she was telling me a story about her life, just like any other day. I thought to myself, *why don't you just shut the fuck up?* Carly, that really took me by surprise, because I loved this lady. I decided right then and there that was it. I knew it was time to say goodbye before I said something like that out loud one day."

I've often thought about Haley's story over the past ten years and wondered if that day would ever come for me. I can say with conviction, I still love what I do and I love my clients and our conversations. I can never imagine that happening.

I look back over the years on the clients who have passed away. This is one of the hardest things for me to go through. I get so attached to my clients, that when death happens, I feel such an enormous sense of loss. Clients who were my age when I first started in the nail business are now getting older just like I am. I had several clients pass away last year alone, including Patti after her valiant struggle with ovarian cancer.

One in particular was a widow named Mildred. My first three years in Park City she became a regular client. Mildred not only drove to her appointments regularly, but she also drove back and forth to California and Las Vegas on a regular basis. One day Mildred came in and told me about one of those Las Vegas trips. She went with her boyfriend, Norman. I was so excited and happy for her and she confessed how nice it was to have a companion again. They traveled together and seemingly had the time of their lives.

A couple more years passed and she came in for her pedicure. Her son had bought her an iPhone. It was the first one I had seen. She told me about all of the features and how much fun she was having learning all about it. She showed me the camera and some of the pictures she had taken of their travels. I was impressed with the quality of these photos. My little flip phone's camera didn't even come close to this.

"Do you want to see a picture of my little boyfriend, Norman?" she asked?

I had never met him or even seen a photo yet, so I excitedly answered with a smile, "Of course. I would love to!"

"I have Norman as my screen saver," Mildred said.

*How cute,* I thought.

She turned her phone for me to take a look, and there on her phone was a picture of a white standard poodle! I looked at her quite puzzled. "Wait! Norman is a…dog?" I asked in disbelief.

"Well, yes," she answered. "What else would he be?"

"All of these years I thought Norman was a real boyfriend!" I exclaimed.

"Heavens, no," she said. "We could never travel that much together if he were."

Shortly after that I got to meet Norman in person, as I began doing her pedicures at her home. She needed to breathe with an oxygen tank, and her use had increased. Going up and down stairs had become increasingly difficult for her. So I went once a month to her place to do her nails for almost five years, and I so enjoyed our talks.

Mildred had been a high school teacher in California and had two children of her own. They both lived nearby and were truly shining examples of how to care for an aging parent. When she passed away at age 93, I was out of town and her daughter called me. We cried together. Upon my return, I went to her daughter's house. She told me she had something for me that her mother had wanted me to have. She gave me the most beautiful jade necklace with matching earrings, locally made by a Park City artist. I was so touched. I think about going to her home and all of the great conversations we had and although my heart is sad at the loss of her, I will always treasure those times.

When a client passes that is right in line with your age, you do begin to question your own mortality. This doesn't happen often, thank goodness, but it does happen. Cathy was a client of mine for many years; she was also my daughter's grade school teacher. We used to have the best conversations. I knew she was ill, but also knew she was a very private person, and I had to respect that. We didn't chat about her illness at all. I would always ask her how she was feeling.

"I'm fine," Cathy would answer convincingly, even when I knew she was anything but fine.

I remember, as she was nearing the end, she kept her nail appointments every two weeks, coming in to see me even at her weakest. Each time, I hugged her and told her to take good care.

Cathy would smile at me, even when I knew she was not feeling well.

Shortly after that, I hugged her tight for what I knew was the very last time, as she left the salon with the help of her sister. Then I went into the bathroom and cried my eyes out. I knew my Thursday mornings every other week at nine were never going to be the same.

And I was right.

# Gimme a Brake

O ne of the most frustrating parts of doing nails is when a client breaks an acrylic fingernail. It is frustrating for both the client and the technician. I always find their reasons for their nail damage interesting.

One day, one of my long time clients started to make excuses as soon as she hit the door. She sat in the chair and continued to blurt out one excuse after the next, as to the reason why she had no acrylic nails left. I listened to her ramble on, as she said they all started to just fall off *all by themselves.*

I calmly looked her straight in the eye and said, "Look, Linda, I've been through two husbands and three children with you and I know what you would do for a Klondike Bar, so do you think I don't know that you pulled off your nails yourself?"

Then we both laughed. And she shut up about her nails falling off.

We, as technicians, can tell immediately if acrylic nails have been picked off, or if they "just fell off."

If they are pickers, more often than not, they don't like to admit it. However, there are those who will 'fess up, even if they are embarrassed about it. I have had both types in my chair.

I had one client who came in and as she sat down, she held up her index finger and said, "This one broke."

I said, "Oh. I'm sorry."

To which she replied with an honest answer. "Well, that's what happens when you chew on them!"

How refreshing! Whether they were just in or it's been a few weeks it doesn't matter. I was at a point with my "sacred schedule" that I had to fit repairs in between acrylic nail appointments, or at the end of the day.

One thing you should know, I've never charged for nail repairs. My thoughts were that clients pay enough for their nails, charging them for a broken one just didn't seem right to me. Often they will slap down a five-dollar bill and tell me to buy myself a cup of coffee and I do appreciate that. However, if they come in with five or six broken nails the day before their appointment that's a different story!

I remember I had a client who needed a repair on her thumbnail. Mandy worked at the airport, and did not leave work until about six, so I asked her to come at seven o'clock that evening. I was fixing her broken nail, and she told me that the brakes were going out in her car, and driving back from the airport she noticed they were worse.

"I'm happy to give you a ride home after your appointment," I told her.

"Thank you," she said. "How about we go for a drink at Adolph's before we head out?"

Adolph's is a restaurant and bar near where I work in Park City. It had been a long day and I had no one expecting me home. I thought it would be good for me. I needed to go out and free my mind from the man I was trying to forget. My thoughts quickly turned to Kathy's words. "Devin getting a divorce will just be the beginning of your problems with him." And I clung to that.

"That sounds lovely,!" I exclaimed eagerly.

It was a Friday night and, of course, Adolph's was busy. We sat at the bar and began a conversation with Mary, a bartender we both knew. A few hours and a few drinks later, a group of men came over to introduce themselves. They were all doctors from various places, here for a convention and some ski time. They had just finished dinner in the dining room and had come into the bar area for a nightcap. They had an early morning meeting at The Yarrow, a nearby hotel, so all except two of the doctors went home. That left Jerry and Denny. They were both very gentlemanly, and each had his own terrific sense of humor.

We got the obligatory small talk out of the way and were soon engaged in a full-on deep conversation. All of a sudden the lights came on. To our amazement the bar was closing. It was already 2:00 a.m.? Jerry and Mandy were in a political discussion about the Clintons, and Denny and I were discussing Mormonism. Being from the south Denny had never met a Mormon and he was curious about the culture.

"Do you wear garments?" he wanted to know.

"No." I answered and chuckled thinking about Devin's.

It's surprising how little people who live outside of Utah know about Mormonism.

Our doctors asked for a lift home since their ride left hours ago. Mandy had thought it was a good idea to go back to their place and continue the Clinton conversation. I was always cautious around people I really didn't know. I found bartender Mary in the back of the restaurant and asked her how well she knew these doctors.

"You think they're safe?" I asked cautiously.

Mary gave me the thumbs up. She had known them all for about five years, since they first started to attend the annual medical conference here.

"I actually know them quite well," she said. "They're nice men. Harmless."

I trusted her judgment.

We all piled into my car, a very small Chevrolet Cavalier, and drove to the house they rented in Deer Valley. The house was dark and quiet, as we went in; they both went into the kitchen to make us all a drink.

I turned to Mandy and said, "What are we doing here? They could be axe murderers for all we know!"

She laughed at me as they returned with our drinks.

We sat on the couch, and the discussions continued. After a couple of hours, I stood up and announced that we had to leave. We opened the door to find about a foot of snow on my car. It had only been lightly snowing when we left the restaurant. We joked about how we had been without a storm since Christmas, which was almost a month without snow.

They both were upset that they were leaving in the morning and had not skied at all this trip due to the lack of snow. Mandy and I started out to my car when Denny asked me to wait, so he could find something to clear the light powdery white stuff off of my windshield. By the time he came out, I had started my car and cleared the windows with my arm. There he stood, broom in hand, staring at my car.

"Wow! You Mormon girls are tough," he exclaimed.

*If you only knew.*

They left the next morning, but not without Denny calling me at work to say goodbye. He asked for my home phone number. I gave it to him.

Thus began a friendship and closeness through daily phone calls. The next three months we spent learning everything about each other via the telephone.

In the meantime, I was still healing from Devin, but my long-distance doctor was a great distraction. My girlfriend, Diana told me jokingly that I needed, what she called a gap filler and I suppose Denny was just what Doctor Diana ordered.

Coupled with me realizing I had to stop numbing my pain at the expense of my liver.

## 34
### Tart Deco

Ɉn March, our doctor dudes, Denny and Jerry, decided to take a ski trip back to Utah for some spring skiing. Mandy and I picked them up at the airport. We wanted to surprise them, so we made signs to hold up as they exited the plane. Back then you could meet the passengers at the gate. We went prepared. I wore a red and black outfit with fishnet stockings attached to a garter belt under my long black coat, and held a homemade sign that read, "Kiss me like you missed me." I also wore the diamond necklace and matching earrings I had received from Missionary Man. Mandy, also a black leather jacket and her pearls of course, was in her Victoria's Secret black leather mini skirt with a matching bustier top, holding her own sign that read, "Till the Twelfth of Never."

As we approached the security area, Mandy walked through the metal detector with no problem. Then I followed. *Beep, beep, beep, beep, beeeeep*!

"Please step aside," the security officer said. She was a large, tough-looking woman with a gun on her hip.

I did as I was told. People stood by watching alongside Mandy.

The security lady ran the magic wand up and down the sides of my body as I held my arms out and up. No beeping. Then she moved it to the back of my upper body and down my spine. No beeping. She walked around to the front and began at the top, and slowly moved the wand down my body, past my chest and stomach. Still nothing. I wondered if I had forgotten that my Altoids were in my coat pocket. As she continued moving the wand down to my legs, she got about mid thigh and then it began; *beep beep, beep.*

"Please open your coat," she commanded. This was a problem, since people were still staring at me. Mandy worked at the airport and she looked at me puzzled, as I shrugged my shoulders.

"Do I really have to?" I asked the security officer shyly and quietly.

"Open your coat," she repeated, but louder and stronger this time.

I slowly undid the belt around my waist and opened my coat. "I'm meeting my husband who has been away," I lied. I thought that made me sound like more of a nice girl, and perhaps less of a tart.

The security officer looked at my outfit under the coat, rolled her eyes and quietly said, "You're free to go."

*Dang those metal garters!* I thought.

The weather can be so unpredictable in Utah. It was mid March and we were having one of the biggest storms of the year thus far. Of course, Denny and Jerry were both thrilled. We laughed about how we thought they came just to see us. They said they did, but had planned this trip factoring in the weather report.

Some mention was made about perfect planning since they had missed out on the snow in January. We all laughed as we drove them to their rental place in Deer Valley to check in.

Later that evening Mandy and I met up with Denny and Jerry for dinner at a very high-end local restaurant. The music was soft and the lights were low. The menu looked wonderful as Denny ordered a bottle of Jordan Cabernet wine to start, which was quite a treat. I had never had it before, but it quickly became my favorite. The waiter took our dinner orders as the conversation turned to skiing in the morning. Denny and Jerry were busy making plans where to ski, weighing out the differences between each resort. Mandy and I excused ourselves and walked slowly towards the restroom. Our waiter flashed us a smile as we made our way to the ladies room.

"What now, Mandy? Are we going to spend the evening with them?" I asked curiously.

"I'm not. I don't feel ready yet, plus I have to go home and take care of my dog," Mandy answered, "but you go ahead, Carly." Mandy had a beautiful golden retriever named Sundance that she absolutely adored and with good reason. Sundance was not only a beautiful animal, but so sweet and well-behaved.

"I don't know if I am ready to jump into bed with Denny either." I answered quickly.

"This is only the second time we have seen them," Mandy added, "it feels kinda weird to me."

"I agree, but I feel like I know Denny since we have spent the last three months talking on the phone *every day,*" I said truthfully.

Mandy knew Denny called me first thing in the morning before work and last thing in the evening before bed. "Well, we have been getting to know each other, but I'm worried about the sex part too," I said with some reservation.

Mandy nodded.

"Do you think they expect us to go home with them by the way we dressed at the airport?" I asked Mandy.

"Who cares what they expect? I'm not ready, plus I can't leave Sundance to fend for herself all night long." Mandy answered.

"Okay, I understand. I'm with you, girlfriend," I said.

We walked back to the table and sat down. I smiled to myself as I noticed our dinner was there. Don't you just love it when you go to the restroom and come back to find your food waiting for you? More wine was poured as we started our meal. The food was excellent! *I would definitely come here again, if I could afford it.*

Denny and Jerry were perfect gentlemen as we made plans to meet them the next morning, so we could have a quick breakfast before skiing.

"Are you girls ready to go?" Jerry asked politely.

"Yes, we are," Mandy and I said in unison.

We walked out to the parking lot to our vehicles, which were parked next to each other. I watched Mandy drive off in her truck and Jerry jumped in the driver's seat of the rental SUV. Denny walked with me to my car and opened the door. I thanked him, and hopped in.

"Are you okay to drive, Carly?" Denny asked.

"Yes, I 'm okay, thank you." I answered.

"Call me when you are home safely, Carly."

I nodded my head yes.

Denny kissed me on the forehead and closed the door. I watched him get into the Jeep Cherokee and they waited until I started my car and drove off.

I arrived home safely and made the call I agreed to make. An hour and a half later we finally said goodnight.

The next day, as we rode up the chair lift at PCMR, I looked more closely at Denny. The sun was out that morning and the conditions were sure to be perfect for spring skiing. And the light was also very good, yet unforgiving. I weakly smiled at Denny as I saw that he had a huge amount of course, black hair growing out of the very top of his nose.

*Hmmmm…* That was something I hadn't noticed before and we had not covered that topic in our numerous phone conversations. I concluded that he must have previously shaved it off when we originally met at Adolph's that first evening. *If he did it then, he could do it again*, I thought, while secretly hoping he would. It wasn't *necessarily* a deal breaker. We all have our "things" that make us unique. I know I certainly do.

After a beautiful day on the slopes, we all walked to the SUV, changed out of our ski boots and into our more comfortable boots.

"Anybody up for an après ski drink?" Denny asked, indicating he was.

"Sure!" we all answered excitedly.

We drove to Adolph's. Once inside Denny asked, "Another bottle of Jordan Cab?"

"Sounds great," I said, thinking I could get used to this.

We finished the bottle and drove back to the rental house.

"Anybody up for a hot tub?" Jerry asked.

Mandy and I looked at each other, a bit wide-eyed.

"What's the matter?" Denny asked.

"No suits," I answered nervously.

"Just leave your underwear on," Jerry suggested.

"That will work," Denny chimed in as Mandy and I walked into one of the bedrooms to change. I felt okay since we both had sports bras on. I looked down at my black g-string underwear as I wrapped a towel around my waist. Mandy followed my lead. We approached the outside hot tub and saw they were already in.

"Close your eyes!" I ordered the boys, and they did just that.

We climbed in next to them.

"You boys mind well," I said half joking as we all laughed.

I am not a big fan of hot tubs, but I was a good sport. I have to admit it did feel wonderful after the day on the ski slopes.

Once again, I looked over at Denny and I rubbed his chest, which was covered in very thick, black hair that resembled a sweater.

"I am very hairy," Denny said with a chuckle.

"Yes, you are," I said as I rubbed the stubble on the top of his nose.

"I was too tired to shave this morning, someone kept me on the phone too long last night," Denny said as he squeezed my thigh under the water. I smiled at him affectionately and he kissed me this time on the lips.

Mandy and I enjoyed a fun weekend of skiing, complete with nice dinners, romantic evenings and continuing to get to know the guys. When they left early Monday morning, I felt like I finally knew Denny. He was a very nice man but had a strong Type A personality. Jerry was just the opposite, down to earth and low key. I was amused at how they would argue over who was paying the check at dinner. Of course, Denny usually won out, while Mandy and I sat quietly after we thanked both of them over and over.

I had an important epiphany that weekend. I was enjoying this part of my life. Denny was just what I needed at the time. I was trying hard to fall in love with him, but my heart was still in pieces. I missed my Missionary Man, but had to realize that what I thought we had never really existed. Truly, nothing about it was real. It was all pure fantasy. I wanted it so badly that I let my head cloud with the promises of a married man and I still felt so bad about myself. I needed to call Kathy, my therapist and savior, to help me get through this. *Had I really sold my soul to a three-piece suit?*

I shook my head and I tried to clear my thoughts. In my heart I knew that on that fateful night in Vegas, Devin became unlovable to me. I just had to face that fact so my heart could heal. It was over, and I realized I needed to forget about Devin and get on with my life.

*There are some things you can't cover up with lipstick and powder!*

# Look No Hands!

I had an early morning appointment on Tuesday that began with my client, Kristie, in tears. She was contemplating divorce. She was concerned about an array of things, one of which was her nail appointments. She thought maybe she should take off her nails to try and save money.

I told her what I always told clients who were worried about the cost of nails.

"You can still come in for your appointments, and I won't worry about getting paid until you're back on your feet."

"Thank you, Carly. When I don't have my nails on, it looks like I have no hands!"

I smiled at Kristie and nodded, "I completely agree."

I know we are all in business to make money, but I also believe we are all here to love and support one another along the way. The problem with taking your nails off is when your life is in chaos you need something to feel good about. A beautiful manicure or pedicure does just that. It provides a measure of emotional comfort and a feeling of well-being. The last thing you should do is stop the things that make you feel good. Not to mention, having someone to talk to about your feelings on a weekly basis can be beneficial.

Kristie and I had some interesting and insightful conversations over the next few appointments. We both expressed our feelings, thoughts, and concerns. She was trying to figure out her next step. I had some experience with being divorced that I shared with her. One of the most important things I feel I learned along the way, as I matured, was if you can possibly keep your natural family together, it makes life a bit easier down the road. Of course, there are exceptions beyond our control, which can make it impossible to do so. I soon found out this was one of those exceptions.

"Max moved out," she said tearfully.

"I am so sorry, sweetie," I said as I rubbed her hand.

I met her husband a handful of times. He was a tall, handsome man, but he had a severe drinking problem.

"He moved down to Salt Lake City with two bisexual women." Kristie informed me.

I listened and sympathized without judgment as she continued to speak, her green eyes filled with tears.

Then when she finished, she looked at me as she asked, "What do you think I should do?"

I answered honestly. "You do realize he is never coming back, don't you? Isn't that just about every man's fantasy? The Beach Boys even wrote a song about it..."Two Girls for Every Boy."

At least that made her smile.

One of my favorite clients is a well-schooled man who only lives in Park City during the winter. He and his wife have both been coming to see me for almost thirty years. I was giving him a pedicure one afternoon while we chatted.

"So Carly, we're building this beautiful home, our dream house in Malibu, so I may need to answer my cell phone during the pedicure." Rex informed me.

"No problem, you do what you have to do. That is part of the beauty of a pedicure, you are hands-free!" I told him.

"Well, thank you," Rex said.

"Tell me about this dream home." I inquired.

"It's going to be close to 10,000-square-feet. We have a great architect who has suggested some very interesting and unique features that I am so excited about."

"Like what?" I asked curiously, as I start his foot massage. I have seen a ton of beautiful homes living in Park City, so I was intrigued.

"You know, Carly," Rex started to say but stopped short to enjoy the massage. He laid his head back on the chair, as he closed his eyes. "I've always had this fantasy," Rex said with his eyes still closed.

I stopped dead with what I was doing. "Now Rex, we've known each other far too long to start that kind of crap."

He opened his eyes and shot straight up off the back of the chair, eyes wide open and his face bright red.

He exclaimed, "No, no Carly, that's not what I meant. I was merely going to tell you about the fantasy of having a large threshold going from the back of the house and directly over a waterfall and coming out the other side on our property!"

We both chuckled as I apologized for my misunderstanding. I was a bit embarrassed, but continued with his foot massage. *How presumptuous, Carly! You should be embarrassed!*

After it was over I thanked him and he thanked me.

"No hard feelings?" I asked still feeling ashamed.

"Of course not, Carly!" Rex assured me.

I breathed a sigh of relief.

"You know, Carly, I get the same services in California, but there is a big difference with you."

"Thank you," I said quickly.

"The difference is like driving a Chevy and driving a Rolls Royce," he added.

"I drive a Chevy, Rex," I said dryly and we both laughed.

## 36
### Love It or Leaf It

In this business, we do meet all kinds of people. I remember one of the times working at Vie Retreat, I had a woman who came in for a manicure. Jessie was a familiar face around town and in some of the aerobic classes I attended, although I had never worked on her before. She was a fun girl, a real pistol, so to speak. Jessie quickly became one of my regular clients. I never heard anything negative or bad about her job, her husband, or her family. Everything was always wonderful in her life. I have to say it was a pleasant hour and a half. I welcomed the change and began to really look forward to our time together.

We became fast friends. She would come and pick me up in her Ferrari, and we would go to exercise classes. I thought that was so cool, as I had only seen a Ferrari on television. Our friendship continued to grow as well as our client relationship. I loved being around such an upbeat positive person.

One day Jessie came in for her usual appointment, still happy. We began to chat as I was doing her manicure. They were planning a family trip to Bermuda and she wouldn't be in for a couple of weeks. I smiled and thought how fun that sounded, as I was cleaning out under her fingernails. The index, middle and ring finger on her right hand were especially dirty. I went under them for a second and third time, finally removing the debris. It was all over the towel that covered my desk, but it wasn't dirt. It was a bit more leafy than that.

I looked at her and before I could say anything she muttered softly, "Pot...sorry."

I laughed as I continued to clean the bits of marijuana leaves out from under her fingernails, hence the happiness!

I also had a woman who came in regularly, who owned a successful sandwich shop in town, and she always came to her nail appointment with her dog, a very sweet and quiet poodle. When I would clean under her nails, I would scrape out avocado. To this day, the mere smell of an avocado takes me back about twenty-five years! It actually took me quite a while to even start to eat them again and that was hard because I do love avocados! I would always think of Bonnie and her great sandwiches...with avocado!

I have always believed in giving business back to people who give business to me. I tried to do this over the years, but once I got so many real estate clients, it became next to impossible. I would have had to buy or sell a house every year to do an even trade with them all!

Okay, that is a bit of an exaggeration, but you get the idea.

I did have one real estate agent client who said she purchased some acrylic nail supplies and was going to do her own nails. She felt I had given enough business to another client of mine who also sold real estate. I didn't see her for about a month, and then she called.

"Um, could you help me with the nails I put on myself?"

"Sure!" I replied. "Come on in."

She showed up at the end of the day and held out her hands. Her nails were approximately a quarter inch or more thick. "I couldn't get them even, so I just kept piling the acrylic on," she said.

I sent her to the paint store to buy some pure acetone. I can't believe that is what I used back then to take off acrylic nails! Not the gentler acetone we use today to remove any kind of nail enhancements. No, this was straight up, heavy-duty acetone.

I told her to get two glass bowls, fill them with enough of the stuff to cover her fingernails, and then cover her hands with a hot washcloth, remove and scrape off the softened product and repeat until it was all gone. Then start on the other hand.

As I said before, it is quite the process and trying to preserve the natural nail and the surrounding skin is a challenge. She said it took over two hours and then she still had to do the other hand.

To make a long story short, she came back regularly to have her nails done after that. She felt bad and confessed that she really thought she could do it.

"It didn't look that hard," she said.

"We all have our specialties," I replied, "I can't sell real estate, either."

But let's go back and revisit the purpose of cleaning under that nail plate. Even if there is nothing under your nails except the lotions and oils you have used on them, a little debris from things like gardening, avocado, mascara, or pot collects under there. Cleaning under the nail really is a must for a complete and finished-looking manicure. Plus, scraping underneath the nail also lets you know the edges are smooth.

Although we are in the beauty business, sometimes that part of our job is not really beautiful. You realize that doing nails is a hard business. Hard on your eyes, your back, and sometimes, your emotional well being. Not to mention the sitting hour after hour. It also requires a tremendous amount of focus. I had the son of Debra from Vie Retreat say to his mom, "Boy, Carly sure has a nice, cushy job, just sitting here painting fingernails all day!"

No clue whatsoever.

# If the Slipper Fits

I t had been almost four months of dating Denny, the doctor, long distance. We continued our nightly phone calls learning more about one another. He commented that he felt bad for me, stating that I had these husbands and men in my life, and nobody had helped me out financially. He was amazed that I had done it on my own, calling me a survivor.

One thing about Denny, he didn't believe in credit card debt. I had only one credit card, and that had a balance of over two thousand dollars. That was unacceptable to him. "You are paying interest on that balance, Carly," he informed me. "Let me pay it off for you."

"No, thank you, "I answered. "I will continue to pay it off myself over time." That was the part he didn't like.

"That is a waste of money," he insisted, as his voice approached a slight increase in volume. "You are accruing 18% interest every month you carry a balance!"

*Oh, really? What a surprise!* I thought to myself sarcastically. "I know, Denny." I replied calmly. (Obviously, I am much braver in my thoughts.)

"Please let me help you," Denny said as he my hands in his, "I can and I am going to do this. I care about you and I can easily afford to do it." And then Denny added, "That's the end of it."

*Well, if you insist.* I nodded my head, sighed, and said, "Okay, thank you."

He folded up my credit card statement, and kissed me on the top of the head, as he put it in his coat pocket.

Once again, Denny's Type A personality won out.

Denny explained that he wanted to help out somebody whom he felt was a nice person and deserved a break. "I just want to sit by the ocean, and smoke my cigar knowing I helped someone out whom I care about. Carly, you deserve a helping hand."

I really don't like owing anyone money, particularly a romantic interest. It just doesn't feel good to me, but he insisted and I reluctantly went along.

Denny and I saw each other that first six months just a few times. I would go to his beach house, located on the ocean in Hilton Head, South Carolina. He was into golf and wanted me to be into it as well. He bought me my first set of golf clubs. Medicine had been very good to Denny. We vacationed at not only the beach house in Hilton Head, but at his family cabin in Wisconsin, and at his primary residence, a palatial mansion in Savannah, Georgia. There were lots of weekend trips and I was having a blast. I felt like Cinderella! Those all-consuming thoughts of Devin that had flooded my mind, were now occasional, and almost non-existent. I was happy that Denny was in my life. But there were some struggles, most of which I tried to ignore, but the signs were there. I wondered if I could deal with someone who had time requirements for getting ready. Coupled with him pushing so hard to get his own way. I knew Denny's Type A personality presented itself quite regularly and I worried it was going to be just one of those struggles. Time will tell, I told myself, hoping I could deal with his strong, and often bossy personality.

As the time passed, I felt an enormous amount of pressure from Denny to get away more. But I couldn't just take off and vacation anytime I wanted, no matter how much fun I had. I had a business to run and clients who depended on me being there. This was hard for Denny to understand, which surprised me. He had his own medical practice with a full clientele, yet he wanted to vacation all the time. I was puzzled, but soon came to realize this man was used to getting his own way. One time, he wanted me to meet him in Savannah and we would drive to his place on Hilton Head Island. "I have some work to do on the beach house, painting and such." Denny said. "I would like to stay for about ten days or so," he informed me.

"I can't possibly get away for ten days, Denny."

"Why not?" he asked.

"I still have to support myself," I answered. "That is a lot of time away from work. I can't miss all of those days, especially to watch you paint," I said with a quick wink and smile. "I could *maybe* do five days, if I incorporated it with my regular days off."

"Okay," Denny agreed.

Wow, how easy was that?

"I'll go for the first five days by myself," he planned. "You fly into Savannah for the remaining five days. I'll pick you up and we'll do a bit of sightseeing before driving to the beach house."

Done and done.

I always wanted to visit Savannah and he knew it. I read a book about the historic haunts of Savannah. It is said to be one of America's most haunted cities and I was intrigued. Since childhood, I have always been interested in that kind of thing.

That and vampire stories!

However, it wasn't long before the real Denny emerged once again! He still couldn't fathom why it was so difficult for me to get away for the ten days.

*Here we go,* I thought.

I reiterated my missing work meant no income.

"How much money do you make in a day, Carly?"

"It depends, it can vary," I answered.

Impatiently he asked, "What is the most you have made in one day?"

At that time I guessed at around three hundred dollars.

With that he took out his checkbook, wrote me a check, handed it to me and said, "Now, you can afford the ten days."

I looked at the check made out to me for $3,000, as he added, "You need to have a life outside of work, Carly."

He had a point. I did agree with that part.

*Hmmm…If I factor in my days off, it makes it somewhat easier, even though I'll have to work like mad before leaving, trying my best to fit everyone in. I am sure I will do the same on my return,* I thought.

What the heck. I want to go.

So off I went to Savannah, Georgia. It was everything that I had anticipated. I really had a fun, interesting time, and I never did have to paint! The nights sitting on the beach were magical and really made the trip memorable.

But the flipside? Spending ten straight days with Denny was beginning to wear on me. I saw firsthand how demanding he could be. I had to ask myself if this was really what I wanted. Geographically, Denny was undesirable, and coupled with his Type A personality, I was in a quandary.

It would be wonderful not to struggle with money, but I am now smart enough to know, there is always a high price attached to "financial freedom."

# Perfect Clarity

enny was slowly becoming more controlling and bossy with me. For example, he started to complain about how long I took to get ready. "From now on, you only have eight minutes to get ready, Carly."

*What? Hair AND makeup in only eight minutes? Are you crazy?* I thought. Now, don't get me wrong, I am not really that high maintenance! I can be ready in five minutes if I have to and I can take five hours if I want to.

Jokingly, I said, "Denny, if I had only spent eight minutes on myself the night we met in Adolph's, you wouldn't have looked twice at me!"

Unfortunately, he wasn't amused, and it didn't end there. Denny paid no mind to my cute comment. Instead, he continued with the time limits and his demands that I get away more with him and for longer periods of time. I found out rather quickly that he would not take no for an answer. He began making plans for my future.

"I want you to move to Savannah," he finally said adamantly.

*Oh no, not this.*

I calmly listed the reasons why I couldn't move. "Denny, first of all, I can't leave my grandchildren. Utah is my home. And what about my business? My clientele?"

"Fine," he interrupted. "I will sell my practice and move to Utah and you won't have to leave. I love it there," Denny continued before I could speak. He was very good at that. "I could retire in Utah just as easily as I could in Georgia," he reasoned. "I will purchase a house in Deer Valley; you won't even have to work. You could quit your job and travel with me and enjoy life." He had it all figured out.

I gasped out loud. "Wait! What do you mean quit my job?"

I literally felt as if my life passed right before my eyes. It was close to having a near death experience! My head spun and I felt faint. *Hold everything!*

"Denny, I need to think about this. Let's not rush into anything."

But of course, he wouldn't listen. He was busy making his plans for our life.

"You need to go home and start to prepare your clients for this life change, the sooner the better. You only live once," he said.

"But I love my clients and my job. I don't want to quit," I said.

Didn't matter. He simply wouldn't take no for an answer.

This discussion took place in the airport on our way back to Utah from the Savannah trip. They called boarding for our flight, and I gathered my carry-on.

"I promise. I'll think about it," I said, just to get him off my back.

Denny smiled and gave me a quick kiss on the cheek as I hurried toward the gate.

*Whew! That seemed to satisfy him, at least for the time being.*

Before entering the long hallway to the plane, I glanced back at him and he looked so happy. I blew him a kiss goodbye and turned around. As the plane took off, I wondered if I would ever see Denny again. I knew I wasn't quitting my job or moving to Savannah or Hilton Head Island. Not even Deer Valley was a big enough carrot, as my thoughts drifted to his proposal of selling his practice and moving to Utah. I shuddered as I remembered a saying I heard years ago, *"The one who has the money gets to be the boss."*

I knew deep down what I needed to do. I felt it all the way to my core.

For now, he was in Georgia and I was in Utah, right where we both belonged.

The next morning I went to work at 7:30. I had some long days ahead of me. That has always been the hard part about going away for any length of time. You are so busy before you leave trying to get everyone in, and upon returning you are just as busy trying to play catch up. Often, I would question if it was worth the few days off.

But I am smart enough to know that it is.

In this business, we have to have time off. We have to take care of ourselves. We get so busy taking care of our clients, that this is something we can forget to do. As I steadily built a clientele to the point it is now, I became so consumed with fitting every single, solitary person in that contacted me that I forgot about myself along the way. I took no breaks in my twelve-hour days, and forget about a lunch hour. I survived on coffee and an occasional apple for years, and it was my own doing. I made the choice to say yes. One of the many benefits of being self-employed is that we are able to make our own schedules, but few of us make it the right way. If you are a people pleaser, as I am, be prepared for this and make the choice to take care of yourself first. Learn to say no.

The conversations I have with clients are not always troubled ones. There are the times when there can be very funny ones as well. I had a client, Joanne, in her early eighties who was telling me about her Restless Leg Syndrome. She had seemingly tried everything. Then her doctor had advised her every night to use a hand held vibrating apparatus on her legs before she got into bed. This seemed to help ease her discomfort so much that she couldn't do without it. Joanne came in one morning about twenty minutes early.

"Carly, sorry I'm early, but I couldn't sleep at all last night."

"Oh, I am sorry, Joanne, are you okay?" I asked.

"Yes, I will be okay. My handheld vibrator for my *RLS, Restless Leg Syndrome,* finally gave out. My legs have been bothering me all night."

She added her doctor had suggested she purchase a leg massager with a stronger motor from a medical supply company, but when she investigated the cost, she was surprised to find it quite expensive. She sighed and said, "I will just see how it goes."

I gave her a sympathetic smile. Joanne never complained about anything and my heart was sad for her as I realized this syndrome must be hard to deal with.

Joanne had a large family who lived close by, and they were very involved in their aging parents' care. Their children wanted to make the rest of their time safe, comfortable and relatively easy. *They could help her with the expensive apparatus* I thought. That would solve that.

One day her daughter, Libby, who was in the nutrition field, decided her mom needed to have a "Blendtec," which is an overgrown blender, according to Joanne.

Libby said she wanted her parents to start blending their protein smoothies with less effort. They sold them at a nearby Costco and they were fairly expensive, but well worth it, the daughter had concluded.

Joanne was skeptical and went back and forth on the subject, realizing she still needed the handheld apparatus for her RLS. Mostly to appease Libby, they decided to take a trip to Costco. Joanne said she was quite surprised at the price of this overgrown blender.

"It's a whopping $350.00," she told me, wondering if it would really make that much of a difference.

Then added, "I think the vibrator has to come before the Blendtec," just as my next client walked in the room. The look on her face was priceless. Timing is everything.

While we are on the subject… there are the clients who decide that when they are in the room with you, nobody else is welcome. Period.

"This is my time with you, Carly."

I get it and I completely understand.

I have a close friend named Tess, who has been a client since I started here in Park City. After her nail appointment, she and I would end the day with a glass or two of red wine until she became a devout Mormon over twenty years ago. We are still very close friends, and she feels comfortable enough to just walk in my room, sit down and wait for me to finish with the client before her. One day I was doing a pedicure on another client, Chandler, who is hilarious, outspoken and irreverent, in a funny but strong way. I was just finishing up polishing her toes, when Tess walked in and sat down at my desk. Chandler flashed her a how dare you kind of look as she stopped what she was saying.

It was quiet for a few seconds when Chandler looked directly at me and asked calmly, "Have you ever been to the Blue Boutique?"

This is Salt Lake City's version of a sex shop complete with adult toys and intimate apparel.

Before I could answer, she added, "I bought this awesome vibrator there, it's so amazing, I want to marry it," she exclaimed loudly.

I kept my head down trying desperately to concentrate on the toes I was painting. Tess stood up and as she walked out, she announced, "I will be out here in the lobby waiting, Carly." Tess pointed to the lobby area.

"Okay Tess," I said as I looked up at Chandler, shook my head and mouthed silently, *"YOU ARE SO BAD!"*

I have a restroom connected with my salon room located in Silver Shears, where I have worked since 2002. Often, clients from the hairdressers come in while I am working and use that restroom. It annoys the majority of my clients so much that one of them actually made a sign that read, *"Private. Restroom is across the hall."*

Yes, it was Chandler, the same client who frequents the Blue Boutique!

I admit I get annoyed, but for a different reason. I need to be in the restroom getting the paraffin wax for the pedicure, changing the water and sanitizing the implements I use. Basically, I need to get ready for my next client. Being on time is important. I don't mind if my next client needs to pop in there before or after we start her appointment. In fact, I have this client, Anna, who had that need before her last appointment. I was in the restroom, running the water for her pedicure, when she came in, pulling her pants down.

"Sorry, Carly, but I have to pee," Anna said rather quickly and matter-of-factly.

"No worries," I said as I stopped what I was doing and turned to walk out.

"Christ, you've seen inside my soul, which is a hell of a lot more intimate than seeing my vagina," Anna informed me.

I stopped and turned the water back on and began to fill the tub for her pedicure as she continued to pee.

"You have a valid point," I smiled, as I knew exactly what she meant.

## 39

## Soulmate

I was still working at L & Company, an established salon and was busier than ever. I didn't have a lot of time to think about Denny's lifetime plan for me. He was still calling me nightly, trying to convince me to move.

I went to work that morning and as the day progressed my friend, Kallie, called. She worked for a real estate company in town. She had developed a slight crush on her broker, Davis, and we (Davis and I) happen to share the same birthday. Kallie made a plan to invite him out for a drink to celebrate our birthdays. I knew Davis a little better than she did, hence the invite.

I reminded her how I didn't like to go out on Friday night. I worked Saturdays back then and needed to be on my game mentally, as well as physically. I (somewhat) jokingly told her how difficult it is to apply nail polish with a shaking hand.

"Can't we wait until tomorrow night, Kallie?" I pleaded.

"No, we can't wait. Davis is going out of town for his birthday tomorrow," she said. "It has to be tonight."

I protested.

"Just one glass of wine." She wasn't going to give up.

Reluctantly, I agreed, but really is it ever just one glass?

"Stay just long enough to break the ice," Kallie said. "It has been forever since I've been interested in anyone and now I am and I need your help, Carly. He could be the one, my soul mate!"

She was right. She suffered through a long, painful, and messy divorce. It took some convincing on her part, but I finally agreed to meet her and Davis at Adolph's for that infamous *one* glass of wine.

The bar was empty on this cool June evening, but it was still early. We grabbed three bar stools and ordered our wine. Mary was bartending that evening when we walked in. "How is Denny doing?" she asked right away.

"He is doing great. Thanks for asking," I replied cheerfully. No sense in telling her what a control freak he was and that I was going to end my relationship with him if he kept pressing me.

"I like Denny so much, he is such a great guy. I am so happy for you," Mary stated equally as cheerful. "When are you guys going to get married?"

I laughed nervously, as Mary sat down three glasses of red wine. I raised mine to toast our birthdays and quickly took the first sip.

Over the course of the evening, Kallie and Davis seemed to be getting along quite well. I had a group of friends arrive for dinner, so I let them chat while I made my way over to their table. I sat down next to Diana. "Where's your boyfriend, sister?"

"Denny is back in Savannah, doing the doctor thing." I answered.

"What is going on over there?" she asked quizzically as her head nodded in the direction of Kallie and Davis. Diana knew them both like everybody else in this small town.

I raised my eyebrows coyly. She immediately got my message.

"Oh, I hope they really hit it off," she said with excitement. "I like them both so much."

"Me, too," I said, "I'll let you get back to your evening."

I picked up my glass of red wine and made my way back to the bar.

Kallie and Davis were both laughing and talking about the real estate business. They both appeared to be genuinely enjoying each other's company. I was excited for her. She had been so sad and lonely for quite a few years and it looked like she was now ready to move on. That evening, on that barstool, flirting with Davis, she actually looked happy. She was relaxed and enjoying herself for the first rime in a long time. I love to see my friends happy. I smiled at her and she smiled back. I was glad I had come out with her that night. *Perhaps her broken heart was healing after all.*

There's another reason I was glad I let Kallie drag me out. We were in Adolph's for over an hour and on our *second* glass of wine, when in walked the man of my dreams. He just didn't know it yet.

He stood at the bar talking to Mary, the bartender. She handed him a glass of Chardonnay. He was so tall and so handsome. I had always liked tall men, being tall myself, and his good looks were certainly a plus. I wondered who he was. I thought I knew most of the men in Park City, but yet I had never met this man. As he sipped his Chardonnay, he turned and walked over to the far side of the bar where we were sitting, and sat down two stools down from us. He propped his feet up on the bar stool next to me. I looked over at his long, outstretched legs, reached over and pinched his big toe through the sole of his golf shoe and said, "Hi."

He looked at me and said tentatively with some reservation, "Hi." Then he stared straight ahead and took another sip of wine.

*Okay…playing it cool. I get it.* I thought. The result? Another pinch and another "hi" from me.

This time, he smiled as he said, "Hi."

His smile was so warm and welcoming. He moved his feet off of the stool and I slid over next to him with my glass of red wine.

"I'm Bennett," I said with a smile.

"I'm Stenmark. And why did you pinch my toe?" he asked curiously.

I had no good answer. I didn't even know myself. I had never pinched *anyone's* toe before. Ironically, when I am not sitting across from a client, I am usually quiet and shy, particularly around the opposite sex. That was really out of character for me.

I simply said, "I don't know, maybe it's fate."

"Fate, huh?" Stenmark replied.

I chuckled and commented on a Bonnie Raitt song that was playing in the bar. "Oh, I love this song, it's one of my favorites!"

Stenmark replied, "What's the name of it?"

"Love Me Like a Man," I answered.

Stenmark smiled as he said, "Great name for a song. So you like music?"

"I love music!" was my reply. As it turned out he was a musician. *Score!*

We spent the next two hours deep in conversation about everything. I felt so comfortable talking to him. He was a good listener and an interesting conversationalist and he was so cool. I soon realized we had a lot in common, and our love of music was just one of the many things. We knew some of the same musicians in and around the Salt Lake City area and that was fun and interesting.

Out of the blue, the subject changed to intelligence, as I started joking about studying for the Mensa test. I always felt a bit embarrassed about the fact that I never graduated from high school, and truly never thought about going back to obtain my diploma. I never felt it was necessary. I was a business owner and a successful one at that, but must have felt a strong connection to Stenmark as I did something I had never done before. I confessed I was a high school dropout, something I only shared with my closest friend in Park City. I never even discussed it with my own children, as I didn't want them to think that was an option.

When I made this confession, he had one of his own. Turns out, Stenmark was a Mensa member. I could tell he was much more intelligent than Devin was and I always thought he was the most intelligent man I had been around.

*But Devin wasn't a member of Mensa!*

Stenmark chuckled and said, "I don't carry the card, too ostentatious."

I laughed thinking, *how cool is that?* He was very down to earth and that was refreshing.

"Do you golf?" he asked.

"Well, Kallie and I signed up for a series of lessons at the city course." I told Stenmark.

"How many lessons did you sign up for?"

"We signed up for five and we've done two out of the five lessons. I broke my ankle playing on my coed softball team in our last championship game the end of the season." I explained with way too much detail.

"Are you going to start back with those lessons this year?" Stenmark asked getting to the point.

"I only had a couple of lessons left when I broke my ankle last year. I don't know," I said adding, "They probably have expired by now. And I didn't really care for my instructor anyway."

"What was his name?" asked Stenmark. I thought this was an odd question, coming from a musician.

"His name was Bill."

Stenmark answered with, "Well, what if I could get those lessons back for you with a different instructor?"

I must have had a puzzled look on my face because he added, "I work at the golf course and actually Bill is my boss."

*Open mouth, insert foot, once again!*

"Oh, no, now I'm embarrassed," I said. "You work with him!"

He laughed. "If you want I can speak with Bill and I think I will be able to get the lessons back with me."

"What do you mean?" I asked him.

"We trade off on lessons all the time," Stenmark informed me.

"That would be cool," I told him.

Kallie and I had signed up for golf hoping to meet nice men with honesty and integrity. *But now it is possible I am no longer looking!* I smiled at my sudden-found confidence as I looked over at Diana, who was waving for me to come back to her table. "Excuse me, please, I will be right back," I hurried over to her table and sat down.

Diana said sternly, "Sister, that is *not* your boyfriend, you already have a boyfriend, and a wealthy boyfriend at that!"

*Thanks for the reminder, Diana!*

"I know," I said just to appease her, but my heart was getting the best of me. Diana and I were close, so close we referred to each other as 'sister' (and still do to this day) rarely using our given names.

But I didn't want to think about Denny right now! I felt bad when I thought about Denny. He was a kind, generous man but I wanted to know more about *this* man. I was intrigued and I really didn't even know why. On other occasions, I usually listened to Diana. I paid attention to her advice, warnings, and predictions. Diana was an old soul who was very wise way beyond her years. I always trusted her judgment and listened intently to her words as she spoke with complete conviction. Diana had an amazing belief system that I greatly admired, but envied at times. There was no denying that, but I still longed to get to know Stenmark better.

*Sorry not this time, sister.*

I walked back and took my seat next to Stenmark.

He smiled as I sat down next to him. I was already convinced this was meant to be.

I thought, to myself, *Denny who?*

# 40
## Bare My Soul

The conversation with Stenmark continued and turned to other topics. Time flew by.

Kallie and Davis decided to go uptown, hear some music and dance while Stenmark and I stayed behind and continued talking. He ordered another glass of Chardonnay. I was still chatting and sipping my second glass of red wine. I told him all about my family and he listened intently.

He also told me all about his life. He was from Minnesota, his parents were from Sweden, and his father owned and operated a barbershop in Minneapolis. His mother was a homemaker and he had two sisters, much older than him. He was basically raised as an only child. He played football in high school and college, then moved to Utah with his first love, and taught skiing at Alta and Park City. He also traveled back and forth to L.A. playing music.

We talked about my four children and I asked him if he had any children? He said he had a son who had turned eight the day before. I listened as he told me all about him and how he loved being a father. I knew he was a good man. I could just tell.

I decided to shift gears, as our conversation continued. I told him all about my boyfriend, Denny, the doctor. I told him I was getting ready for a trip in July to his cabin in Wisconsin. I would be gone for about a week. I told him all about Denny's place on Hilton Head Island and the golfing. I had met Denny's daughter on several occasions, so I told him all about her. I babbled on and on about life with Denny, almost as if I were trying to convince myself that Denny was THE ONE. But it didn't work. I couldn't deny the gravitational pull I felt towards Stenmark.

I looked at my watch and realizing the time, I said I had to go. "I have to work early in the morning," I said.

"How do I get in touch with you about the golf lessons?" he asked.

I reached into my day timer and pulled out my business card.

"There you go," I said with a big smile.

"Great," he said, "I'll see what I can do. I'll be in touch."

"Thank you, that will be fun to start up again," I said with another big smile.

"Bye now," I added as I turned and walked out the door.

I drove home without even turning on the car radio. I was mesmerized by the night, and by him. "You have a boyfriend, you have a boyfriend, you have a boyfriend." I repeated over and over to myself that night in the car, and then again later until I fell fast asleep.

I woke up the next morning, still deep in thought about the night before. I headed out the door for a quick run, before work. I had to clear my head. I arrived at work fairly early, which is not unusual for me. I always liked to be there before my first client walked in. That way I could get the coffee going, turn on the music and just spiff things up. I always felt it was important to be ready, so it doesn't look as if I just woke up!

Fortunately, I didn't have a hangover that morning. I learned early on, that drinking to excess doesn't mix well with doing nails. The smell of the acrylic is nauseating enough. Plus, if you feel the need to confess that you are hung over to these clients whom have now become friends, be prepared for backlash. That can be the kiss of death, so to speak. Fast-forward two weeks after your confession and you're likely to hear, "My nails didn't hold up, of course you were hung over the last time!"

The lesson here is this: If you're going to over indulge, do it on Saturday nights when you can lay in bed all day Sunday, and eat everything in sight, trying to make yourself feel better.

# Find a Short Cut

My first client the morning after meeting Stenmark was Stevie, a pretty blonde with a Type A personality. She is very funny and always tells the best jokes. She always arrives early, looks at her watch, looks at your clock, then back at her watch and asks, "Are you on time?" I try so hard to be, and since she was the first of the day, I was.

Stevie and I began to chat, as I started her pedicure. She had just returned from a long road trip with her husband, and filled me in on all the details. She asked if I ever listened to books on tape.

"No," I shook my head. "I like to listen to music," I told her.

She then began telling me about a book on tape that she had picked up from the library. She said about halfway into it, it became so erotic that they had to pull off the highway. "We pulled into a vacant campground, and instead of having a picnic, we had a poke-nic, then continued on our way!"

My next pedicure appointment was Marsha, a second homeowner. She came in maybe two or three times a year during the ski season. She was elderly and recently widowed. I really enjoyed our talks and our time together. She too had just returned from a road trip with a few of her girlfriends. "I have to tell you what happened on our way home," she said.

"What happened?" I asked, a bit worried about these elderly women traveling alone.

"Oh, nothing bad, Carly. We stopped in a restaurant to have lunch in a place called Snowflake, Utah."

I was curious. "Where is that? I've lived in Utah my whole life and it doesn't ring a bell."

"It is about four hours from here. We found it by accident trying to find a faster route," she answered.

I wondered if she was confusing it with Snowville, Utah, which I had heard of.

Marsha continued with her story. "Well, this place we stopped was a quaint old diner, of sorts. We noticed a couple of young men probably in their late twenties sitting at the bar enjoying their lunch. The waitress inquired where we were from," said my client. "When we answered 'Park City,' one of the young men from the counter overhearing the conversation turned around and said, 'You're not here to have lunch, you're here to buy the place!'"

We had a chuckle about the misconception that a lot of people have if you live in Park City. I told her I always used to say, "I'm the poorest person who lives there."

We both had a good laugh.

As I began her pedicure, she confessed that she couldn't get in to see me before she left and had to go to one of the Asian salons. "I cheated on you, Carly. I had to go to one of those 'fast foot' places here in town."

The reference to fast food made me chuckle. Inexpensive, unprofessional and lacking in quality came to mind.

"Oh, Marsha, I understand," I said hoping everything went well. I'd heard the stories so I had to ask, "Was everything all right?"

"Well, they finished me in thirty minutes flat, so I pulled out my book and began to read while I waited for my polish to dry."

I smiled and said, "Good girl."

"But I looked over at the woman next to me and noticed they were dipping her feet into the paraffin wax when I realized I didn't get the full treatment."

"Oh, that's too bad. That's the best part," I said sympathetically.

"I was a bit irritated. I didn't know I needed to ask for it. I am so used to you doing it automatically," Marsha added, "until they came back to remove the wax from her feet."

"Why? What happened then?" I asked curiously.

"They put the used wax from her feet *back* into the paraffin tub!"

"You're kidding," I said in disbelief, "yuck!"

"No, I'm not. I was so happy I didn't get the wax dip," Marsha said with a sense of relief.

"That's really disgusting," I said trying to control my feeling of repulsion. Since the market has been inundated with new salons popping up all over Park City, I've tried very hard not to speak badly about them. But when I hear something like that, it completely unnerves me.

It's unfortunate that a few bad salons can give the good salons such a bad name. It is really frustrating and hard when bad salons are in the news. Clients come in understandably worried about what the news investigates. It is important to keep 'in the know' about these things. That way I can reassure my clients if they happen to ask me about using Windex instead of Barbicide in the sanitation jars, for example, or even the reusing of the paraffin wax! If a client asks me, "What is MMA liquid," I better know the answer and the reasons it is not legal. I believe it is my responsibility to know how to keep my clients safe. I can't tell you the number of people who come in for a pedicure and have never been asked if they are diabetic prior to getting one. It blows me away! I have to protect my clients and protect myself, not only healthwise, but legally, as well.

I also need to know when I'm out of my element. I am a not doctor. One of the first things I did was find a good podiatrist in the area to whom I could refer clients. I am here basically to beautify and soften the feet, not to perform surgery!

# 42
## Lost Labyrinth

I enjoy meeting the husbands, significant others, and life partners of my clients. It's nice to put a face with a name behind the funny (and serious) stories I hear. For example, I have a close client and an even closer friend who is absolutely hysterical. Zena has been one of my longest known clients and of course, we became close friends almost immediately. She is only a couple of years older than me, but wise beyond her years. I love her philosophy on life. Zena meditates daily and attends spiritual seminars and she is able to do readings for others. I do believe she is very talented, gifted, and psychic. I have traveled with her and for me it is quite the ethereal experience. I have to say, I have learned so much from Zena over the years. I have confided in her, and asked for her advice and opinions. When I ask for her input, I'm prepared for a very direct and honest answer, like it or not. I remember once a long-time Park City resident happened to follow Zena's manicure appointment. While waiting for her nails to dry, Zena and antoher client, Hellen began to chat about the upcoming Mayoral election.

"Why don't you run for Mayor?" Hellen asked Zena.

Zena laughed and shook her head, "No way!"

Hellen was curious and asked, "Why not? Are you afraid that people don't like you and you will lose?"

Zena laughed even harder as she answered Hellen. "It's not that they don't like me. They just don't understand my honesty about their stupidity!"

As I said, you can always count on an honest answer from Zena!

Zena is a weekly manicure that I always look forward to. She usually comes in with lattes in hand for us to enjoy during her service, which is nice. I guess you could say we have weekly coffee for a *half* hour or so.

Once, on a day she planned to leave town right after our appointment, Zena left her place in a rush as her husband followed her out and asked, "Where are you going? We're leaving soon."

"First, I'm going to get lattes, and then I'm going to see Car," she told him. Zena continued, "I will stop and walk the labyrinth before our long drive up to Idaho."

Her husband replied with, "Everything in this town revolves around Car. In this town, Car always seems to come first."

Zena left him with a smile and a wink, jokingly stating, "That's right, and don't you forget it!" Then Zena added, "I'll be back in a half hour...or so."

I have another long-time client and friend, Jody. She is also an amazing, kind hearted and wise woman. She taught me the meaning of "pick your battles." I often think had I met her before my first divorce, I could have saved myself a ton of grief! We both have the same religious upbringing, although she stayed in the LDS church and is still a member in good standing and I am positive she obeys *The Word of Wisdom*! Jody used to envy my trips to a certain degree, as her husband is retired and hangs around the house. Whenever I left on fun trips, she would give me a job. "Be sure and have a cheeseburger, fries and a glass of chardonnay by the pool, and think of me."

And I would do exactly that.

Jody had a funny story that she shared with me. Before she married her retired husband in the Salt Lake City Temple, she would go to the Country Club to have lunch. She would order her "healthy" lunch and a glass of white wine. She would then ask the waiter to please put the wine in a coffee cup. He did. As she sat there enjoying her lunch, she called him over and asked him for a dessert menu. As she pondered her choices, she asked the waiter for a cup of black coffee. He wrote it down, and stoically asked her, "Would you like that in a wine glass?"

You have to love a good sense of humor.

One day, I received a phone call from Pamela, a client of thirty-plus years, who moved to California a couple of years prior. "Hey Carly, I am going to be in town for a few days. Would you like to meet for dinner and a glass of wine?" she asked.

"I would love to!" I replied eagerly, I've missed you, Pamela!"

"Great, what day works the best for you? I am here Monday through Thursday this week."

"I could do Tuesday after work," I told her eagerly.

Pamela was just as excited as she asked, "Will six o'clock work for you?"

"That will be perfect. See you then," I answered.

We agreed to meet at a local restaurant close to my work.

I walked in close to the agreed time to find Pamela sitting at a table with a glass of wine for both of us. I smiled as I greeted her since it had been a couple of years since we had seen one another, we had a lot of catching up to do.

After about three hours of talking about kids, grandkids, pets, and just life in general, we walked out to the parking lot. As we stood by my car, saying our goodbyes, both of us teary-eyed, Pamela confessed, "You know it's funny, Carly, I've lived in Park City for over thirty years, and when I came back I told my husband the only person I really want to see is Carly."

I was stunned and flattered. Pamela had a ton of friends and I felt so honored. I gave her a hug as she continued on. "I miss our talks about our ups and downs in life. And I miss your sense of humor, Carly."

"I've missed all of that, too," I admitted, and hugged her again.

In this business, we build some strong relationships that can become everlasting, and truly in the scheme of things, I whole-heartedly believe, that's really what it is all about.

I was told years ago by quite a few of my clients, that their husbands often refer to me as, "Carly, who does your nails."

Some of these men became clients, some of them became friends, and a handful of them I have never met. I've spoken to them over the years by phone, so it feels like I know them, but it is always fun to put a face with a name. For me, I am often reminded of a profound saying from Maya Angelou that I came to love, especially as I matured in life: *"I've learned that people will forget what you said, people will forget what you did, but people will never forget how you made them feel."*

And there it is once again. We need to remember we *are* in the feel good business and, treat people accordingly.

# Attached at the Chip

I t was a beautiful, sunny June morning, when I received a call on my cell phone. It was Stenmark, the music guy I had met the night before in Adolph's.

"Hey, Bennett. I spoke with my boss, your previous golf instructor. I can do the remaining lessons with you, if you would like."

*If I would like! Uh…yes!* "Really? That would be awesome," I said calmly trying to hide my enthusiasm.

"Okay then, Monday at three o'clock? Isn't that your day off?" he asked.

I wondered if I shared my days off with him Friday night, but then remembered his father was a barber. By and large, all of us in the salon business are off on Sundays and Mondays.

I answered, "That will be perfect."

I thought about Denny and felt a quick pang of guilt.

Somewhere in my mind, I told myself that I could go and just take the lessons. But I knew deep in the back of my mind, I couldn't. Stenmark had been on my mind non-stop, and I wanted to see him, wanted to get to know him better. I wanted more of the conversation that I had ended so abruptly that night, when I left Adolph's, kind of wishing I could forget him, but deep down knowing that was impossible.

I went down to Salt Lake City to get my snow tires taken off of my front-wheel-drive car early Monday morning. My golf lesson was at three o'clock. My heart pounded with the anticipation of seeing the man I couldn't get out of my head. The tire place was crowded. Everyone had the same idea that day. I watched the clock, frantically, getting nervous that they wouldn't finish my car in time. I sat nervously fidgeting with my cell phone trying to keep my mind on clearing my voice messages, but the truth was I couldn't wait to see him again.

Finally, I realized I wouldn't make my golf lesson and I was crushed. They had not even started on my car and it was one o'clock! I called him and a sigh of relief came over me as I got his voice mail. (I didn't want to have to cancel on him in person.) I left my message, and then dealt with the tire people. I was upset, but then I realized how busy they were and decided maybe I should have made an appointment. *DUH!*

The next day Stenmark called and we made another appointment for my lesson the following Monday, my day off. The week was filled with such uneasiness. One day, I wanted to see him, the next day, I wanted to cancel. I was so torn and filled with conflicting emotion. I didn't know which way was up. My head told me to stay away, but my heart told me to go ahead. I couldn't believe that I felt such a strong connection to a stranger. I thought, *how crazy is this?* But I couldn't deny the strong pull I felt, so I embraced it.

When the next Monday rolled around, I headed to the golf course. *It's just a golf lesson,* I told myself. Denny was a golfer. We could golf together next month when we were at the cabin. I tried to convince myself that's all it was, but deep down I knew it was so much more.

My lesson with Stenmark was good, but I was terrible at golf. He said he could help me, and I believed him – mainly because it was a way I could spend time with him without questioning my motives. I wondered if he felt the same way. I knew it was so much more than golf lessons. Thoughts of being in his arms began to invade my concentration and if you have ever played this silly game, you are very much aware of the focus it requires.

"Let's go practice some chip shots," Stenmark said breaking my concentration and snapping me back into the game of golf.

"Okay," I said cheerfully. *What the heck is a chip shot?*

We worked on "chipping" for about an hour. It was so hard. My chip shots were going everywhere except anywhere close to the pin! Suddenly he broke my train of thought.

"Are you focusing, Bennett?" he asked curiously.

"I'm trying," I sort of lied.

I was focusing alright, but it had little to do with my chip shots and everything to do with him.

"I think that's enough for today. You seemed to be losing your focus," Stenmark observed.

If he only knew!

I think I was improving a fair amount after an hour on those chip shots, considering my attention was not on golf. I couldn't change the direction of my thoughts completely as I knew I really liked spending time with him. That was becoming far more important than golf, and all consuming.

But the words of Joan Armatrading's song "The Weakness in Me," popped into my thoughts. *Was this true love I felt?* I wondered.

Suddenly Stenmark said my name. "Bennett? Where did you go?" he asked.

"Oh, sorry, I was just thinking about something I need to do," I said avoiding his questioning stare.

"Do you want to run to Adolph's for a glass of wine?" he asked.

"I can't tonight, a couple of my friends are throwing me a birthday party in about two hours. I need to go home and get ready, sorry."

Stenmark smiled, "Happy Birthday," he said. I looked in his eyes and he looked a little disappointed. I felt the same way.

Thoughts of inviting him to my party didn't really cross my mind, but then I knew it was not a possibility, this was strictly a girls' party. But still I was a bit sad to miss the wine, conversation and mostly the time with him, but I also enjoyed my girl time, too! It was a party with only three of my closest friends attending. Diana being one of them. She and I still needed to talk about my love life, as I hadn't really made time to tell her what was going on. This might be a dreaded conversation, but a much needed one. Out of all of my friends, I could always count on brutal honesty from Diana and sometimes I feared that, but more often than not, I needed to hear it. Diana was always the voice of reason.

I thought back on the time another client and close friend invited herself to my birthday party when she ran into Diana at the local grocery store. Diana calmly told her, "No, it's only a little group of us. We do this every year for Carly."

Then she called me and said, "Sister, we can't have anyone else at your party, it will change the dynamics of the group!"

Yes, I knew better.

"I would love a rain check though." I said trying to sound upbeat.

"It's a deal," Stenmark said.

I had two lessons left, so we made an appointment for next Monday at three o'clock. *I can do this,* I thought. I can finish up the lessons and that will be that! But I had to ask myself, "*Will that really be that? Was I still trying to deny what this really was?*" Yes, but I was only fooling myself.

Fortunately I was blessed with an extra busy week and Monday arrived quickly. I dashed off to my lesson. This time, I could get the ball in the air, so I was making a little progress. He was excited, but I wondered how much better I could get in one more lesson. I thought maybe I would need to pay for a few more lessons. But do I dare? There was definitely a mutual attraction between us. We were so comfortable with each other. It was as if I had known him all of my life, as if our souls recognized one another.

The lesson ended, and again he asked me about going for a glass of wine to celebrate my improvement.

I had to say no.

This time, it was Cassidy, my granddaughter's birthday and I had to go back down to the Salt Lake Valley for her party. Even though I was secretly disappointed, a small part of me was relieved. I jumped in my car and headed down the hill, thinking of him and next Monday, but wondering if me being a grandmother would scare him away. He did have a funny look of surprise on his face when I had said my granddaughter.

Next Monday would be my last lesson. Thoughts of the lessons ending filled my head, causing time to drag on, even though I was busy at work. Stenmark called during the week, and left a message to confirm Monday. Twice. This made me smile. I liked hearing the sound of his voice and was looking forward to my lesson.

Monday couldn't get here soon enough. I was supposed to practice in between Mondays, but so far that hadn't happened. I was also playing on a co-ed softball team on Mondays and time was limited…or so I told myself. I played sports all of my life, and I never had to practice! I thought I was a natural athlete. Practice was foreign to me., but this sport was hard! When I played basketball, baseball and girl's football at West High, I did the required practice time during school hours. I kicked ass and I had the trophies to prove it!

Fortunately, the week was busy and Friday morning was finally here. My eight a.m. arrived her usual ten minutes late. Her name is Beth and she is quite the character! Beth had been on my waiting list for this Friday morning time slot. Finally the day came and I called her voicemail to tell her the slot was available and ended my message with a quick see you then. Beth was thrilled to get the time she was praying for as she walked in that first Friday exclaiming her excitement. "Car, Car! I can't believe it! Who died?" she asked.

I looked at her with tears in my eyes and said, "Actually my client, Dave."

That stopped Beth right in her tracks as her standard comment to other people was usually, "Someone has to die before you can get a standing appointment with Car!" Poor Beth!

However this morning in particular, she arrived as bubbly as ever. "Do you have any coffee made?" she asked.

"Yes I do and I have some vanilla flavoring, if you would like," I answered.

On occasion, Beth would bring lattes in for us and hers would have vanilla in it, so I figured this would make her happy and I was right.

Several months passed and we continued our Friday morning appointments complete with coffee, hers with vanilla syrup and mine black. Beth traveled with her own very large coffee cup and always had at least two cups of coffee, sometimes three while I did her nails. She had just started a new job three months prior to getting her preferred standing time with me and she was happy!

This particular Friday, as I went to refill her coffee cup, I opened the cupboard where the vanilla syrup was kept and noticed the almost empty bottle. It had appeared there and I assumed it belonged to one of the hairdressers.

"I will have to find out who brought this in so I can pick up another bottle, it's almost gone," I said. "Let me see it," Beth said as she held out her hand.

As I went to hand it to her, I noticed a small little sticker on the bottle and I almost fainted! It was from the State Liquor Store!

"Oh, No! Beth, this has alcohol in it! It is a liqueur!" I shouted.

"Are you kidding me, Car?" Beth said wide-eyed.

I handed the bottle to her as I apologized over and over. "I'm so sorry, Beth!"

She began to laugh hysterically, " No wonder I love my job on Fridays!"

I answered her with, " I hope you still do."

Good Lord, Carly!

# Shatter the Scales

*E*ach and every day, I am so grateful for the clientele that I have. I express my gratitude in several ways. One of the ways I do this, and you might want consider this as well, is that I hand write personalized thank-you notes that cater specifically to each client. But the most important thing when I do it is that I am completely sincere. Because I *really do* appreciate these clients. I have supported myself all of these years because of their continued patronage. When I owned Sisters Salon writing thank-you notes was a requirement of the staff. We printed up the cards, and whenever a client came in, the stylist would send a thank-you, letting them know how much we appreciate them choosing our salon. It always paid off with loyal customers. Weigh it out for yourself. If you try it, I think you will agree.

One day, I chatted with one of my clients and I told her how much I appreciated her business. "I realize having your nails done is not a necessity, so I'm thankful you come," I told her.

The client replied with, "You're right, the nails aren't a necessity, but the conversation is."

Coincidentally, a few hours later, I was doing an acrylic nail fill on another client, when a friend of hers, who is also a client of mine, called the client in my chair on her cell phone and because I had her hands, she put her on speaker.

She answered and said, "I'm sitting here with Carly."

The woman on the other end of the line replied, "Oh, my favorite person," to which she replied, "Everybody's favorite person."

*Big, appreciative smile on my face.*

Along with the conversation, I also realize that the work I do has to be perfectly done. I don't think clients would stay with a nail technician if the work was shoddy, no matter how good the conversation was. They do go hand in hand. (Pun intended.) I admit I have learned a few tricks of the trade, along the way. For example, I do get clients who want me to choose the color that I think looks best on their fingers and toes. In the beginning, I would look at the color of their lipstick and go from there. If no lipstick was worn, I looked at the colors they chose to wear. Finally I figured out, and eventually perfected, matching colors with a client's skin tone. But relying on makeup and clothing is a great little helper until you get to that point, and fortunately it didn't take long to do so. I always suggest a couple of colors, and then before I polish, I lay the bottle against the skin, and can usually tell by that. I polish one finger or one toe, depending on the service, and ask them what they think. I always tell them, "I want you happy. After you leave here, I don't have to look at your fingers and toes, but you do!"

However, I once tried something new on a client who always lets me choose her color. She comes in every two weeks for her pedicure and any color I choose is okay with her. If I'm hesitant, she reminds me, "Carly, it is only two weeks! I can live with anything for two weeks."

This particular appointment, it was close to the fourth of July. I had purchased the new "shattered" polish from OPI. The idea of this was that you painted a regular color on the nail, and then instead of a second coat of the same color, you painted the "shattered" color over the top. Then as the polish dried, that top color would literally shatter, giving it a cracked look and the color underneath would show through. I did a red color on the bottom, and then painted the blue shatter polish over the top. It started to separate, and the cracked look was absolutely horrific. I started to remove it, and she was fighting me every step of the way, saying it was okay.

"Well, it is not okay in my eyes," I told her. "You can't go around with your toes like that!"

She argued with me saying, "It's only for two weeks."

I stood my ground and said, "This is my work and I can't have people seeing your toes like this. I am sorry but I have to redo it."

She agreed, which surprised me, since she is a retired attorney who enjoys a good fight, so to speak.

I was prepared for a very good argument as to why I should just leave it alone. I concluded that it must have really looked bad to her, but she didn't want to hurt my feelings, or maybe it really didn't matter to her.

But it mattered to me, and hopefully it will matter to you.

After all, do you really want to send someone out of the salon with their polish looking like Stevie Wonder did the polish job?

# 45
## Not Charmed by a Snake

I had a client that I was very close to, who has since moved to Costa Rica. One day while doing her manicure and pedicure, I told her something about me that only (some of) my family knew.

When I was 18, in August of that year, I moved to Tennessee with my first husband, Steve, who was in the Navy at the time. Our first child, Sean, was only eight months old when we moved. We rented out our house and left Salt Lake City. The three of us drove across the country to our new home on a Naval base located in Memphis, Tennessee. I was young and it was my first time being so far away from my parents, to the point that I became very lonely and homesick.

Steve was young as well, and began to spread his wings, so to speak. He stayed out all night with his new Navy buddies, while I was stuck at home with a baby and no friends (I knew no one in Memphis). Steve worked in the bakery on base at kind of a grunt job. His hours were the typical bakery hours. He left home at 10:00 p.m. and was supposed to get off work at 4:00 a.m. However, he made friends and hung out with them after work, arriving home much later. One morning, I was up feeding Sean when Steve walked in at 8:00 a.m., four hours late!

"Where have you been?" I asked.

"I went to a friend's house to have a beer," was his reply.

We were both so young and we never drank alcohol, so I was surprised, but continued to feed the baby. Steve went to bed. I called my mother and she told me to let it go. "Steve will snap out of it," Mom said reassuringly.

Well, he didn't snap out of it.

Steve continued his absentee behavior after work, although he did ask for our anniversary off, and the three of us went out for a nice dinner. But his friends were his priority now.

Finally, I was fed up. "Why are you not coming home?" I asked. "You go out every single night, Steve!"

Steve answered with, "No more Mr. Nice Guy!"

*What did that mean? Was he just quoting the Alice Cooper song?*

Turns out, he wasn't. Steve continued to party with his friends and finally I couldn't take it anymore. I called my mother and she sent plane tickets for Sean and I back to Salt Lake City. Our house was rented for another few months so we stayed with my parents waiting for the lease to expire.

The holidays were upon us, and I prepared to move back into our home in January, even though Steve stayed back in Tennessee. I had put a thirty-five-dollar entertainment center on layaway at the Kmart located in Bountiful, Utah. The layaway was about to expire, so I asked my mother to watch Sean, while I went to pick it up. Of course, she was more than happy to help out.

As I left Kmart, with this huge box in my cart that I could barely see over, I thought *this is going to be fun to put together.* And then out of nowhere a very nice-looking guy held the door open for me as I struggled to get through it. "Oh, thank you," I said.

The stranger flashed a smile my way, but it was not genuine. In fact, I found it very off-putting and forced. It made me uneasy and I felt a shiver run through my body.

"Would you mind giving my car a jump?" he asked. "It won't start and I think it's the battery. I have the jumper cables."

"Where's your car?" I replied.

The stranger pointed to the back of the dimly lit parking lot to a light colored Volkswagen Beetle, sitting all by itself.

*There was something about this man that was completely unnerving to me. I couldn't put my finger on it, but I was literally shivering and not from the cold. I could feel a wickedness about him, but I didn't know why. He was a very good looking man with a boyish face, but deep down I knew he was pure evil. His blue eyes were as empty as his stare. This complete stranger seemed to look right through me and that troubled me. He was soulless and I knew it. I had to think fast. Be careful who you trust Carly, remember the devil was once an angel. I must follow my instincts and trust my suspicions of this insipid creature.*

*Monsters are real and they look like people.*

Without missing a beat I said, "My husband went to get the car, then we will drive over and help you." It just came out, I couldn't have controlled it or stopped it even if I wanted to and I didn't. This stranger gave me a chill down my spine and I wanted him to go far away.

I noticed a quick but fleeting agitated look on his face. Then all of the sudden it was as if his mood changed and he responded with a charming smile that I didn't fall for. "It will only take a second," he said quickly with a reassuring tone.

I shivered inside, wanting to scream at the top of my lungs and make a run from this nefarious soul. I managed to quiet my thoughts enough to calm my voice. "I will get my husband," I said in the most confident tone I could muster up.

I proceeded to walk slowly in the parking lot towards my car, stopping intermittently to readjust my purchase as it was cumbersome, but truly I was stalling as the stranger watched me intently. It felt like he looked straight through me and I shuddered as I glanced back at him. I pretended to look for *my husband*, who of course, was still in Memphis.

It was getting dark and the cars driving around the parking lot all had their lights turned on as I continued to walk to my empty car.

Suddenly, the stranger was gone.

I looked over at his Volkswagen only to see the lights come on as he effortlessly drove out of the parking lot and off into the darkness. I knew that often, if a battery sat for a while, the car would start up unexpectedly, so I chalked it up to that. I loaded the box into the back seat of my car to find it wasn't heavy at all, but then again, it was a thirty-five-dollar entertainment center! I jumped in my car quickly and locked all of the doors.

I arrived at my parent's house safe and sound, but still couldn't shake the intense feeling of being completely paralyzed. The guy in the Volkswagen had terrorized my soul. I couldn't put my finger on why I felt so creeped out. I was safe now but inside my internal alarm was still ringing loudly. I told my mother about him and our conversation. I also shared the uneasiness I felt about the stranger, and about how relieved I was when I saw that his car started up and I witnessed him drive away.

My mother said with a concerned look on her face, "Good, honey, always pay attention to those feelings. They are there for a reason."

This I knew. It had been drilled in my head all of my life.

That was pretty much the end of it, however those icy cold blue eyes still haunted me from time to time.

It wasn't until a couple of years later, while visiting my parents that I saw the stranger again, this time on the television. I recognized him immediately, as I pointed to the TV. "That's him, Mom! That's the guy at Kmart I told you about, Oh my God!"

I was literally shaking.

My mom stood up and put her arm around me. "Are you sure, honey?"

I was so overcome with emotion that I began to cry, "I am positive."

My mother and I hugged each other as I sobbed uncontrollably, realizing my fate could have been sealed. The stranger's stare had haunted me all this time, and to see him again was almost too much to bear.

My father came into the room and asked, "What the hell is going on in here?"

My mom began to explain as she held me tight.

"That's the son of a bitch Carly told me about in the Kmart parking lot," she blurted out, pointing to the TV.

My dad listened to the news story in which we learned that the police had finally caught serial killer, Ted Bundy.

Without a doubt, the man in the Kmart parking lot who tried to lure me to his car was Ted Bundy. I was not a television watcher back then, I only listened to music on Stereo X, (a popular radio station, one of the first FM classic rock channels in Salt Lake City). This was the first time I had actually seen the stranger, since that night at Kmart.

"We need to call the police, or the National Enquirer or something," Mom announced.

*The National Enquirer?* My mom had lost it.

My always-reasonable father said, "Just hold on, everybody calm the hell down right now! We are keeping this to ourselves. This guy keeps getting caught and escaping."

"But he is in custody now," my Mom countered.

Dad replied with, "For now!"

After much discussion, we agreed to keep this revelation to ourselves. Ted Bundy had not succeeded in his attempt to kidnap me and we were all worried about him escaping again.

"What if he comes back to find Carly, the one that got away?" my father asked.

That was our family secret. I was so young at this time, I never questioned my parents' advice and fortunately Ted Bundy never escaped again. I don't think I would have been able to handle the guilt if he had done so and killed another girl.

It wasn't until many years later, when my son, Ricky, who was twelve years old at the time, was studying the execution of Ted Bundy in a class at school, that I revealed to him my haunting experience. Ricky's large blue eyes stared intently at me as I spoke, his dark pupils growing wide and dilated. I loved those eyes.

"But Mom what would have happened to all of us if you would have gone with him?" he asked.

I answered, "Well, the only one who would be here would be Sean and I suppose Granny and Grandpa would have raised him."

A few weeks after that daunting night, I found out I was pregnant with my daughter, Chantele. That anniversary night back in Memphis that Steve had requested off was the one night in the month that he was home! Steve and I divorced upon my return from Tennessee and Chantele was born the end of July. I didn't know it at the time, but I figured out I was close to three months pregnant the night my path crossed with Ted Bundy. *How scary!*

Suddenly, I snapped out of my own thoughts and back to reality when my son, Ricky, threw his arms around me and cried.

"Oh, honey, it's okay now," I said trying to comfort my sensitive son.

"But Mom we have been learning about his life in school. He was on a good path to be an attorney at the University of Utah!"

"I know, son. Something must of just got screwed up in his head," I told him.

Ricky sat up and said, "My teacher told us that he started looking at a lot of pornography."

"Yes, I heard that as well." I said, agreeing with my son, but wondering what else he had been told. I knew of the necrophilia, but was truly unprepared to have that discussion with my young son.

I calmly switched the topic. "Also, he was mean to animals when he was growing up," I said in a way to diffuse the other topic, as my son loved animals.

"Eww...that's awful, Mom."

"Ted Bundy was a sick man, Ricky."

"I feel sorry for the animals," Ricky said in his own naïve, sensitive, and young way.

I shook my head and gave him a sympathetic smile.

Ricky went to school the next day and shared my story with his class. His teacher called me a few days later and asked me if I would be willing to speak to the class about my experience. I agreed. The following Monday, I went to school after the lunch break and addressed Ricky's class. I explained my story in great detail, and added the importance of trusting your instincts and listening to your mother!

Thank you, Mom!

# Truth or Dare

*Y*ou know, clients can become friends rather quickly, with or without sport activities to help move the friendships along. My social life is my clients. I get invited to dinners, parties, fundraisers, and other activities on a regular basis. I really enjoy this part of my job.

I also enjoy the interesting and humorous things clients say. In fact, over the years I have jotted these things down so I wouldn't forget them. I have a client who comes in and wants to discuss politics. YIKES! I just listen as I work on her nails, and then try to ease into another subject.

I am not always successful at this.

We are on opposite sides of the fence, so to speak, when it comes to politics. When I tried to tell her that (in a positive and kind way), she glared at me and sternly stated, "We are all in the same boat, Carly, and we all better start rowing!" She looked kind of mean when she said it.

But as I finished her manicure, she looked down at her hands and said, "Oh, my hands look human again, how do you do it?"

I smiled at her and answered, "Thank you, that makes me feel so good!"

She then answered back with, "Not as good as it makes me feel!"

Funny thing is, that morning she was supposed to come in at 10:30 and did not show up. I usually give clients about ten minutes before I call them to ask if I messed up (a much better way to say it, than to accuse them of forgetting their appointments). When I finally did call her, she was mortified, as she usually is very prompt. I happened to have a cancellation later in the afternoon, which I offered to her, and she accepted.

She came in apologizing and asked, "Guess what I was doing when you called?"

"I don't know," I said.

"I was watching a television program on how to improve your memory!" she answered excited.

The irony was not lost on me.

Over the years, I have heard and experienced some very funny things. Candy, a client of mine broke her leg skiing. After she felt a little better, she called me for a pedicure and manicure. We finished her service and Candy told me her husband had driven her and she would talk to him on the way home about booking her next appointment, as she needed to see what his schedule was. I had never met her husband before and after a few months she began to drive herself, as her leg was healing nicely.

Candy came in one afternoon and told me her husband had dropped her off and asked what time should she call him to pick her up. I told her and he arrived promptly, just as I was charging her credit card for her service. She introduced us and he commented on how he used to complain about Candy spending so much on her salon appointments. Then he added, "Her mood is so much better when she comes home after spending a couple of hours with you, it is totally worth the cost, so thank you, Carly."

I have a relatively new client named Hope. I just met her three months ago, and she comes in for monthly pedicures. She usually pays with a credit card, and after her second visit to the salon, I received an email message from the credit card company saying that a customer had left feedback on my account wall. I looked at the comment and was so happy to read these words, "Thank you Carly, you are the best. A great pedicure and a therapy session. What a deal!"

I actually had another client, Cherie, dispute her charge on her credit card. I called her after receiving an email from the credit card company to ask if there was a problem with her service. She said she had not disputed the charge, but then she stopped short. "What is the name of your business? Is it just under your name?"

I explained it was under my business name, More Than a Manicure.

She said, "Oh dear, on the credit card statement it only said *More Than a Man*. Good thing you called before my husband came home, I was ready to start questioning him!" We both laughed, and then she added, "I'll send the credit card company an email to let them know it's fine." The next time Cherie came in, she apologized and said how embarrassed she was.

"No worries," I told her and began her pedicure. After finishing, we moved to the nail table to start her manicure. She is not a very talkative client anyway, so I worked and she sat there with her eyes closed. "I'll just take a power nap while you make my hands beautiful," she said.

I turned down the music and went to work. After I finished her manicure, I whispered quietly, "We're all done."

She opened her eyes and asked, "Oh, no is it really all over?"

"All over but the crying," I said as I patted her hands, referring to her paying the bill for the service, as a joke.

She frowned. "Darn it," was her reply, as she took out her credit card.

As I have said throughout this book, I have many clients who have become very close friends, which makes work more fun, as well. One of those clients/friends is Suzanne. She is fun-loving, kind, and very cool. One day, I started her pedicure and she told me how much she loved her toenail color and wanted to do the same one this time. I couldn't remember what it was, so I set the cotton I was using to remove her color off to the side of my table. I am pretty good at guessing and finding the color again, but wanted to save the cotton soaked pad in case I needed to match it up.

While dipping her clean, pedicured feet in the paraffin wax, she asked if I could help her make a ringtone for her phone. She wanted the song, "Coconut" by Harry Nilsson. I told her to search for the song as I was taking the wax off and starting her second massage.

After Suzanne found her song, she tried to figure out how to purchase it. She couldn't remember her password and was quietly talking to herself about what it could be.

I stood up and walked over to my polish rack, but she was growing frustrated and mumbling to herself, "What could it be, dammit, what is it?"

I picked up a couple of colors and looked at the names. I finally decided on one and asked her, "Could it be Pink Flamingo?"

She gave me a funny look and said, "No! My password wouldn't be something that dumb."

I paused and said, "No, not your password, the nail polish color we used before on your toes." Then we both laughed.

She sent me a text message later that evening telling me she found her password and the color on her toes was perfect!

Another client of mine is such a sweet lady. Her name is Barbara and after every appointment she sends me a text message telling me how much she loves her nails and thanks me for doing them. This is so nice to hear, or shall I say, read? I do appreciate all of my clients as they make my job so much less of a job. I look forward to the time we spend together. By and large, the majority of my clients make me feel so proud of my work. Well, at least 99.9 percent of them do.

I believe the greatest achievements in life, are not accomplished alone, but with the help of other people. I try to surround myself with positive, uplifting people, and as a result the job of doing nails becomes less of a job and more of an appreciated art form.

# I Heart My Instructor

have to admit as I was waiting (not so patiently) for my next golf lesson, I realized I had completely forgotten about my Missionary Man, Devin. My feelings for him had completely faded. Even though he broke my heart, occasionally my mind wandered back to him and I played out the life I imagined I would've had with him, sometimes even while I was with Denny. But that never happened when I was with Stenmark.

Devin had called several times over the last few months, leaving messages expressing sorrow and his need to see me, but I never answered, thanks to caller ID. I smile now as I think back about my strength in that situation. I have dealt with hard things in my life, and felt completely lost at times, but I am a survivor! This I know. Of course, having something (or someone) else to focus on certainly helps. Saying goodbye to the past had become solid ground for the future, at least for me. Devin was now my past, and Denny was quickly getting to that point, as well.

These random thoughts flooded my mind. Stenmark could be the man in the songs, the man I had always dreamed of. I suddenly realized I hadn't been in love with Devin at all, I was in lust and I knew Denny was a gap filler, just what I needed at the time, but this man, my golf instructor, I realized was my one true love, my soul mate and my future.

Lucky for me, he liked to prop up his feet!

Monday's golf lesson was finally here. *How can a week take so long?* I asked myself, as I drove to the golf course.

He greeted me with that beautiful smile. "Hi, Bennett," Stenmark said. "How are you?"

"Great!" I replied. "How are you?"

"Better now," he said with a wink.

My heart skipped a beat as I smiled and thought, *WOW!*

I tried to shift my focus to golf as the lesson began. I wondered if I would ever get the hang of this silly game after I did my practice swing.

Stenmark stood a few feet in front of me, his arms folded across his chest. "Step up and pull the trigger."

I did as instructed, swung hard and totally missed the ball! That was embarrassing!

"And stay in posture," he added.

I laughed nervously and tried it again. Success! The ball flew into the air about a hundred yards. *It's a start*, I thought. The lesson continued and the hour passed quickly.

"Let's grab a cart and play a couple of holes," Stenmark offered.

"What do you mean?" I asked, somewhat confused. I barely got the ball into the air and now I was to play on the real course?

"Yes, just a couple of holes, that's all," he answered.

We hopped in the golf cart and sped across the course to an open hole. I was going to play golf! I was a bit nervous, but I loved sitting so close to him as we pulled up to the tee box. Stenmark jumped out of the golf cart and grabbed a ball out of his golf bag, along with a tee, and pulled out his driver. He did a practice swing, stepped up to the ball and pulled the trigger! I watched the ball sail out of sight.

"Nice shot." I said, as he sat down in the cart and drove to the ladies' tee box.

"Your turn," Stenmark said.

I quickly jumped out of the cart, and gathered my ball and tee. He came around to the back of the golf cart just as I started to pull out my driver. I reached for the club and my hand was shaking like a leaf.

"What's the matter?" he asked with a very concerned look on his face.

"I'm scared," I replied softly.

He chuckled. "You'll be fine."

I slowly walked up to my tee box, and set up. I stepped back and did my practice swing, brushing the ground perfectly.

"Just like that." he said, reassuring me.

I focused on my ball. *Keep your head down, load the right side, swing the club back, hinge, hips first, let the arms drop down and through the ball, and for God's sake stay in posture, Carly!* I took a deep breath as I brought the club back slowly. Trying my best to do it correctly, I said a little prayer. I swung hard…and I missed! I looked at Stenmark sheepishly.

He smiled. "That's enough for today," he said comfortingly. "Let's go get that glass of wine."

I happily agreed.

Adolph's was busy as usual when we walked in and took a seat at the bar. The bartender, Mary brought over two glasses of Chardonnay, as she gave both of us the hairy eyeball. I knew what she was thinking. She politely asked what we were doing.

I answered first. "I just had a golf lesson."

Mary asked, "How'd you do?"

"Room for improvement," I said, smiling at my golf instructor/man of my dreams.

Stenmark added, "She is doing great."

Mary smiled knowingly. "Golf is hard." But then she offhandedly added, "When is Denny coming back?" I knew she and Denny were friends and I certainly didn't want anything to be weird between Mary and me.

"Actually, I'm going to his cabin in Wisconsin next week to play golf," I said cheerfully.

Her eyes lit up. "Oh good, please tell him hello from me."

"I will for sure," I said with a big smile.

Mary excused herself as she hustled off to take care of her other customers.

Stenmark lifted his glass of wine. "Let's toast to you making time to practice your golf before you go to Wisconsin to play." We touched glasses and each took a big drink.

The next hour we discussed golf and the importance of practice. He also schooled me on the rules of golf. Even though it was all golf talk, I so enjoyed listening to him. I have to say, he really knew his golf rules. I probably wouldn't remember all he told me, but it didn't matter. I loved just being with him.

We finished our wine and I looked at my watch. "It's eight o'clock, I better go home," I said hesitantly.

Stenmark motioned for Mary to bring the check as he took out his credit card. After he paid the bill, he held the door open for me and we headed out towards the parking lot. When I clicked my car door to open, Stenmark asked when I was leaving for Wisconsin.

"Next Saturday," I answered.

"When will you be back?"

"The following Saturday."

For a spilt second, I looked at him and thought he looked a bit sad. Our eyes met, he reached down, cupped his hands around my face, and planted a kiss on my lips that almost brought me to my knees.

"Well, have fun," Stenmark quietly added. Then he casually walked to his car, hopped in and started the engine. I just stood there and watched as he drove off. I waited until his blue Montero was out of sight before I left.

Driving home deep in thought, I turned on the radio, full volume. Never underestimate the therapeutic power of driving and listening to very loud music! I couldn't help but think... *Now what, Bennett?*

# Bite Your Tongue

y first client was at seven the next morning. I dressed quickly for work. This week was going to be busy, since I had to prepare for my golf trip to Wisconsin. When I arrived at the salon I got everything ready for my first client. I hoped everyone would be on time today, so that my day would run smoothly. When booked solid, it only takes one person early in the day to mess up the rest of the day's schedule. Tardiness can really throw everything off.

I always chuckle to myself when I think about one particular client of Rebecka's. Her name was Jamie and she was habitually late. It used to drive my sister crazy. One day she was waiting for Jamie to arrive, getting more and more irritated as the clocked ticked. "She is fifteen minutes late for a half hour appointment!" Rebecka announced with a huge degree of warranted aggravation.

I shook my head, just as Jamie rushed in apologizing profusely, throwing off her scarf and setting down her Gucci handbag.

"I am so sorry, Rebecka, now I am going to make you late for your next person."

"No, you're not, because I canceled you," Rebecka announced calmly.

Jamie just stared at Rebecka.

I lowered my head and began filing quickly, acting like I was unaware of the uncomfortable conversation unfolding. Rebecka was being assertive all on her own and I was proud of her. Even without a purple jacket. (Remember my infamous purple power-color jacket I always wore when letting an employee go?) Rebecka had the power and was in control of the tough situation!

"What do you mean?" Jamie asked with a look of surprise on her face.

"Just what I said," Rebecka replied flatly.

After a few more uncomfortable seconds, Jamie gathered up her matching scarf and purse and without saying a word, walked out the door. Just in time to pass my sister's next client walking in seven minutes early. That was that!

I also remember another time Rebecka had a late client and once again she was understandably annoyed. This time the client didn't show up. Her name was Linda and she had a habit of being what we call in the business a *no-show*. She always paid for the missed appointment, but even so, it's still frustrating.

"She better be dead," Rebecka groused in her humorous way.

Well, she was.

Sadly, Linda had been killed in a car accident earlier that day. Poor Rebecka cried her eyes out.

It is hard to keep on a very tight schedule with clients who are late; fortunately it is just a few of the clients. By and large, most of my clients are on time for their appointments. Things happen that cause tardiness on occasion, and of course, I understand. But if you are way late and you come rushing in with a Starbucks latte in your hand, you better have one for me, too!

Launa, my first client of the day walked in, five minutes early as I snapped back to reality. I love this client. She unfortunately lost her husband a few years back, but now was dating a wonderful man, who absolutely adored her. I enjoyed her stories of this budding romance and was so happy for her. Everybody deserves someone who makes them look forward to tomorrow. Launa put her feet in the water.

"Carly, I have to apologize in advance, my feet are really bad this time."

"Not to worry, this is my job." I said. Extra soaking required today!

I did let her feet soak for a little longer than usual. I poured us each a cup of coffee and began her pedicure. She was spot on… her feet were terrible, but the conversation was interesting as usual.

"I am so happy you could take me today," Launa said. "I am going to London tomorrow to meet my future in-laws."

"Launa! You are remarrying?" I asked excitedly.

"I am, in London," she answered with a big smile.

I had to stand up and give her a big hug. I was thrilled for her. When we switched feet, I noticed that her big toe nail was coming off. "Launa, I need to trim this down, if that's okay with you," I said, continuing with, "if I don't, I am afraid you will catch it on the sheet and rip it all the way off."

Launa answered with, "Well, you are right there next to a doctor, so whatever you think, Carly."

I laughed as I trimmed the loose toenail carefully. *I love that my clients have such trust and faith in me.*

As I have said before, I think it's important to work hard and truly strive to build your business and have the confidence in your ability by doing the things that matter. I haven't always done it right, either. I have struggled and made those bad choices, just like you probably have, especially in my younger days. To be old and wise we must first be young and stupid, I guess! I am not a perfect person, as you must have figured out by now, but I have learned along the way. I've learned that working hard for something you love is called passion. I have always believed in following your heart, because your heart will never lie to you. That's your mind's job! In the end, it's completely up to you to decide what you want, believe you'll get it, and then live like you already have it.

Trust the process.

# 49

## Glow the Extra Mile

$O$ver the years, I have been blessed with clients who became close friends. One of those friends was Carrie, who had a six o'clock appointment with me one evening. She was both a manicure and a pedicure this particular night, so coupled with conversation, it was nearly eight thirty when we said goodbye. As I was straightening up my room before driving home, my phone rang. Caller ID told me it was Carrie, so I answered, "Hi there. Is everything okay?" I asked, worrying that she had messed up a nail putting on her seatbelt.

"Carly, when I walked out of the salon, there was a strange-looking man sitting on the lawn in front of the salon. I sat in my car for a couple of minutes and when I pulled out of the lot, he was still there." I listened intently as she continued. "I drove around the block and he is still there, so I am sitting in front of the salon. Take your time cleaning up, I will wait for you, but I want to drive you to your car."

"Okay, thanks," I said.

I finished my cleaning rather quickly and walked outside to her car. The man was still there, just sitting on the lawn. He probably was harmless, but again one never knows. I was grateful for her concern for my safety, and thanked her as I got in my car.

I told another client about this story the following morning. She looked at me and said, "Do you want me to come back later and walk you to your car? I have a free night!"

I laughed and thanked her. "No, I will be okay, I am not working too late this evening." I always felt safe living here in Shangri-La.

Carrie called me later that day to ask me about doing a fun filled weekend with her in a couple of weeks to benefit the Make-A-Wish Foundation. "The weekend starts with a nice dinner and wine tasting on Friday night," she said. And then added, "It ends on Sunday afternoon with a hot air balloon ride and lunch afterwards."

"I would love to do that, Carrie, I have never been in a hot air balloon."

Carrie was surprised, "Really? How long have you lived here?"

"I know…" I knew hot air balloons were a big deal in Park City. "Is it safe?" I asked cautiously.

"It is safe, Carly. I actually used to crew for a company back in Kansas. It is a really fun experience, especially if you have never done it before."

"Okay then," I agreed, "it's a date!"

We will have fun," she said. "Call me when you're back from your trip to Wisconsin and we will firm up the details."

"Okay," I said with a fair amount of hesitation, being the thrill seeker that I am (not)!

# No Baggage Please

The week flew by, with not much time to think about or do anything but work. Stenmark called and left a couple of messages, wishing me a safe and fun trip. Also reminding me to keep my head down and stay in posture while golfing. That made me giggle. I hoped to be able to speak with him before I left, but I had no time. Friday night, after a phone call from my friend, Mandy, who worked for Delta Airlines, I decided to go to the airport and try for an earlier flight. I was pass-riding, thanks to Mandy.

"Carly, the red eye flight tonight looks wide open, much better than your early morning flight," Mandy said.

"What time will I arrive?" I asked.

"The flight leaves at twelve-forty a.m. and arrives in Green Bay at five-thirty-five a.m.," she said.

"Sounds painful, Mandy."

"You can sleep, but don't forget to change planes in Chicago."

*Like I can ever sleep on a plane.* "Let me call Denny and make sure he is willing to pick me up that early," I replied.

"Okay, call me after you speak with him, and I will list you on the flight this evening. Your chances look much better," she added.

I thanked Mandy as she reminded me, "Don't forget you only need a carry-on, not a bunch of baggage."

"I've got it, already packed, thanks girlfriend," I told her.

Well, Denny was elated that I was coming in earlier. "I will *absolutely* be there to pick you up," he said excitedly.

"Are you sure you don't mind?" I asked.

"Carly, I am up early anyway."

As it turns out, I did get on the flight. I was off to Green Bay, Wisconsin. I couldn't sleep on the plane, as expected, so I had time to think. Thoughts filled my mind, but not about my trip. I admit it, I was thinking about my golf instructor. Consequently, I was wide-awake when I changed planes in Chicago. It was a quick plane ride to Wisconsin and my plane arrived on time.

As I exited the aircraft, Denny stood there smiling, eager for a heartfelt reunion. My conscience got the better of me and I thought what a bad person I was. *Denny is a nice man and he's good to me. I should try harder to make this work.*

He had a big smile on his face, even though we had a two-hour drive ahead of us to reach the cabin. "How was your flight?" Denny asked as he threw his arms around me.

I answered cheerfully, "It was good."

"Did you sleep?"

"Off and on, I said, I have a hard time sleeping on planes." *Could he tell that I wasn't into this trip?*

"You should take an Ambien on those flights, like I do," Denny suggested.

"No, I am scared of Ambien," I said, eager to keep the conversation platonic. "When I was in the middle of my divorce from Clark, a doctor prescribed Ambien to me. It wasn't a good experience."

Thankfully, Denny was curious, "Why? What happened?"

"I arrived home from work, turned on the television as I got ready for bed. I took half of an Ambien, and realized I hadn't really eaten much of anything that day, so I got up off of the couch and went to the pantry. I opened a box of cinnamon graham crackers, took one out and decided I needed some protein, so I put some peanut butter on it."

As usual, Denny chastised me, "That's not much of a meal, Carly."

I sighed and continued, "I know, anyway...I sat down on the couch, took a bite of my *meal*, and started to watch a bit of television. I woke up the next morning to *Good Morning America* on TV, and the graham cracker sitting on my chest with one bite out of it!"

"You're kidding," he said, "I have never had a problem with it!"

"At least, not that you know of, right?" I said half teasing. "I've heard some scary stories about people being in an Ambien state and not realizing they were out and about, even driving!"

"Seriously?"

I nodded as we drove on. *What else could we talk about? I didn't want him to ask me what I'd been doing lately.*

# "Berried" Secrets

We stopped at a restaurant in a quaint little town for a late breakfast. The perky waitress brought us menus and we ordered coffee.

"I called and made an earlier tee time for us," Denny informed me as we studied the menu

I almost choked on my Altoid. "This should be an interesting game," I told him, "being that I am a new player functioning on little or no sleep!"

Denny laughed. "You will be just fine. You have been taking quite a few lessons, right?"

*Indeed I have, but that's my little secret.* I smiled at him as I peered over the menu.

"I will help you, as well," he reassured me.

Thankfully, the perky waitress came back. "Here you go," she said as she delivered the coffee. "Are you ready to order?"

I looked at her nametag, as Denny pointed to me. "Hi, Christy," I said, "I'll have a cinnamon graham cracker with peanut butter on it, please."

I watched Denny for a response.

Denny narrowed his eyes at me. I could tell he wasn't amused by my attempt at humor.

"That's a little joke between us, Christy," I said laughing. "I'll take a ham and cheese omelet, no potatoes with a side of your fresh berries please."

Denny, still not amused, said dryly to me, "That's better." Then addressing Christy he added, "I'll have the same." *Was this how it was going to be the whole trip? Me pushing his buttons, and him showing how displeased he was by my behavior?*

Our breakfast arrived in a timely fashion. We ate and then took off for the golf course. It was a beautiful course and an even more beautiful day.

I played the best I could, but my heart wasn't in it. And my mind was preoccupied. I had Stenmark, my golf instructor, on the brain. I thought of his calm demeanor, his caring blue eyes, and that smile. I thought of the way his cologne smelled. I felt guilty feeling this way. I brushed away those thoughts of *him*. *This just isn't fair to Denny*, I silently told myself as I picked up my ball and moved it next to Denny's. I remembered that it was important to keep up pace of play. However it was turning out to be a very long eighteen holes.

And an even longer trip. I needed a distraction.

Thankfully, Mandy (the one who worked at the airport) and Jerry were arriving the next day, so I had that to look forward to.

Denny and I headed to a nice restaurant (at which he'd made reservations) after our day on the golf course. I showered and as

I began to get dolled up for the evening, Denny came into the bathroom, completely dressed and ready for dinner, including cologne. There I stood with my bathrobe on, wet hair and no makeup. I looked at him surprised, wondering if I had mistaken the time.

"What time is our reservation?" I asked as I turned down the music on the clock radio.

"Seven o'clock," he answered.

I looked at the time on the clock radio. It was barely five thirty.

"We have to leave by six-fifteen," he said with a worried look on his face.

"I'll be ready, don't worry, Denny."

Impatiently he asked me, "How much longer?"

*Oh no, not this again*, I thought. I turned the radio back up and said, "Six songs."

Denny walked out of the bathroom. I sighed and thought, *Here we go with the time constraints*. I proceeded to get ready...*quickly*!

And then, true to my word, I walked out of the bathroom at six-ten.

I held my hands out to the side and exclaimed in my best French accent, "*Je suis prête!*"

"Oh, you *are* ready. You look beautiful," Denny complimented.

"Thank you, sir," I said with a smile as I bowed.

Denny kissed me on top of the head.

"I don't want to mess up your makeup, so you have to start over," he said irritated, clearly not an attempt at humor.

He was serious, *serious as a heart attack*! I chose to ignore his snide comment.

We walked to his BMW. He opened the door for me, and as I got into the car, I thought, *What a gentleman he is*. Denny always opened the door for me. *That was another nice thing*, as I tallied the score in my head. Not a fair comparison, however. There are no doors on golf carts!

Denny was happy as we drove to the restaurant. He presented me with a wonderful, romantic dinner, complete with a bottle of Jordan Cabernet, of course. Throughout the evening I tried my hardest to keep my mind on Denny, but thoughts of Stenmark kept rushing in. I was clearly confused. I wondered if I could get used to this type of life with Denny, or was I too far down the rabbit hole? I wasn't sure, but one thing I did know, I never could do anything with half my heart!

## 52
## Spoken from the Heart

$a$fter dinner, Denny and I returned to the cabin and had a nightcap (gin and tonic) to wind down. "Before Mandy and Jerry get here in the morning, I think we should talk," Denny said.

*Uh-oh, here it comes.* "About what?" I asked nervously. But I knew.

"Have you given any more thought about our life together?" Denny asked.

I took a big gulp of my drink and swallowed hard. "Um… you're talking about moving, right?" I asked anticipating the answer.

"Well yes, but to be honest I really don't want to leave Georgia, at least until my daughter is out of high school," he confessed.

"I see," I said. *I will just let him talk and go from there.*

Denny continued with, "Your children are all grown-up and on their own, so moving for you would not be that hard."

"What about my grandchildren, Denny?" *Seriously? Does he believe being a parent stops once they become old enough to vote?*

He answered swiftly. "You said it right there; your *grandchildren*." I didn't understand where he was going with this logic until he continued to press his point. "I never really knew my grandparents, did you? We never grew up around them, we visited on holidays and such, but that was it. That's the way it is supposed to be, Carly. I would *let you* fly to see them on special occasions and some holidays."

I gave him a concerned look. "*Let me?*"

Denny stood up to freshen our drinks and offhandedly said, "You know what I mean. Flying is expensive, you just couldn't fly back and forth on a whim, Carly, that's all I meant."

*C'mon, Carly be honest with him.* I knew I needed to be in all fairness to Denny and myself, but I admit, I was scared. It was the whole confrontation thing. *Maybe* *after* *this trip, I could find the courage to tell him how my heart felt.* I rationalized my feelings, telling myself, this relationship was never the way it was supposed to be, even before I met Stenmark. There was no real connection, no fluttering butterflies in my stomach or deep longing to see Denny when we weren't together, like there was with Stenmark. I had to accept the fact that, as sweet and kind of a man as Denny was, I was nowhere near feeling about him the way I felt when I knew I was in love.

Suddenly, I realized, Denny *was* a gap-filler. Diana always said after a bad break up, you needed a gap-filler until you either heal or meet someone else. She was right! Denny was my gap-filler. I was so broken-hearted after Devin, I needed to move on and Denny, without knowing, helped me to do just that. *Holy shift!*

I decided it was time to be honest with Denny, But I really didn't know what to say. *Was I really going to break up with him tonight?* Maybe this weekend was not the time.

"I know it's hard for you to understand," I started, "since you still have a teenager and no grandchildren, so let me try and explain how I feel."

Denny nodded giving me the go ahead.

"Something magical happened deep in my heart when I became a grandmother. I don't think you or anyone can fully understand that feeling unless you experience it firsthand. I want to be near enough to watch my grandchildren grow up. I want to spend time with them, nurture and love them. I can't be that far away from them."

Denny just stared at me like I was speaking another language. Clearly, this is not what he expected. "I reiterate, they are your *grandchildren*, not your *children*."

"I realize that, Denny, but I need for *you* to understand something. You cannot possibly know the amount of love I have in my heart for them, because you have never had grandchildren." I wondered if this would be my out. It was the truth, after all. I couldn't imagine not being close to my grandchildren and I thought about a quote from Margaret Mead: *Everyone needs to have access to both grandparents and grandchildren in order to be a full human being.*

Denny stood up and fixed his third gin and tonic, "Do you want another drink?"

"No, thank you, I'm okay with the rest of this one." I said, but knew I probably would need another one if I wanted to speak from the heart. *Yikes!*

Denny sat down in the chair across from me, which told me he wasn't happy with my answers to his questions.

"So…what now?" he asked.

I took a deep breath. *No time like the present, I guess.* I didn't want to hurt Denny's feelings, but this was the time. I knew I could do it without being cruel. That was not my nature, so I asked him, "Do you love me, Denny?"

He looked surprised as he moved back over to the couch. "I care for you deeply, Carly, I don't believe you can fall in love with someone this quickly. Love takes time. We have only known each other six months, and have only been around each other three times in that six months, so no, I am not in love with you… yet."

*Since he doesn't love me, this might be easier than I imagined!* "I feel the same way, Denny. You are a wonderful, kind and generous man and I feel so fortunate to have met you, but I am not in love with you either."

He stood up without speaking and walked into the kitchen and poured us both another gin and tonic. He held out the glass and as I reached up for it, I saw there were tears in his eyes.

"I'm sorry," I said sincerely, as he wiped his cheek.

"So am I, Carly, but I think we could grow to love one another if we lived together and were around each other more often."

"Maybe so, but what if it never happened after we both uprooted our lives?" I asked. I could feel the tears starting to sting my eyes, as well.

"I really do care so much for you, Carly, I really do feel it could develop into a real love."

*This is tough stuff!* I began to feel nauseous. I told myself to keep it together.

Denny was still wiping his eyes, while drinking his fifth gin and tonic.

*Shouldn't he pass out soon?* "Denny," I said as I swallowed hard, "I have always felt it should be there, right from the get go, don't you?"

He smiled but he looked so sad, it made my heart hurt. "You are just such a perfect girlfriend, Carly. You are beautiful, kind and so sweet. I love how you always pull your wallet out even if we are only getting a newspaper and a cup of coffee. You don't ever just expect me to pay. It is so refreshing."

*Great. Now I feel worse, who is this man? He isn't being bossy or demanding. He doesn't appear to be mad or angry. He is being so kind. Where is the Type A man I wasn't in love with?*

Denny continued. "I have dated a lot of women and without fail, every one of them just expected me to pay. Not one of them *even offered* to pay. It was as if they stood there, waiting for a handout. But not you. That's why I say you are so perfect for me as a girlfriend."

*Wait, what? THAT'S why you care so deeply about me??*

"I couldn't imagine ever breaking up with you. Well…unless you gained weight, then I could. That's a deal breaker."

*Aw…there he is! Denny, the man I never fell in love with!*

"Well," I said, "thank you for being so sweet." No point getting into it. I was in the middle of nowhere and giving Denny a piece of my mind about his shallowness would do no good for either of us. I thought about how my weight goes up and down and figured I dodged another bullet.

"Denny, I think I should leave in the morning." There. I said it. *Finally!* And it felt good. Before he could respond, I quickly added, "I could catch a flight back when you go to pick up Jerry and Mandy."

"Okay." Denny agreed sadly.

"I will call Mandy in the morning and have her arrange my flight back to Utah." I was actually starting to feel excited about going home sooner than expected.

"That sounds good, Carly. I will sleep in one of the guest rooms. We should leave by six a.m. in order to avoid the traffic.

I nodded my head. My expression was sad, but my heart was RELIEVED!

Denny walked over and kissed me once again on top of the head, and said, "Good night, sleep well."

"You, too, "I said with some relief, even though I still had a sick feeling in the pit of my stomach.

# 53
## "Red-y" to Roll

I dressed for bed, and surprisingly, I slept. I knew in my heart I did the right thing for both of us. It wasn't fair to Denny *or me*. He deserved someone who was focused only on him and that certainly wasn't me.

I woke up exhausted the next morning. Sleep really doesn't help if your soul is tired, but sleeping is nice. You get to forget about everything for a while. I dressed quickly and called Mandy.

She sounded like she was in shock. "What do you mean you are leaving? What happened in the first day and night?"

"Mandy, we had a heart-to-heart talk last night after dinner. I told Denny I wasn't in love with him and he told me the same thing," I said.

She couldn't believe it. "You are kidding me, right?"

"No, not kidding. Denny slept in the guest room last night. I need you to list me on the first possible flight to Salt Lake City this morning. We leave soon for the airport."

I could tell she was disappointed. "Okay, I'll call you back."

I gathered up my things and put them in my suitcase, just as Denny knocked on the bedroom door.

"Are you up?" he asked as he opened the door. I quickly stuffed my red silk nightgown into my bag as I looked up and said, "Good morning."

Denny looked as if somebody took out his eyeballs with a spoon and stomped on them. My guess was Denny was hung-over. That assumption was confirmed when I followed him into the kitchen and saw the empty bottle of Bombay gin.

"How are you doing this morning?" I asked. I tried to sound cheerful, but not *too cheerful*. We still had a drive ahead of us. I wasn't home yet.

"Just fuckin' great," he grumbled sarcastically. "How are you?" Obviously, Denny was not as cheerful as I was.

I took a deep breath. "About the same." That was a lie, but I couldn't tell him how relieved I was when he was feeling so low. I am not that cruel. But honestly, I was so happy I was going home early. *This is becoming a habit, but at least I was flying on a free pass this time.*

Mandy called as we were en route to the airport. "I booked you on the flight that looked the best, I think you will get on for sure, but it is not until three-twenty. The others were full."

I didn't care what time the flight was, I just wanted to go home that day. "Thank you, Mandy, that's great," I reassured her.

"Well, how are you guys this morning?" she asked.

"Pretty chilly," I answered. Mandy chuckled at my humor.

Denny chimed in, "Tell her I will see them this evening. I'm looking forward to it."

"Did you hear Denny?" I asked.

Mandy quietly answered, "Yes. Tell him we are, too."

"I will and thanks again," I said, and hung up.

Denny stared at the road, and without turning his head, he asked me, "What did you tell Mandy?"

"I told her the truth."

We drove the rest of the way in silence. It was a long, strained uncomfortable ride back to the airport. I prayed I could fall asleep, as I laid my head back and closed my tired eyes.

"We're almost there, Carly."

I opened my eyes and looked out the window just as Denny pulled up to the unloading zone. He parked close to curb, jumped out quickly and opened the back door. Grabbing my luggage, he walked quickly to the sidewalk.

I opened my own car door for the first time since we'd been together, and slid out of the car. *So much for chivalry.* I walked over to Denny and looked him in the eye. In return I got the usual kiss on the top of the head. "Goodbye, Carly," he said flatly.

I told him goodbye, picked up my carry-on, and walked fast through the revolving door, which felt like my life right now. I didn't look back.

# Straight Up, No Sugar

The airport was busy, as I hurried to the gate. I had three and a half hours before my flight. That gave me a lot of time to think and that is exactly what I did. I thought about how sad Denny looked this morning and my heart ached. I am kind and soft-hearted, however I just couldn't in good conscience, stay with a man I wasn't in love with. But I still felt bad for hurting him.

Only a short five months ago, I tried to fall in love with him. I honestly thought I could and I really wanted to. Denny represented an easier life for me. I began to think more about the future, particularly as I started to get older. I loved my job, but it was hard work, it wasn't as simple as just sitting there all day painting fingernails to make ends meet. Often I lived paycheck to paycheck and, I am not going to lie, sometimes it was a struggle. Denny was more than financially stable and that was foreign to me. I thought about what a kind man he was and how I enjoyed his sense of humor, how he spoiled me with trips, nice gifts and expensive dinners…even paying off my credit card.

But then I remembered how he could be bossy, demanding and controlling. I realized even if I hadn't met Stenmark, being with Denny would have been another mistake. I never make the same mistake twice. I usually make it five or six times, you know, just to be sure. Especially when I fall in love.

The flight to Salt Lake City was uneventful, and of course, I was unable to sleep. I took off my headphones when we touched down. *Thank God for music, it has always been my escape.* I gathered up my things quickly, and as the plane stopped, so did my heart. *What now? Do I call Stenmark and tell him? No, can't do that. Sounds too desperate, I could scare him away.* I walked through the airport at a fast pace, out the door, and there sat the long term parking bus. No waiting this time. The driver helped me as I struggled with the wheels on my luggage, up the steps and into the bus. *That was nice.*

I smiled and thanked him, then sat down, still deep in thought. Lot six came up quickly. I exited the bus with another smile and thank-you. Once again the kind driver helped me with my luggage.

I walked to my car still in awe of what just happened in the last 24 hours. *I'm grateful to be out of a loveless relationship, but now what?* I thought. And as I went to open my car door, I saw propped on top of the handle, a white golf tee. After I left the airport, I drove through Salt Lake City, and up Parleys Canyon to Park City, holding the tee in my hand the entire way home. It was almost ten o'clock at night. I decided it was too late for a phone call, coupled with the fact I wasn't due back for five more days. I took a quick shower, hopped into bed and turned on music. I tenderly tucked the white golf tee safely under my pillow and drifted off to sleep listening to Mary Chapin Carpenter's song, "Passionate Kisses." *Just Perfect.*

I had the best night's sleep I had in a long time, and woke up refreshed. It wasn't until then that I realized my cell phone was still in my luggage. *Coffee first, then I will unpack.*

As I sipped the hot coffee, I thought about a client of mine, Sophie. She shared a story with me one day while I was doing her acrylic nails. She told me, "I pour myself a big mug full of coffee and drink it all day," Sophie said.

"Ew, I do not like cold or even warm coffee. It has to be really hot," I said.

"Oh, I just microwave it all day long," Sophie replied.

"Do you use cream or sugar in your coffee?" I asked thinking that would taste gross microwaved.

"Cream, no sugar," Sophie answered.

I shook my head, "Doesn't that make it taste funny?"

"No, not that I have noticed. Of course, I try not to forget about it and have it boil and overflow. Are you a coffee snob, Carly?" she asked jokingly.

"I guess I kind of am," I replied seriously.

Sophie went on to say, "One day, I had just filled my huge coffee mug, when my son called from school. He had forgotten his backpack with his homework in it, and needed me to bring it to school, so I did. But while I was in town, I went to pick up the mail, go to the market and fill up the car with gas, all of the errands I was going to tackle later that day."

"Well, yes, since you live in Jeremy Ranch, that makes sense," I said.

Sophie continued. "When I arrived home, my husband was upstairs doing some work from home. I popped my large mug of coffee into the microwave while I put away the groceries."

"Oh, no did it overflow?" I asked.

"No, but it was starting to boil. I got it out just in time. Anyway…I started with my housecleaning as I drank the coffee. Over the next two hours, I reheated it three or four times as it cooled down," she said.

I was curious, "How did that taste?"

"It actually tasted fine, until I got to the last couple of sips. It started to cool, so I took a big gulp of the last bit of coffee. I felt something weird in my mouth, so I walked over and spit it in the kitchen sink. I looked and there were toenails and fingernails in my coffee mug."

"What?" I shouted, almost gagging at the thought.

"Yes, my husband had trimmed his toenails and fingernails while I was gone. He said he saw the cup sitting there and thought he would just throw them in, instead of leaving them on the carpet."

I almost felt ill. "He didn't think of putting them in the trash? That is so disgusting," I exclaimed, grateful I was no longer married.

"I know, right?" Sophie said, then added, "and to think I cooked them with the coffee a few times that morning in the microwave."

"Not to mention, he is still alive," I added. Ugh! We laughed about it, but I still found it hard to believe a grown man would do that!

# 55

## Regret is Overrated

I went back to the job of unpacking, realizing I hadn't even turned my cell phone back on. I dug it out of my bag and turned it on. And there it was; twelve missed calls, and eight voice messages. I started to listen.

The first one was Devin, wanting to meet with me to return some of my things. The remaining messages were from Denny, asking me to call when I got home. I thought about the "things" Devin wanted to return and the only thing I really wanted back happened to be a frame of eight pictures of myself. I had made this for him for Christmas one year when he made the comment of wishing he had known me sooner. "I want to know what you looked like from the very start," he said one night over dinner. That was when I decided to surprise him with pictures from birth to present day. Of course, those were the only copies I had of the photos, so I did want them back, even though I was filled with dread at the thought of seeing him again. *Why couldn't he stick them in the mail like I did his stuff?* I even sent him a manila envelope filled completely full of new cards that I purchased specifically for him. Yes, I was big on sending mushy greeting cards! Devin left me a message the day he received the manila envelope letting me know he got my "care package."

Anyway, I called Devin back to suggest he mail me my things instead of coming over.

No answer.

I looked at the clock and saw it was approaching eleven o'clock. *Devin was probably in church, being the devout Mormon that he is.* I left a message asking him to pop the pictures in the mail and he could throw away anything else I left behind. Whatever else there was, a toothbrush and maybe a shirt or two, possibly some makeup, I had replaced all of that by now.

I thought how time had flown since Devin and I had been together. Devin's birthday was in October and I met Denny in January, it was now close to July, so it had been awhile.

I took a deep breath, time to tackle the second caller, Denny. *Look at you, Carly, just tying up those loose ends!* Yes, that is what I thought, but I sat there, fingers crossed, hoping for another opportunity to leave a message, simply stating I had arrived back in Utah, safe and sound. *The end.*

"Hello?" Denny answered.

*Shit!* "Hi, Denny," I said. "I wanted to let you know I'm home safe."

"Did you get my messages?" he asked flatly, with no emotion in his voice.

I answered, "I left my phone in my bag last night, and just turned it on. I saw that you called and just called you back."

"So, you didn't listen to the messages?" he asked in only the way that Denny can ask.

I rolled my eyes. "No, Denny, I just called you back."

"Well, I think we should talk," he declared, as if we hadn't already. But before I could utter a word, he started in. "Carly, I have done nothing except be nice to you, and try to help you out. I can't believe you've had these men in your life before and not one has helped you financially."

*Here we go again.* "Denny, we've been through all this," I said rather calmly, even though I was frustrated. "I appreciate everything you've done for me. Please don't think for a second that I don't…"

He interrupted me before I could finish my thought. "Carly, I want to be with you, what can we do to make that happen?"

I thought about what it would take… *a lobotomy, maybe?* "Denny, we aren't in love," I said stating the obvious with a bit of hesitation.

"We haven't known one another long enough to determine *if* we are in love or not. We need to give it another shot, don't you think?" Denny pleaded.

My heart sank. I thought we were done with this. *I was done with this.* I didn't know what to say. But before I realized it, I blurted out, "I am so confused." I regretted it as soon as I said it. That was the wrong thing to say.

"I know you are, that's why we need to try again. I am going to send you a check made out to Kathy, I want her to help you figure it out," Denny said with an air of confidence.

Kathy was the counselor I saw when Clark and I were going through our divorce. Counselor Bob had moved to Seattle years ago and I was happy to have found Kathy, who was such a gem. I had complete faith and trust in her, so much to the fact that every man I dated after Clark, including Devin and Denny, had to see her, too. It was a pre-requisite!

"Okay, thank you," I said, thinking it was a complete waste of my time to try and argue with Denny. It was his money, and a few sessions with Kathy couldn't hurt!

"I will send the check today, so watch for it, and you should call her today and get on her books for every Monday," he instructed.

"I will, Denny, thanks again, bye now," I said.

"Goodbye for now, and don't forget to call Kathy," Denny reminded me once again.

"I won't," I said. "I really need to go now, but thanks for…"

"Do it right after we hang up, Carly," Denny demanded.

"Okay, Denny, I will." *If you ever let me hang up!*

"Good girl, love you."

*What?* My mouth dropped as I hung up the phone. *Love you? Oh, Dear Lord!* I quickly hung up the phone without another word.

# 56
## Steel Waters Run Deep

I called Kathy, as instructed. Since the last time I saw her, she had moved to a private college, and I was unsure if she was only counseling students who were in school there. I got her answering machine and left her a voice message. "Hi Kathy, it's Carly. I was wondering if I could make an appointment with you? I know you're at Westminster College now, but was wondering if you are only seeing students or will you still take one of your old fucked up clients?"

I hung up the phone, just as Devin called back. I was on a roll, so I decided to take the bull by the horns, and answered his call.

"Hi, it's me," Devin said softly.

"I know," I said matter-of-factly.

"Carly, I can't mail all of this stuff to you, there's too much. Can we meet at the Soup Kitchen today? I'll give it to you there."

*Bull by the horns, Carly; why not get this chapter closed?*

"What time?" I asked with a sigh.

He sounded surprised. He was probably shocked that I agreed. "Um…in about an hour?"

"See you there in an hour and a half, and don't forget my pictures."

"Okay." Devin said.

I hung up the phone and then I screamed. *I can't believe I am going to meet that hypocrite!* I hurried to get ready, and boy was I ready!

I dressed as if I was going to meet my worst enemy, and on some level, I was. But, I have to say, it was a good day, and I looked great. You know how some days you just look better than others? Well, luckily this was one of those days. Just as I was ready to walk out the door, Kathy returned my call. "Funny message, Carly, and yes I will see you, she said half chuckling, does Monday at 2:00 work?"

"Perfect, I will see you then," I said, watching the clock. I had twenty minutes to get to the soup kitchen. Oh, well, Devin can wait. I want this over.

I started my car and drove *under* the speed limit, not so anxious to reach my destination, but anxious to have it be done once and for all. I pulled in the crowded parking lot and got out of my car.

I slowly walked into the Soup Kitchen and there he sat. I hadn't seen his face for so long, I forgot how handsome he was, at least on the outside.

*Do not pay attention to his looks,* I reminded myself. I walked over to his table and sat down, immediately noticing a gold band on his left hand.

*Are you kidding me right now? What the...*

Devin interrupted my thoughts, but I was seething inside. I stared at him trying to control the blood that was boiling in my veins.

"Hi Carly, you look great."

*I know!*

"Thank you," I managed to reply trying to remain calm and unaffected by what I saw, and pretending I hadn't noticed. *I will not give him the satisfaction.*

"Do you want some tomato soup?"

*Oh, trying to play the 'I know you' card.* Tomato soup is my favorite.

"No thank you, I have to get back up the canyon. Is that my stuff?" I asked pointing to a small basket at the end of the table.

*I am pretending not to notice your wedding ring. I don't care about you anymore and I will not give you the pleasure of wondering if I do.*

"Yes," he said as he took my hands in his and continued as the ring stared me right in the face. *Keep it together, old girl.*

"I am so sorry, Carly. I love you just as much as I always have, even after all of this time. When you walked in, I was stunned."

*What an asshole!*

I fired back quickly, "Oh, like I was when I walked in your room in Vegas." *Dammit, I didn't want to go there! That looks like I give a shit and I don't! I don't!*

"Please stop," he said, "I've apologized numerous times for that. I am still kicking myself in the ass, I'm sorry! I don't know what else I can say. I know you have probably moved on, but I would like to be in a place of still being able to call you and talk to you, see how your life is going, tell you about my life. I'd like us to be friends."

*Oh, would you now?* Fat chance.

I pulled my hands away, stood up, and picked up the basket and rummaged through it. *Oh, good the pictures, still in the frame, are in there.*

"Please, Carly, I don't understand why we can't at least be friends."

I could no longer take it. I screamed at him, "Friends? Seriously you want to be friends? You broke my fucking heart and now you want us to be friends?" Suddenly, you could hear a pin drop, no more slurping from the soup patrons. Devin was just as quiet. I am usually so soft-spoken and kind, but I just lost it. I shook my head and continued, "I trusted you, but now your words mean *nothing* to me because your actions spoke the truth. *Un*-believable."

"Carly, I'm sorry please don't hate me," Devin said with tears in his eyes.

"I try not to carry any hate in my heart for you, Devin. I loved you once and as much as I can't stand to admit it, I probably still have some love for you." I drew in a breath as I closed my eyes. I opened my eyes as I exhaled and said sternly, "Stay the hell away from me, though." I looked Devin right in his tear filled eyes and felt complete repulsion. I knew in my heart that I despised this hypocrite inside and out.

I turned and walked out to my car and thought as I put the basket on the front seat. *I know I'm not where I need to be, but thank God, I'm no longer where I used to be.*

I drove up the canyon thinking, *one down, one to go*, as I knew in my heart, Denny would not let go easily. *But, you are stronger now, Carly. The things I used to trip on, I walk over now! I am stronger! That was hard, but I did it and the truth is I feel empowered. I am no longer sad, scared or hurt. Not anymore. I have grown too strong to ever fall back in his arms again. And now, I will do what is best for me.*

I turned on the radio only to hear "It's My Life" by *No Doubt*. I turned it up full volume and sang along at the top of my lungs the rest of the way home.

# Got My Groove Back

I called Stenmark to get on his books for a golf lesson. I got his voicemail and left a message. I was trying for the following day, since I was already scheduled for a day off due to coming home early.

He returned my call promptly. "I thought you weren't back for another day," Stenmark said.

"No, I am back now." *No point involving Stenmark in my life's drama. Not yet, anyway, but I did need to be honest at some point. Just not right now.*

"Great! I don't work tomorrow, but I could come up at five, then we could go for a glass of Chardonnay."

"Perfect, see you then, Stenmark."

"Wait! Bennett, how was your trip, how did you play?"

"I was functioning on no sleep, so golf was tough. I shot a 124."

"That's not bad considering you're new at the game."

"Room for improvement," I said. And then added, "By the way, I got the 'calling card' you left on my car door handle."

Stenmark laughed and said, "It wasn't me."

"Very funny," I said. "See you tomorrow at five." I set down my cell phone and wished it was today at five. I could use a distraction.

I decided to finish my errands. I went to the post office box to find a package sent overnight from Denny. I sighed as I opened it right there, and inside was a book titled, *The Highly Sensitive Person in Love,* and a thousand-dollar check made out to Kathy, my counselor. I stared at the book for a couple of minutes and wondered if it was meant for me or for Denny. I opened it to find he had handwritten a couple of small paragraphs. I walked out to my car and sat down to read his words.

*Dear Carly,*

*I found this book and as I skimmed through the pages, I had an epiphany and I realized something about myself. I am in love with you after all. I think I am just too sensitive of a person to let my feelings show. You asked me once if I had ever had my heart broken. My answer was no. I remembered you looking surprised and asking me not even when my marriage of fifteen years ended? My reply was the same.*

*After seeing a different version of myself right there in black and white, I decided you were right. I have had my heart broken and I made it seem like I skipped through life untouched. That simply was not true and I apologize. It hurt and it hurt because it mattered. And now, my heart is broken again. Please read this book and then we will talk.*

*Love, Denny.*

Oh, this one is going to take some time.

I consoled myself by thinking at least he doesn't live here, but seriously wondered what the heck happened to that pillar of strength? *I am woman, hear me roar! Yeah, right.*

As anticipated, the phone calls from Denny came several times a day. And as such, they were no longer missed calls, they were long, detailed messages and they were nice messages, which made it more difficult to stand my ground. Fortunately, I kept my mind occupied during the day, but still I would let it go to voicemail. I just wasn't ready to deal with it. *Here I go again.* Life status: Currently trying to hold it all together with one bottle of nail glue!

However, I had a golf lesson to look forward to…and a glass of wine!

I slept fitfully, but what did I expect? I was excited to see Stenmark, but still I was lying in my bed dreading the thought of talking to Denny. Why did he have to find that darn book? I used the excuse of not loving each other pretty heavily in my argument three nights ago, basing nearly everything on that one truth without knowing he would have an awakening! I didn't want to hurt his feelings or be unkind. That simply is not my nature, but I knew deep inside I had to end it and end it fast!

*You are one decision from a completely new life, so carry on, Carly!*

# 58

# The Game of Golf — No Holes "Parred"

I arrived at the golf course right on time and was greeted by my golf instructor, "Hi Bennett, how are you doing today?"

"I am doing great, how about you?" I asked with a smile.

"I'm well, thanks, shall we get started?" he asked.

Now that the pleasantries were out of the way, the lesson began. I was in my golf posture, looking at the ball, when he walked over and stuck a blue baseball cap on my head, backwards.

"How can you see anything with your hair hanging down in your face? Don't even try and tell me you can see the ball. I know better," Stenmark joked...sort of.

I laughed. I had to admit it was a better view of the ball, and of him standing across from me. (Actually he started a new fashion trend with me, I still to this day wear a baseball cap when I'm golfing. And I still wear it backwards!)

"Yes, Stenmark, that is much better, thanks."

He flashed that smile and gave a wink. I loved that!

"Am I ever going to improve enough to play an actual game with real people?" I asked.

Stenmark laughed and assured me, "You'll be shooting par before you know it." *I seriously doubt that, but I like his optimism.*

The lesson was good and I did feel some improvement in the silly game, but today I was looking forward to the end of the lesson.

"Do you want to do next Monday?" he asked.

"I have another appointment Monday at 2:00," I said.

For a moment I thought seriously about cancelling it, when reality slapped me in the face. I needed to keep my appointment with Kathy. I thought of Denny and realized how much I needed help in dealing with my breakup. "How about early morning?" I asked.

"No, I have junior camps in the morning," Stenmark answered.

Then he added, "We'll figure something out, now let's go for that glass of wine."

I agreed and off we went to Adolph's in our separate vehicles.

The usual suspects were sitting at the bar, the same faces drinking their beverages of choice and chatting with Mary, the bartender, when we walked in. Mary greeted us as she poured two glasses of Kendall Jackson Chardonnay and sat them on a small table in the corner. We sat down as she smiled and walked away. This time there was no mention of Denny.

Stenmark lifted his glass and said, "Here's to your improvement today."

I clicked my glass with his and we took a sip of the cold, buttery and very refreshing wine. It was yummy. I usually drank red wine, but I truly enjoyed the Chardonnay, and I enjoyed being with Stenmark.

*So now what?*

It was like he read my mind, "Where do we go from here?" he asked.

"I was just thinking that myself," I answered half scared to know the answer.

"Bennett, after I left you the last time, I went home and just laid in bed looking up at the ceiling, unable to sleep."

"You mean the night after the kiss?"

He nodded.

"Me too." I answered honestly.

"Let's go someplace where we can talk." Stenmark said as he motioned to Mary for the check. We walked outside into the crisp air and got into his car, he pulled a CD from the backseat and stuck it in his car stereo. "Do you know who this is?" he asked.

"Garth Brooks?" I guessed.

Stenmark laughed and shook his head, "No, it's me."

He had an incredible voice and those song lyrics were so clever, and poignant. Being a songwriter has always intrigued me. I've always loved the play on words.

"Did you write this?" I asked.

"Yes."

I listened carefully to the lyrics, some of which were, *'It's funny how one night somewhere can affect how you're thinkin', that one night with you almost changed my feelings about love.'*

I looked at him and listened more intently to the upcoming chorus, *'So we've gone from strangers to lovers to strangers, new friends to good friends to not friends at all, but loving so fast and so hard posed a danger of turning strangers to lovers to strangers.'*

We looked at each other and I don't think either one of us could deny the attraction.

"I actually recognize that song," I said, breaking his intense stare.

Stenmark seemed surprised. "Really? You've heard my song?" he asked.

I answered honestly, "Yes. Wasn't it on the jukebox at the biker bar on State Street? I can't really remember the name of the bar."

"It was called Rocky's," he said with a smile, "and yes, it *was* on the jukebox there. Good memory, Bennett." He then added casually, "I can't believe you know my song."

"It's a great song, very clever and true to life. Was it a hit?" I asked in all seriousness.

Shyly, he answered with a soft, quick, "Yes."

*How cool was this? I believe I not only found the man in the songs, but the man who writes the song...and it wasn't Barry Manilow.* "That's impressive," I said, kind of star struck.

He shrugged it off. "Thanks." He was so humble! That was refreshing.

"So...how *was* your trip?" Stenmark asked.

"I came back early." I answered tentatively, wondering if I should really go there this soon. I was nervous and I was scared, but there was no denying we had a connection.

"I noticed," he said with a grin.

*Here goes nothing!* "Yeah, it was a hard trip." I began slowly. "Denny can be so intense at times. He is a nice man but..." I stopped pondering my words and picking them oh so carefully.

Stenmark looked at me with anticipation. "But what?" he asked.

*Just say it, Carly!*

I blurted it out, "He's not you."

*There, I said it!*

Then he leaned in and lifted my chin up. He kissed me softly on the lips and I kissed him right back, and it was once again magical.

"So, is it over now?" Stenmark asked.

"I think so," I said. "To be honest with you, Denny wasn't happy with me when I left, but he did agree that we were not in love." I continued on, remembering that long evening. "He drank close to a half bottle of gin during and after our conversation and we slept in separate rooms that night."

Stenmark raised his eyebrows, "Really?"

I wondered if he was surprised about the gin, the sleeping arrangements or both.

"Yes, and we got up early the following morning and he took me to the airport, so that was kinda that." I said desperately hoping that was the end of it.

He kissed me again. Then he said the words I had dreamed about. "Well, good. I'm glad because I think I'm falling in love with you."

I felt the same way, but nonetheless, hearing the words caught me by surprise. "Me, too," I said biting my lower lip. *Oh, wow this is really happening! We're already wet, and now we're gonna go swimming, metaphorically speaking, obviously!* I couldn't help but feel relieved that part was over but now I was on a roll. "There's something else I need to tell you about," I said.

"You're pregnant," he said trying to add some levity, I'm sure.

I laughed as I began my Las Vegas story.

Yes, I told him all about Devin and the hooker.

Stenmark looked at me and said, "I promise to never hurt you, Bennett."

And I believed him.

I was praying that all of that was truly out of the way so I changed the subject to something a little more benign.

"So, who do you like music-wise?" I asked.

He began to name some of my favorites.

Our music interests were virtually the same, and other than my late husband, Rick, I never met a man who enjoyed the same music or even knew a lot of the artists I listened to. Lucinda Williams, Steve Earle, The Warren Bothers, John Hiatt, and Guy Clark just to name a few. I found it interesting that we knew some of the same people in the music scene in Salt Lake City and that was fun to talk about and I absolutely loved that we had this in common.

But as stimulating as the conversation was, it was getting late. Finally I said, "I better go home, I have work early in the morning."

"Hey before you go, it just so happens, The Warren Brothers are playing at The Westerner Saturday night, would you like to go?" The Westerner was, and still is, a popular bar in Salt Lake City, and the thought of going there to listen to music with Stenmark thrilled me.

"I would love that, they are one of my fav's," I said.

"Same here. I'll talk to you before then and we can make plans. Maybe go to dinner before the show?" Stenmark asked tentatively.

"That sounds great." *Wow, dinner and a show. A real date!*

We said our goodbyes and I walked to my car. I opened the door and turned back as I quickly blew him a kiss. Stenmark waited until my car started and I turned on the lights, before he drove away with a quick honk of his horn.

# Aim to Misbehave

I was so happy when I walked into the salon the next morning, and it was obvious. My first client of the day, Joyce, came in for her regular standing pedicure, perfectly on time. "How was your vacation, Carly?" she asked.

"It was fun, the weather was beautiful," I answered not wanting to go into much detail.

"So, are we going to lose you to the state of Georgia?" she asked.

I laughed and answered honestly. "No. Denny is a nice man, however he can be pretty intense. It's fun to go on these trips, but he isn't the one."

Joyce said, "You never really seemed over the moon for him, not like you were for Devin, even though he never remembered your birthday."

*This was true.* "Yeah, I know, I really wasn't into Denny, but Devin was a psycho," I said half joking.

We both laughed. I nervously changed the subject. "What have you been up to, Joyce?"

"Golf and work, my two favorite things, what about you?"

"I've been working hard on getting my book finished," I said hoping to get off the subject of my love life.

Joyce looked surprised as she asked, "What book?"

"Oh, I'm writing a book about my life as a nail technician with funny stories about clients, my life and such."

She looked at me in amazement and said, "If I would have known you were writing a book, I would have acted out and misbehaved a little more."

We both laughed. "You're funny, but guess what? You still have time, it's not finished yet."

Then with her dry sense of humor she added, "I'm not that funny today, 'cuz I'm tired."

I told her to close her eyes and take a little nap. Joyce took my advice and slept through the rest of her pedicure.

My next client, Grace was an interesting woman. Grace had never been married, and had no children and she was not a warm person at all. She was very business-like and always brought a stack of paperwork in with her. This made the time fly by for me, because there was no talking, so I just focused on my work. And today was no different. Grace was a strong woman who could be difficult, but I've always had a talent to see beyond some of those tough exteriors once you get to know someone, often they really aren't as hard as that outer shell initially appears.

"Hi, Grace," I said cheerfully when she came in.

Her response was rapid. "Hi." She pulled a stool over next to her chair, piled her paperwork on the top and we both went to work. She shuffled through her papers, turning them over as she finished with each and every one.

I was busy filing her acrylic nails when one of the hairdresser's next clients walked in with her five-year-old daughter. "I am so sorry I am late," said the client, "but my babysitter did not show up and I hope you don't mind, I had to bring my daughter with me." The slim brunette was exasperated. "I know it's a perm today, but I brought things for her to do and she is really quiet and good."

"No problem," I said, and made room for her daughter.

Grace never even looked up.

The hairdresser started her service and the little girl sat down to read her book. After about a half an hour, it appeared the child was getting bored. She walked over to my nail desk and without saying a word she just watched me work. I smiled at her and, of course, I didn't mind, plus she was adorable. A couple of minutes passed, but still the curious little girl just quietly stared at me doing acrylics. Finally, Grace looked up at the child and said in her own dry, flat, and emotionless tone, "Go away."

I almost died! *Good grief, Grace.*

The little girl walked away without saying a word, and sat down next to her books. She picked one up and began reading again. I kept filing and Grace kept reading and turning the pages over, stacking them on top of each other until the pile slid off onto the floor.

"Fuck!" Grace yelled, staring at the mess. Her pages were all over the floor. She was trapped with the stool in front of her and her hands were in my possession. I couldn't believe Grace's language! I am no prude by any means, in case you haven't figured that out by now, but there was a young, sweet, impressionable child in the room and I was embarrassed. Her mother just sat there with her nose in a fashion magazine, forgetting she even had a daughter, it seemed. I don't mean to judge, but geez!

Quickly, the little girl jumped out of her seat and began picking up the papers, straightening them into a nice, neat pile, as she sat them atop the stool.

"Oh, thank you," Grace said acting annoyed at herself. "That was nice of you," she added quickly in her own insincere way.

The little girl said, "That's okay, just don't drop them again." Then she went back to her seat and sat down. *Touché!*

I have to say even Grace laughed, and that is most definitely a rarity!

# 60
## Never Ask Permission

I must admit it was so nice to have my work as a distraction, especially given my present circumstances with men. I knew my phone had been ringing off the hook, as we used to say, but this was a cell phone…no hook. I ignored it all day, only answering the salon phone.

But once work was over and I was home, THEN it was time to deal with it all. I poured a glass of Chardonnay and thought of Stenmark. Thoughts of him happily tumbled around in my head…until I looked down at my cell phone. Several missed calls and fourteen voice messages, split pretty evenly between Devin and Denny, with Denny ahead by four. *UGH!* I took a big sip of wine and pressed 'listen.'

Let's see, Devin was still wondering why we couldn't remain friends and Denny was wondering if I received *his* care package. I erased all of Devin's messages except one, the last one. I must admit I was intrigued because it started with, "This is the last time I will call you." *Let's hope so!* I listened further. "You made yourself clear at the Soup Kitchen, so I will not bother you anymore and I will stay away from you. But I promise you, I will call you once a year, every year, from here on out, on July 31st." That was the anniversary of the day we met. *Oh, great something to look forward to every year.* I stared at the phone and I shook my head.

Then I called Denny. He answered. "Hi Denny," I said, "I wanted to let you know I received your package, thank you."

"Did you make an appointment with Kathy?" he replied eagerly.

"Yes, I did. I am seeing her at two this Monday." I said annoyed, as I rolled my eyes. *Don't be bitchy, Carly.*

"I was thinking," he said.

*Uh-oh,* I thought.

"You should take the book in with you and show it to her. You have my permission to let her read what I wrote inside the book."

"Okay, I will." *Something I already had planned to do, anyway. Now I have Denny's permission.*

Denny interrupted my thoughts. "Carly, have you given any thought to my words?"

"Of course I have, but I really would like to speak with Kathy first." *Just because you have had an epiphany, doesn't mean the same holds true for me.* "Denny, I am just really confused." I lied and I admit it. I knew where I wanted to be and it was not with Denny. I longed for Stenmark, but I couldn't find it in my heart to hurt Denny. I wanted to let him down easy with the help of a trained professional, Kathy. I truly had made my decision, and just wanted this loose end tied up once and for all.

Much to my surprise, Denny acquiesced, "I understand," he said. "I will talk to you on Monday evening after you see Kathy."

*Geez, couldn't I please have a few sessions with Kathy under my belt first?* "Okay, Denny, talk soon. Thanks again." I hung up the phone. *I am such a chicken. But at least, he didn't say he loved me this time,* I thought with relief.

I went to bed early and woke up before the alarm. Maybe my brain was getting used to me rising at five a.m. I decided to go to the gym. It had almost been a week and I was hoping to get back into the habit. I enjoy working out, not only the physical benefits of it, but the emotional benefit for me was huge. I remember when Clark and I were in the throes of divorce, I wasn't working out much. I just worked to try and keep my mind busy. One afternoon, I went to see my family physician. I was feeling pretty low and a bit depressed.

The doctor walked in and asked, "How are you doing, Carly?"

I answered with some smart ass sarcasm, "I'm doing fine right up here on cloud nine." *Good thing Dr. Quinn knows my humor.*

He smiled, "What's going on?"

"Honestly, I just can't seem to get rid of this dark cloud looming over my head," I told him.

Dr. Quinn asked me, "Have you ever taken anything for your feelings of doom and gloom?"

"Just Percocet once in a while," I said with a grin. Dr. Quinn laughed, but just to make sure he understood, I said, "I am joking."

"Well, seriously Carly there is this new anti-depressant out called Zoloft, and it is really wonderful," he offered confidently. "So much so they call it the happy pill."

"What are the side effects?" I asked cautiously.

Dr. Quinn said, "Not nearly as bad as Percocet can be," then he winked. He had been my doctor for over twenty-five years and I always enjoyed his sense of humor.

"Many experience weight loss." *Sold! I'll take it!* "But the two main side effects are one, you can't drink with it."

"Oh." *That's not good.* "What happens if you do?"

"Well, first of all, you should never drink with any anti-depressant, because as we know, alcohol is a depressant itself. But if you do drink with it, one of two things can happen. You will either get drunk immediately, like on one drink, or you will drink and drink and never feel drunk until it hits you *hard.*"

*Hmmmm…That could be bad or that could be fun!*

Dr. Quinn continued, "The second thing is you can't have an orgasm on it. You will feel like you can but you never will be able to achieve it."

*Well now, that's a real deal-breaker. I'm out.*

"Do you have any questions, Carly?" Dr. Quinn asked.

"Yes, I guess I am somewhat confused. If you can't drink on it, and you can't have an orgasm on it, why do they call it the happy pill?"

He smiled slightly, not wanting to seem unprofessional. "Why don't we try it for a couple of months and see how it goes?"

"Well, I am not in an intimate relationship right now, and I am not a big drinker anyway, so why not?" I told him and he wrote me a prescription for three month's supply. However, after about six weeks, I couldn't stand the way it made me feel. I felt like I was outside of my body, watching my world go by. I felt as if I could care less about life.

I called Dr. Quinn and he advised me to wean myself off of the "happy pill" slowly, which I did. And I haven't tried another anti-depressant since.

# 61
## Files Over the Edge

I woke up the next morning promptly at five a.m. ready for the gym. It felt good to jump on the treadmill. I knew I had a full day of acrylic nail fills ahead of me and I was ready.

My first client of the day was Shauna, a petite runner herself, who had recently moved here from Ohio. I began to remove her nail polish and I stopped and reached in the drawer to pull out her envelope containing her own nail file. She looked at the envelope, curiously.

"What is that with my name on it?" she asked.

"Oh, that's your nail file." I replied.

"You have a nail file for every one of your clients?" She seemed surprised.

"Yes, I do. These gold wooden boards are not sanitizable, so I don't re-use them. They can get human tissue and nail filings on them and that would be nasty."

"That's cool, I have been getting my nails done for over twenty years and no one has ever had a separate file for me."

"Well, maybe they have a different opinion than I do about it, but until they come up with a tough file I can use on acrylics and sanitize, I will continue to do it this way."

Shauna asked, "Isn't it pricey?"

"Yes," I answered, "but I figure, it's cheaper than a hospital visit for an infection."

"That's true, but how many fake nail people do you have?" Shauna asked.

"Basically, about a third of my clientele wears acrylic nails." I added, "There used to be more until the recession in 2008, close to ninety percent of my clients wore them. Now they either have gone *au naturale* or they use the gels."

Shauna nodded, "I have a friend that gets her gels done back in Ohio. She is addicted to technology and has a manic attachment to her iPad, doesn't go anywhere without it, even to get her nails done."

I laughed, "That makes it so hard. I had a client who answered her phone every time it rang, and it rang a lot. One day she messed up her nail polish three times when she put her cell phone up to her ear next to her long hair. Patiently, I fixed her nail and on the fourth time, without looking up I said, 'Touch it and you're dead, Joan,' she finally let it ring." I think she knew one more time would push me over the edge!

"I know what you mean. I was sitting in a nail appointment with my friend and her gel nails were wrapped in the foil. I looked over and she was using her nose to swipe her iPad!"

I laughed so hard with Shauna. "Enter the age of technology." I concluded.

"That's for sure." Shauna agreed.

My next client walked in and Shauna said, "You just have one right after another, don't you?"

I thought of The Rawhide song from TV, "Rollin,' Rollin, Rollin'." "Yes, I pretty much do." I have often said, "I think I could do this in my sleep or at least in the dark," I told Shauna.

She nodded her head in agreement because there was no denying I was always busy.

Stenmark and I had our very first date that night and I was beyond excited. I dressed in my best cowgirl attire for the concert at The Westerner, which included a denim mini skirt with red cowboy boots, no hat. That was the best I could do, I wasn't really a cowgirl, but I did love The Warren Brothers. Unfortunately, the concert began earlier than expected, so we skipped dinner, which was fine. Anytime, I can skip a meal is always good by me, as I have never been much of an eater.

The concert was phenomenal, one of the best I had seen. Or was it just the company? I won't lie; I don't think I had ever felt this at ease with a man. Stenmark was just so comfortable to be with. I did feel badly about him driving me back up the canyon to Park City, even though he lived in Salt Lake City. "I am so sorry you have to drive back and forth." I said sincerely.

Stenmark replied, "I could always spend the night with you, neither of us works tomorrow."

*Tempting, very tempting.* "I'm sorry, but I have church early in the morning," I said with a smile.

A puzzled look fell over his face.

"Rain check?" I added.

"Absolutely," he answered as he pulled up to my condo.

We both leaned in and kissed goodnight.

I went to bed and thought about the evening. I also thought about our many conversations, realizing that we literally have no secrets between us now. I'd fessed up about my married Mormon boyfriend who enjoyed the company of hookers. I gave Stenmark all the dirty details concerning the Las Vegas incident. But I'd also involved him in the drama over my break up with Denny as well, every last detail of it He now knew everything about my ex-loves and it felt like I was no longer teetering on the edge of sanity, which was a huge relief. Over the course of just a couple of months, we shared everything about our lives, our families, our jobs and even our lovers, past and present. It felt good.

*This man was sodium pentothal in human form.*

# Up at Noon

I finally drifted off into a very deep, happy sleep. I had amazing dreams that I didn't want to end. When I finally woke up and looked at the clock, it was almost noon *Dang it! Church started a half an hour ago. Guess I missed it, again.*

My friend, Carrie, called later that afternoon. She was ready to talk about our upcoming fun weekend. "Are you ready for our Make-A-Wish weekend that starts this Friday?"

"I am really looking forward to it, Carrie, thanks again for inviting me." Then I added, "What is the plan?"

"Let's meet at the Yarrow Friday night at six, then we all get into a limo and go to the restaurant together for the wine tasting dinner."

I was really excited, "That sounds fun."

"That's only the beginning, Carly. After dinner, the limo picks us up and we go to Stein's and stay overnight in the lodge." Clark and I stayed there once and the rooms were the size of my condo. They were beautiful.

Carrie continued, "We each have our own room, too."

This was sounding better and better but it didn't end there.

"Then in the morning, we all get picked up again and go to a spa for massages, facials, manicures and pedicures."

*What! Manicures and pedicures! What a treat for me! I do not like to do my own nail care services. I was beyond ecstatic!*

"That sounds like so much fun, Carrie!"

"Well wait, Carly, there's more." *Isn't there a television commercial about just that? Adding more and more onto your purchase! But, wait...*

"I think they will do our hair afterwards, too."

"Carrie, would you mind if I went to Rebecka for that part? No one can style hair like my sister!"

"Ohhh, let's call her and see if she can style both of us afterward, I love the way she does my hair, too."

"Okay, I will take care of that part." I offered. "What's up next?" Carrie continued,

"Then we go to The Blue Boar Inn for dinner and we each have our own room there Saturday evening. And then Sunday morning at six a.m., we get on the hot air balloon and ride over the mountains to Snowbird resort."

"We're going all the way over there in a hot air balloon?" I asked, surprised.

"Don't worry it will be safe and so beautiful!" Carrie reassured me.

I sighed as she finished up with, "Then we go back to the Inn and all of us will meet for brunch, then go home. Which means we need to drive our own cars there."

"How many of us are doing this?" I asked.

"Eight of us, you're my date," Carrie said with a laugh. "I'll be in touch before Friday and we can decide where to meet."

"Sounds good," I said. As we hung up I thought, *this will be a blast, but I am a bit worried about the three-hour hot air balloon ride. Come on, Carly, time to step out of your comfort zone! I am going to do this and I am going to enjoy it! I've been told that life begins at the end of your comfort zone and I was beyond ready for a new beginning! I was ready.*

# You Only Live Twice

The week flew by, as it tends to do when you're chained to your desk, metaphorically speaking, of course. I wanted my big Make-A-Wish weekend to come quickly. I was anxious to have this time for just fun. I wouldn't have to think about anything, but enjoying myself, and being with one of my favorite people. Carrie and I started out as client and manicurist and quickly became fast friends. She is one of the most caring, kind and generous women I know, and to top it off, she is incredibly bright! I loved spending time with her and I knew we were going to have the time of our lives that weekend.

I went home a little early on Friday to pack and prepare for our trip. Carrie called just as I was just loading my overnight bag in my car.

"Let's meet at the Yarrow," she suggested. "The limo is picking us up at six-thirty to take us to the restaurant, so will six work?"

"Yes, that's perfect. I will see you there." I looked at my watch, it was 5:30 and I realized I had time to make a couple of calls. I called Stenmark.

"Hi, what's going on?" he asked when he answered his phone.

"I wanted to let you know I'm going to be unavailable until Sunday night. I'm going on a weekend trip for the Make-A-Wish Foundation with a girlfriend of mine."

"Oh, where will you be?" Stenmark asked.

"Kind of here, there and everywhere."

"Will you have your cell phone?"

"Yes, I will have it, just not sure of the reception."

Stenmark sounded a little disappointed as he told me to "Have fun and be safe."

I told him I would. We hung up and I thought I should make things easy on myself and let Denny know, too, just in case there was no cell service. I was happy I got his answering machine. "Hey, Denny, I just wanted to let you know, I'm doing a fundraising weekend with a girlfriend of mine and we will be out of cell service range from tonight until Sunday late afternoon." *Whew! That's done. Now I am off to enjoy myself with no worries!*

The weekend finally started! Carrie and I had so much fun. Saturday morning our spa day had made us feel like beauty queens. Rebecka did our hair and makeup and, as usual, she did an incredible job. We were ready for the limo ride to the Blue Boar Inn.

The dinner at the Blue Boar was fantastic and the wine was superb, as we sat at our table enjoying the company and the conversation. Carrie excused herself when her cell phone rang. She was only absent for about five minutes when she returned disappointed. "Carly that was work. I have to fly out first thing in the morning. I need to leave here by about five a.m. tomorrow. I am so sorry."

"It's okay. But that's really early, should you leave tonight?"

We both had driven over to the Inn separately, so I guess that means I could still sleep in tomorrow. I had my own car and honestly, I wasn't too disappointed about missing the hot air balloon ride.

"No, Carrie said, "you should stay and do the balloon ride, particularly since you have never been in one. It is really fun."

"I know, but since I don't really know the other people, and you'll be gone, maybe I'll skip the ride and get home early."

"Carly, you should do it. Remember I told you I used to crew for a company? It is really a fun experience. Just because I have to work, doesn't mean you shouldn't enjoy the rest of the weekend."

I thought about it. And I remembered about that big step out of my comfort zone, so I agreed.

We said goodnight and each went into our own rooms. I opened my door and was amazed. I was in the gorgeous Victorian-themed room. I wondered what kind of room Carrie got and hoped it was equally as beautiful.

I set my alarm and fell fast asleep.

The next morning I heard my alarm and thought it couldn't already be time to get up. I just fell asleep. I looked at the time and yes, it was five-thirty in the morning. That went fast! I guess it does when you go to bed after one!

I got ready, stuck a tin of Altoids in my pocket, and headed downstairs. Carrie had already left for the airport. *Oh man, I guess I really am going to do this hot air balloon ride with people I don't know.* I walked over to my group and said hello. I really did not know any of these people, so conversation was scarce. However, I did notice, three women who were friends dressed to the nines! Their hair was done, full-on makeup applied, and they wore chic sweaters with leather pants! In fact, all the women in the group had very nice leather purses and matching boots. *I wish Denny could see this. He thinks I am high maintenance.*

The Inn provided coffee and bagels for us while we waited for the balloon to fill up. It was nearing the end of October and the air was crisp. I could see my breath, as we all climbed into the basket. It was roomy, but tight quarters as there were nine of us, including the pilot (John), and the co-pilot (Jillian, his girlfriend).

John gave us the rundown. "Hot air balloons are safe. The only two things you have to worry about are power lines and water. We will stay away from both, so not to worry." And then he added, "Has everyone been on a balloon ride before?"

The women casually reapplied their lipstick as they bobbled their heads *yes.* All the men nodded in agreement, as well.

I piped up. "I haven't and I am happy we won't be going near the water, because I can't swim." (Those of you who know me, know I am deathly afraid of two things, the water and clowns.)

Jillian reassured me, "Don't worry."

I smiled and thought, *Oh, thanks. Now I feel SO MUCH better.*

We took off. I must say it was quite a thrill. We went around the Heber Valley and then headed towards Park City. The view was breathtaking. One of the women, Donna, had an expensive Nikon camera and she snapped photos like mad. We approached the Jordanelle Reservoir and I got a little worried. *Shoot! Were we going across the Jordanelle? Are you kidding me? Last I checked, that's WATER! Calm down, Carly, remember a comfort zone is a beautiful place, but nothing ever grows there. I know, I know I am supposed to be stepping out. Trust me, I am stepping out big time!* My heart pounded and I felt nauseous. I looked at Donna and her date, Jim. They were both leaning way out over the side of the basket snapping pictures. Donna turned to me and said, "Carly come here and look how beautiful this is. The reflection of the balloon against the water is spellbinding."

I was literally glued against the opposite side of the basket, but Jim insisted, "Come on, Carly, you have to see this!"

*You can do this.* I surprised even myself when I peeled my backside and hands off the basket and walked over to join Jim and Donna.

"Lean over, its beautiful," Donna encouraged.

I did. And I must admit, the reflection of the colorful balloon against the water was unbelievable. My folded arms lay on top of the basket and I really started to enjoy the view…even though we were dropping lower and lower.

Wait a minute! Why are we getting so close to the water? We are not supposed to be this close to the water, are we? John said we would not even be near the water. He knows I've never been in a balloon before, he knows I can't swim, what is happening?

# 64
## Skinny Dipping

*S*uddenly, that side we were on went into the water and started to sink. Quickly, the three of us went to the opposite side as the basket rapidly filled up with water. I was paralyzed. I watched the icy cold water get higher and higher. It was up to my knees, then my thighs. I held my hands up into the air and watched as the water continued to fill the wicker basket. *Dear God, please help us! Please protect us. Please, please, please!*

I remembered in a flash what I learned about flying. If you hit turbulence, always look at the flight attendants, if they don't look nervous, there is nothing to worry about. I quickly looked at John and Jillian. They both had a look of complete terror on their faces. John was frantically pulling on some kind of chord.

"C'mon, c'mon, c'mon get up! Get the hell up!" he screamed.

I looked down. The water was at my waist and approaching my chest at a rapid rate. My arms were still above my head, high in the air. I closed my eyes and thought, *This is it, Carly. The basket will go into the water, as it sinks, the balloon will come down on all of us. Those who can swim will try to swim out from under it, but the water is freezing, so hypothermia will set in before they will be able to do it. We are all going to die, unless something miraculous happens fast.*

I prayed and prayed for God to help us. I opened my eyes for what I thought was probably the last time and saw John pull on the chord three fast times in a row when suddenly the basket came up out of the water and surprisingly, water started to flow out of the woven basket. *Thank you, God.* Everyone cheered as John guided the balloon to a dirt access road next to the reservoir. John called the balloon crew to bring the van.

Suddenly, gunshots rang out around us. It was Deer hunting season. We landed in the middle of a licensed hunting ground. *Great.*

The van arrived quickly. We all determined it was not our day to die, thankfully. All of the women piled in, and the driver put the heat on full blast. The men helped the crew fold up the massive balloon and I watched the whole cleanup in awe. I think I was in shock. The other women pulled out their prized possessions, makeup bags, cell phones and the rest of the water-logged contents from their expensive leather purses. *I bet my Altoids are soggy. But we are all alive and I am so grateful to God. Thank you, thank you, and thank you! We are all so lucky and right now my comfort zone looks pretty damn good. I really should go back to church.*

We drove back to the Inn in silence. Finally, one of the men said, "Remember, we still have the champagne brunch in an hour, so let's all get ready and meet downstairs to wrap up this weekend." I seriously thought about skipping the brunch, but decided I could use a glass of champagne.

I got out of the van with a quick "Thank you" to the driver, and sloshed to my room. I was soaked from my chest down. I removed my jacket, took out my Altoids, poured water from the tin, and then threw the whole mess into the trash. I started to undress for a shower, but have you ever tried to get skinny, tight, wet jeans off by yourself? I'll tell you what, it's like wrestling with Satan! I pulled and tugged, and finally a good fifteen minutes later, they were off. But I was out of breath and exhausted!

At the brunch, the waiter poured us all a glass of champagne. John held his up and said, "Here's to life. May we always be as grateful for it, as we are right now in this very moment." We were all in complete agreement, as we clicked glasses and guzzled every last drop. No sipping for this terrified but grateful group!

# 65

## Bond with Whomever

When I arrived home, I took a long nap in my own bed and it felt so good. I slept for three hours. When I woke up, I decided to call Denny, since he had been blowing up my cell phone. I had another sixteen calls from the weekend! It would be a quick conversation, so I could spend more time on the phone when I called Stenmark.

However, the phone rang before I could call. Of course, it was Denny. I told him what happened.

"Didn't you have a life jacket on, Carly?" Denny wondered.

"A life jacket? I was in a hot air balloon, I didn't think I would need a life jacket!" I answered in amazement.

Denny had no good answer. "You just need to be more careful," he chastised.

*Oh. Okay Denny.*

We hung up. I called Stenmark and told him the same story. He had a totally different reaction.

"Bennett, are you okay?" he asked.

"Yes, I'm fine. I just will never go near a hot air balloon again," I said.

"What was he doing that close to the water, anyway?" he asked.

"The way it was explained to us, John, the pilot, said they sometimes go over the water and do what is called a splash and dash, meaning they barely skim the water. I think what happened was since this ride was a donation to Make-A-Wish, just like the whole weekend, there were nine of us in that balloon when he tried to do his fancy move. It was just too much weight."

Stenmark agreed.

"Anyway, I was so scared, I even told our pilot I couldn't swim, but he did it anyway. That was mean."

"Wait," Stenmark interrupted, "what do you mean you can't swim?"

"I don't know how to swim," I confirmed.

"Bennett, I am going to teach you how to swim. Everybody needs to know how to swim, you have to know how to save yourself!" he said.

*Whatever.* I went along with him omitting the fact I was scared to death of the water. I went to work the next morning anxiously awaiting my first client, Franny.

"Hi Franny, how are you doing? Thank you for coming to see me!" I said as I gave her a hug.

Franny was my client when I worked for Vie Retreat. She wasn't a regular standing, but I enjoyed her and the conversation was always good. I ran into Franny in the grocery store a couple of weeks ago and we caught up. "Franny, it's been forever!" I exclaimed. I was so happy to see her.

She threw her arms around me, "It *has* been forever," she admitted.

"I've missed you. When can I come and see you for a manicure?"

I handed her my business card, which by the way, is a perfect example of why you should never be without business cards! "Franny, my book is at work, but I will be there in the morning. Give me a call and we will set something up."

Franny was excited. "I'll call you first thing in the morning," she said with a big smile.

"Great, I look forward to it!" We hugged and said goodbye.

Unfortunately, Franny had to wait about a week, but I finally got her in. And now that she was here in my chair, and I saw her on a regular basis, we talked a lot about her life. Franny had five grown children. Her husband passed away twenty years ago, when their kids were just teenagers. Ironically, her sister-in-law also passed shortly after Franny's husband, which left her husband's brother, Paul, a widower. Two years after they both suffered the loss of their mates, Franny and Paul bonded, and interestingly enough, married each other.

I remember the conversation well.

"Oh, Franny how sad, but how *interesting*," I said.

"Well, Carly, we both had children that needed two parents and it has worked out very well for everyone."

"Yes, but Franny…isn't it kind of weird?"

"Oh, honey, it has been so long now. I don't ever recall it being any different."

So now Franny was back, almost twenty years later, and she looked just as she always did, absolutely great!

We sat down at my table and I began her manicure. That day, there were a couple of young boys, about six years old in the salon. At this time we had a small television and videos (back in the day) for kids to be entertained while waiting. As you can imagine, Franny and I had quite a few years to catch up on, and as we were laughing and talking, one of the boys came into my room. He took hold of the door handle and pulled it closed while saying, "I can't hear my cartoons!" Then he slammed the door completely shut. Franny and I just looked at each other stunned. Without a second passing, Franny said, "God forbid, he can't hear his damn cartoons!" I laughed and changed the subject, which is something I have gotten very used to doing in my chosen profession.

"So. Franny, how is Paul doing?"

"Oh, Carly, Paul died six years ago," she said casually.

I frowned. That was news to me! "Oh, I am so sorry, Franny."

"Well, he was old! Hell, Carly he was over ninety!"

Not knowing what to say, I simply continued to file her nails. There was quite the long pause. Finally I stopped filing, looked up and asked her thoughtfully, "Any more brothers?" After a second, we both broke out laughing. "I'm sorry, Franny," I said. "I couldn't help it."

Franny couldn't stop laughing, tears streamed down her face, but she managed to say, "It's okay, Carly, that's why I always love coming to see you, that great personality of yours!"

I finished her manicure and we re-booked her for once a month, manicure *and* pedicure.

"A half an hour is not long enough," Franny said as she opened the closed door of my room and walked out.

# Don't "Bossa-Nova" Me Around

As the weeks passed, Stenmark and I grew closer and Denny was becoming a distant memory. Kathy, the counselor, told me exactly what I needed to hear. In the end, I had to do what was best for me. It was a slow walk from the bottom to the top, but I was making the hard climb. Denny, however...not so much. He still called trying to convince me how happy I could be with him. It was late one evening and my phone rang. I answered and yes, it was Denny.

"Hi Carly, how are you?" he sounded so upbeat.

"I'm doing fine. I've just been busy. How about you?" I asked.

"Busy doing what?" Denny asked, not so upbeat.

"Uh, nails," I said, cautiously. "And in the evenings I've been making scrapbooks for my kids with the thirty-six photo albums I have in the top of my closet." *Why am I explaining my evenings to him? You know why, Carly? To avoid conflict, why else? I am such a chicken!*

"Good, that will keep you out of the bars. But I have an idea," he said with a fair amount of excitement.

*Oh, Dear Lord, what now?* Trying to add some levity to the conversation, I asked, "You want me to make you a scrapbook, as well?"

Denny was not amused. "No, I want to come and accompany you this Monday to see Kathy. You are still going every Monday, aren't you?" Denny wondered.

"Actually, I was just with her last Monday." I was nervous for his response.

"Why aren't you going every Monday, like I told you, Carly?"

"You know, Denny, I have been, but I also have been taking golf lessons on certain Mondays. Monday is my only day off, so I have a lot to fit in," I said with a bit of a smarty-pants attitude.

Denny's long pause told me he was not happy with my direct answer, and his response confirmed it. "You have had enough golf lessons, Carly. Besides it is October now." Denny informed me, as if I didn't know how to read a calendar.

*Oh, there is that bossy, my-way-or no-way guy! Shoot. Did I really think he was going to change? A leopard doesn't change its spots, so goes the saying. But, Carly, do you really want him to be different now? The answer is no. I do not. I am not in love with him, don't plan to be in love with him, and truly was never in love with him. The Nick Lowe song popped into my tumbling thoughts, "Cruel to be Kind," but how can I? I am not a mean person, and I don't want to be a bitch about it! Why can't you just accept it, Denny? Let it hurt, let it bleed, let it heal, then for hell's sake, let it go!*

I suddenly was snapped back into Denny's reality.

"Carly, did you hear me?" he asked sternly. He sounded like he was reprimanding a child.

"Yes, Denny, I heard you." *Loud and clear! Just say it, Carly.*

"Well, what do you think about me coming out there to see you?"

*Here goes nothing!* "I think it will be a waste of time. I'm still seeing Kathy because I'm conflicted, Denny," I courageously continued on before he could say a word. "Kathy has already cashed the check you sent. I don't think it will do any good for you to join me in my sessions. Wasn't the money for *me* to see Kathy and have her help *me* figure out what I want and need? I don't want you to come and sit there with me and tell her what it is that you think I want or need." *Oh, that was brave of you! Keep going you are doing so well. But why am I shaking?*

"Wow, remind me never to get you mad at me," Denny replied. Then he added, "Okay, we will do this your way, Carly. I won't come, but you have to keep me informed weekly on your progress. And I want you to see her every week, like we talked about."

"Okay, I will, thanks," I said with some resentment. *I just want to get off this phone and out of this conversation, because it is making me crazy!*

The previous evening's conversation was still fresh and in the forefront of my brain. I wished he would meet someone else and fast! *What about that neighbor of his I was always hearing about after her husband died suddenly? What was her name? Oh, yeah, Judy. What about Judy?* Then it hit me. *Now, I remember, Denny told me she was too overweight and had a dog. Denny had a strong dislike for heavy women and any type of pet. I remember his feelings about weight gain, but I forgot about the pet thing. Who doesn't like a dog or cat? That's another reason, Carly. Write that one down, too! The list grows daily at a rapid rate.*

The following morning I called and got Kathy's answering machine.

"Hi, you have reached Kathy Thomas. I am with clients at the present time. Please leave your name and number and I will call you back. Thank you, and have a nice day."

"Hi Kathy, it's Carly, can I please get back on your books for every Monday until Denny's money runs out? I would like to speed things up a bit and Denny is strongly suggesting I see you each Monday. Thank you." Fine. Now I can get through this faster, and hopefully prevent Denny from coming to Utah.

My first client of the day was my accountant, Nancy. She had two young boys about three or four years apart, James and Chip. Nancy wore acrylic nails and often, she would bring the boys in with her, but today she was alone.

"Where are the kiddos?" I asked her.

"Oh, they're at home with my husband today," Nancy said, "but I have a funny story to tell you." Nancy continued on, "When we were in church on Sunday, the boys sat next to each other and they got a little loud, so I separated them and I sat in the middle."

I laughed, "I remember those days."

"After about five minutes, James reached for my hand and told Chip to hold my other hand," Nancy told me.

"Oh, that was sweet," I said with a smile.

"Then James asked me if they could 'play Carly' and they began to pretend to take off my nail polish, file my nails, rub lotion on my hands and finished with pretend polish on my fingernails!"

"Oh, that is adorable, Nancy."

"It was so cute, and it kept them occupied and quiet," she said.

"Wow, it sounds like they really pay attention to the way I do your nails. Maybe they'll become nail technicians!" I said, as we both laughed.

I finished Nancy's fingernails and we rebooked her for two weeks. She left the salon and I checked my messages. I had three new ones. The first was from Kathy.

"Yes, Carly, you can come into my office every Monday at one o'clock. I will put you down, and if for some reason that doesn't work, please call me back as soon as possible. If it does, no need to call. I will just see you on Monday. Thank you."

*That should make Denny happy, and hopefully keep him in his own state.*

Speaking of Denny, the next message was from him. "Carly, call me when you get a break."

I decided to call him right back and get that off of my plate and off of my mind.

Denny answered, "Hi Carly, how are you?"

"Fine. I just got off the phone with Kathy. I'm on her books every Monday at one o'clock"

"Great! That is great news," Denny said overjoyed. "Let's speak every Monday night and you can give me a synopsis of your therapy session."

"Okay, sounds good." I said. It is just so much easier to go along with Denny, this I have learned. "I have to get back to work now, Denny."

"So do I, I will call you tonight," he said.

*Good. He's out of the picture for the time being.*

My next client was Mindy, a pretty brunette who also wore acrylic nails. She sat down at my desk and said, "I have a kidney infection that is killing me this morning."

I was sympathetic. "Oh, sweetie, I hate those. We better hurry and get you finished so you can get home and back in your bed."

"Yes, I was up all night long and when I got out of bed this morning, my husband asked me why I was up so early and if I felt better. I told him I was still in pain and that I called in sick to work. But I was going to get my nails done first, and then go to back to bed."

I smiled and said, "You just sit there and rest, I will hurry."

Mindy did just that. After she left, I wondered what her hubby thought about her coming in for her nail appointment when she was so ill. I laughed to myself because I knew!

## Deer Valley Spice

My next client was a new client from New York. Her name was Gloria and she'd been referred to me by another client. I had sent her a friendly reminder the day before. Often, I would have someone new on my book and they wouldn't show up, so I wanted to make sure this was not one of those times, especially since Gloria was a two-hour appointment.

She was right on time. I started her pedicure as she read her book. After I finished up, we moved over to the nail desk. She wore gel nails, so I began to wrap them up in the foils used to remove the gels, also sometimes called shellac. We were about half way through the process when the power went off. If you know anything at all about the gel or shellac nails, you know they cure with a light, so electricity is a must. Gloria wore bright red polish and I had her right hand cured to the first coat of color. Her left hand had only the base coat on and it had been cured. "Darn it," I said, "it usually comes right back on," I informed Gloria.

"I am in no hurry today, Carly,"

I was happy about that, but still I wanted to find out what was going on with the power. "Oh, good, but still, I'll call the light company and see if there is a problem." I picked up my cell phone and called, "It's busy, that's not a good sign," I said.

"What do we do now?" Gloria asked.

"Well, now we talk and get to know one another!" I said, as I patted her hands. And talk we did.

I found out she lived in Deer Valley part time and her husband had recently been diagnosed with terminal cancer.

"Oh, Gloria I'm so very sorry, That has to be hard."

Tears welled up in her eyes as she said, "Yes, it is the pits."

I sensed the need to end this topic so I did.

"The power should be coming on shortly, then I will get your nails taken care of," I told her in an upbeat, confident but caring tone.

The power was off for a half an hour, which felt like an eternity. Fortunately, I called my next person to reschedule her appointment. I didn't want to have to rush through Gloria's nails.

After the power returned, I finished with Gloria.

She held up her hands and looked at the bright red polish, "They look beautiful, Carly, thank you." I stood up.

"You are so welcome." I told her, "It was so nice to meet you. Thank you for coming in, Gloria."

She stood up and gave me a big warm hug.

"May I please rebook with you every two weeks for the next couple of months?" Gloria asked.

"Of course, thank you," I replied.

After that, she returned to her home in Manhattan professing her loyalty once she returned next summer. Sadly, her husband lost his battle with cancer and he passed away. I sent her a note expressing my sympathy but I never heard back from her. She and her husband loved skiing and being together in Park City. Maybe it was all just too painful for her to come back alone. I get that.

I do want to remind those of you out there, especially if you are just beginning your career as a nail technician, it is important that you not only suggest, but also encourage clients to rebook with you, or offer them standing nail appointments. That way you always know how much money you are going to make in the upcoming weeks or month, depending how you calculate your budget. Your clients will appreciate it, because it's one less thing for them to remember to do (book an appointment). And if they don't have a standing appointment, they might have to wait longer than they want until they can get in. The nails do fall apart if they go past their balance point.

Being in a resort town, we have our summer and winter clientele. I find it fun to have these clients return year after year. One of those seasonal clients is a lady from Nashville. Her name is Dina and she has the full-on southern accent. I have enjoyed her as a friend, client and golf partner for over sixteen years. The last time she was in the salon, we had a fun conversation and I knew this time would be no different.

"Guess what, Carly?" Dina asked in her southern drawl. She always had interesting stories, so I was curious.

"What?" I asked eagerly.

"You will never believe what happened last weekend. A man stopped by our house here in Park City and asked if we knew who owned the big lot next to us. I told him that we owned it, then he offered us a huge amount of money, in cash, for our lot, way above the market value."

I knew that particular lot and it was indeed huge.

"What did you tell him?" I asked, even more curious than before.

"I told him, you *can't* have that lot. That's my dog, Shaggy's, yard."

I smiled as I listened to that smooth, southern drawl, and could only imagine the look on the interested buyer's face.

I cracked up. "Only in Park City does someone have an acre lot of prime real estate for his or her dog's yard!" We both laughed.

I just finished up with Dina when my next client, June, walked in. June and her husband were from Florida and this was her final time with me this year. The last time she was in, I told her to watch out for deer on her way home. She lived at the top of Deer Valley.

"I know, I see them all the time along the side of the Mine Road after they've been hit. We've seen them run fast in front of us, too."

"Yes, they do that. We call them suicide deer." I told her with a giggle.

As I began her pedicure this afternoon, she told me an interesting story. "You will never believe what happened as we drove up the Mine Road yesterday."

"What happened, June?"

"Well, Syd and I were talking and all of a sudden there was a loud thud on the passenger side of the car." I raised my eyebrows in surprise, and June continued on. "We stopped and got out of the car, and there was a deer. The poor thing was lying in the road. Syd and I started to walk towards the deer, which was only about four or five feet back. All of the sudden, just as we approached it, the deer jumped up and ran off back up the mountain and out of sight."

"Wow, I said amazed, "was it hurt or bleeding at all?"

"No, he wasn't limping and there was no blood anywhere. What do you think that was about?" June inquired.

"First attempt, maybe?" I said with a sly grin.

She looked like she didn't get it at first. But then the light bulb went on and she laughed hysterically. The suicide deer.

"It must have been, because it actually just ran right into the passenger door, cost us over two thousand dollars in damage!"

We finished up with her pedicure and hugged goodbye until next summer.

After she left, I had a few minutes to myself. I went deep in thought to reflect on the end of summer. I hate this time of year. These part-time-resident clients have become my friends and I always feel sad when they all go home. I can say in all honesty, I miss them so much when they leave. But I am beyond grateful when they all return and I get to see them again.

My last client of the day was Carrie, my friend who took me on the infamous Make-A-Wish weekend. I always looked forward to seeing Carrie, but this day was different. All day I had anticipated her coming in for one specific reason. I wanted to let her know how my first experience in a hot air balloon turned out. I couldn't wait to relive that!

"Hi, Carrie," I said as she walked in the salon, "good to see you."

"It's good to see you, Carly, so…how was it?" she asked excitedly. I'm sure she was all set to hear how hot air ballooning was my new passion, thanks to her.

"Sit down and I will tell you all about it." I said, as I motioned to the chair. And I did; every last gory detail.

By the end of my story, poor Carrie was in tears. She is a very sensitive girl anyway, but she was literally sobbing. "Oh, Carly, I am so sorry," she managed to spit out between sobs. Carrie had lost her husband to suicide, not quite a year ago and that had understandably devastated her, and left her emotionally raw. She continued on. "I don't know what I would have done if anything would have happened to you, especially since you didn't even want to do it. I talked you into that balloon ride."

I felt bad she was taking my experience to heart. "Carrie, it's okay. All's well that ends well, so they say. We all survived, thank God."

It was a pretty solemn appointment after that.

The next day Carrie popped in. "I made this for you," she said, as she handed me a framed picture of the two of us taken at the restaurant that Friday night.

"Oh, I love it, thank you, my friend."

Carrie hugged me and said, "That was before you had your near death experience."

I laughed and nodded my head, "Indeed it was."

# 68
## No Room for the Blues

*S*tenmark and I began spending more and more time together. I was still seeing Kathy, and she was helping me muster up the courage to tell Denny that it was truly over once and for all. "Really, Carly, it's not fair to Denny to let him hold out hope where there is none."

I nodded my head in complete agreement.

"Just be honest with him," Kathy reassured me. "And I would do it sooner rather than later. Denny deserves that."

I took a deep breath and exhaled. "You're right, Kathy. I'll do it this week. When I see you next Monday, it will be done."

"Good girl. If you need help, just write it all down and practice what you want to say until you feel comfortable."

"Okay, I will do that, thank you, Kathy. I'm just feeling so low right now. This is really hard," I said with my head hanging down.

"You know, Carly, I can write you a prescription for an anti-depressant to help you through this," Kathy said, pen in hand.

"No, I already tried that years ago. I will just run," I said thinking about the *happy pill*. "I'll see you next Monday as a free woman," I confirmed with a grin.

Kathy smiled and patted me on the back as I walked out of her office. I knew what I had to do. On my drive up the canyon, I decided to practice my talk with Denny. I even turned off the radio. I was serious. I began my breakup speech, "You know I have been struggling with this, Denny. I have seen Kathy for months now and she has really helped me. I think you are a great guy, but I am not in love with you. I'm sorry to be so blunt, but I feel the need to be honest." Oh, Lord, my heart was pounding and I was only practicing! But even though I was scared, I continued with my practice. "You even told me three months ago that you didn't love me. We haven't seen each other since that night, and I find it sort of hard to believe that you fell *in love* with me during my absence."

*Does that sound okay? It sounds really good. Continue on, Carly. Let him have it now!* There's that angel and devil again.

"Denny, I think it's best that we both move on."

*Don't forget to tell him about Stenmark,* the devil said.

*Ohhhhh!!! Should I really bring that into my breakup speech? I am trying to be honest, but what if he freaks out on me and starts to yell. Maybe I don't include that part just yet. I've only kissed Stenmark. I don't need to make it sound like it's a full-on love affair, because it isn't.*

*Not yet anyway,* laughed the devil.

*You don't need to bring up Stenmark just yet,* said the angel.

*Oh, how I love her!*

"Anyway, Denny, you are a wonderful, generous, and funny man. You deserve someone who loves you and wants to be with you. I don't want to leave Utah, as we have discussed ad nauseam. I never wanted to hurt your feelings, but I can't continue in this relationship. I talked with Kathy about this and she convinced me that I must speak honestly about this to you. I've seen Kathy every Monday and I've come to realize with her help that it's time for us both to move on." *Oh, shit! You have to just do it, Carly, you just have to and the sooner the better for not only Denny, but for you.*

In my heart, I know I'll be just fine. I just have to rely on myself, after all, I know me better than anyone else. I know I'm strong enough to do this. Denny was what I thought I wanted. I was trying to force myself to fall in love, but I just couldn't get there.

*The time has come to sever it once and for all,* said the angel on my shoulder.

But then the devil on my other shoulder reminded me of all the things Denny had to offer, especially a financially worry-free, life. *You are going to regret this, Carly.*

I went back to my speech. I rehearsed it over and over all the way up the canyon. I took the Park City exit and decided I had it down, at least for tonight. I turned on the radio. Jackson Browne sang, "Tender is the Night." I felt a momentary touch of sadness, as I listened to the song. I pulled in the driveway and opened the garage, parked my car carefully and turned off the lights. Then I sat there in the dark until the song ended, something I have always done. I turned off the radio and I said a little prayer. Something I've been doing a lot lately.

*"Dear God, Please let the spirit of your love and light be with me and with Denny as I breakup with his ass. Let me have no regrets for doing so. Help me be empathetic, kind and caring. In the name of Jesus, Amen."*

Then I thought about the reason dead people receive more flowers than the living, because regret is stronger than gratitude. No regrets. I made a vow to myself to express my gratitude to Denny when we spoke.

# 69
## Enuf is Enuf

I wanted things to go smoothly. I prayed before I even got out of bed the next morning, and this time I was truly sincere, no joking around. I knew it was time to say goodbye. It was important for me to know that.

Sometimes holding on hurts so much more than the letting go part. Kathy told me that so many times. I just prayed that Denny felt the same way. I prayed to help him not to try and hang on like Devin had done all of those months. I've always felt that the men you leave don't really miss you until you move on. They'll try to come back into your life once you're on a new path, clipping along at a good speed, but you've already learned how to live without them, just like I did with Devin. I thought he was the man I would end up with, but as time passed, I met Denny. When I let Devin know I had met someone else, he transformed into a "Klingon," big time.

That was one of the biggest reasons why I wanted to keep Stenmark out of this breakup. I knew I was falling in love with him. It wasn't planned, it just happened. Sometimes you fall in love with the most unexpected person at the most unexpected time and that is exactly what happened. Stenmark and I were connected in such a way that it was hard to explain. I looked at him and saw the rest of my life right in front of my eyes. I believed that meeting him was fate, becoming his friend was a choice, but falling in love with him was beyond my control. Aren't the best relationships the ones you never saw coming? I believed with my whole heart that Stenmark and I were soul mates, that we were a couple before we met. It was meant to be and I knew it deep in my soul. Loving him was like breathing. I just couldn't stop.

But he still had to see Kathy with me and pass that infamous test.

I went through another workday. That evening, I spoke to Stenmark and told him my plans with Denny.

"When are you doing this?" he asked.

"Tonight, right after you and I hang up," I answered.

"Good, it's about time." That was his response!

"Okay, well, with that said, would you be interested in seeing Kathy, my counselor, with me on Monday?" I just threw it out there before I even realized what I said or how it sounded. *Holy shit! I can't believe that flew out of my mouth! I wonder what he thinks about that one!*

"Sure, what time?" he asked.

"One o'clock," I answered feeling a bit uneasy.

"I have a meeting at the ski school in the morning and after that I could meet you there. Where is her office?" Stenmark said, without any hesitation whatsoever.

"Westminster College." I answered quickly.

"Alright, I will meet you there. Good luck with your talk with Denny," he said encouragingly. "I'm sure you will do just fine. Let me know how it goes." I thanked him and hung up.

Before my moment of truth with Denny, I took a quick shower and put on my pajamas. Afterward, I poured a big glass of Chardonnay, picked up my cell phone and dialed Denny's number, hopefully for the last time. He answered. I took a deep breath and gave him the break up speech I had rehearsed all night long, throwing in Kathy's name as often as I could.

His only response was, "I can't believe I paid all that money to Kathy, so she could convince you to break up with me."

And then…silence.

I looked at the phone thinking it had dropped the call. But no, Denny had hung up. I was surprised and grateful at the same time. No argument, protests, or pleading from Denny. Wow, *that was easier than I imagined.*

I called Stenmark to let him know the deed was done and there was no bruising. I thought for sure it would at least leave a mark.

"Good, are you okay?" Stenmark asked.

"Yes," I answered. "I'm happy it's over. One less thing to think about," I said.

He agreed. "Do you want to go to the ski swap this weekend?"

"Sure, I'll go to the gym early on Saturday morning, then after that?"

"Let's go as soon as they open. It gets crowded," Stenmark informed me.

"Perfect," I said, excited to spend the day with him. We said goodbye and hung up.

We spent that weekend together and I knew I had found the man in the songs.

In my heart I didn't think Denny would give up that easily, and I was right. The phone calls began three days later. I received a Kim Richey CD from him in the mail with a Post-it note attached, telling me to listen to the song, "The Moon and the Sun." I was curious and so I did exactly that. The song was all about the moon trying to chase the sun and not being able to catch it. I understood where he was going with it, but it didn't change the way I felt about him.

It was the twenty-six phone calls in less than a week that really made me pay attention. I thought if I ignored them, they would stop, but they didn't. Finally, I listened to a long message he left very late one night, after a good portion of a bottle of Bombay gin, I assumed, by the sound of his slurred words. "Carly, this is Denny. I did everything I could to make you love me. I took you out to nice places, took you on wonderful trips, and paid for everything. I bought you a set of golf clubs and that wasn't cheap. They were top of the line golf clubs. I even paid off your credit card and you never paid me back for any of that. You took advantage of my generous nature."

*Took advantage of what? Are you kidding? Paid him back? Oh, here we go. I knew this would happen!* I couldn't even finish listening to his message. I was fuming as I dialed his number. I could have sworn there was steam coming out of my ears, I was *that* angry.

Denny didn't answer so I left *him* a message. I wanted this over once and for all. I took a deep breath. "Denny, it's Carly. I guess you're going to make me be a bitch about this and I hate that. But I am at my wits' end. I don't know what else to do. To start with, if you don't stop calling me, I will call the police and turn you in for stalking. I have saved all of your messages, all twenty-six of them, which is probably the only proof I need." I shook as I spoke. This is the very last way I wanted this to end.

"Furthermore, how DARE you accuse me of taking advantage of your generosity, I told you several times I wanted to pay you back. I even insisted on it, but you told me no." I was seething as I reminded him of his own words. "In case you have forgotten, Denny, you told me all you wanted to do was sit by the ocean, smoke a cigar and feel good that you helped a deserving person out. What happened to that? I am so angry with you right now. How dare you throw that in my face? You told me you wanted to do all of it, the trips, dinners, golf clubs, and the credit card. All of it! I knew this would happen when it finally came to a halt. This tells me you had a hidden agenda all along, and that irritates me even more. Your message makes me feel like you did all of the things you did to buy my love. You insisted on helping me and I believed you when you said no strings attached. Now you try to make me feel like a complete loser with your accusing words. I should love you because you helped me out? The Beatles wrote a song called 'Can't Buy Me Love.' Why don't you try listening to it, Denny!" I was on a roll.

"I am tired of your coherent and incoherent messages, as well as your phone calls at all hours of the night. This is beyond ridiculous. Shit, the breakup is lasting longer than the relationship did!"

I slammed the cell phone down on the couch. I was so angry. *I would rather struggle every single day of my life than to ever give a man the power to say, "You wouldn't have that if it wasn't for me."*

I was still mad when I woke up the next morning. I assumed Denny got the message, since the phone calls did stop. *Thank you, God.*

However, about a week later, I went to my post office box and it was stuffed full. I gathered my mail up in my arms and I made a vow to pick up my mail more often than every two weeks. I walked over to one of the tables, dropped it down and began sorting. No need to keep the junk mail. There was a long business like envelope that was very thick. I recognized the handwriting, and knew it was from Denny. I wasn't in the least bit curious. I didn't even open it. Instead, I walked up to one of the clerks. "Excuse me sir, but do you have a red pen or pencil?" I asked.

The postal worker rummaged through a drawer. "I only have a red felt tip marker," he informed me.

"Perfect," I told him and scribbled in big letters, "Refused!!! Return to Sender" underlining all of it three or four times with the bright red marker, complete with several exclamation points!

I handed it to the clerk and said, "I am refusing this."

He looked at it, raised his eyebrows and said, "Yes you certainly are."

# 70

## Thanks a Latte

went to work the next morning with a new sense of calmness. My anxiety was gone and I felt happy again. My first client of the day was an acrylic nail fill, a woman named Michelle who was a friend of another long-time client. I met Michelle on several occasions and must admit, she scared me to death the first few times. She was a pretty woman with dark hair and eyes. She was heavy set and loud. I certainly would not ever have wanted to get on her bad side. It had been close to a year since our paths crossed, but at a funeral for a friend, I ran into her and honestly, I hardly recognized her. Michelle was now a slim blonde with a smile! If she had not been standing with another one of my clients I wouldn't have known her.

"Michelle…you look great!" I said.

There was a big smile on her face as she said, "Thanks, Carly! I feel incredible. I started Weight Watchers and I joined a gym. It has changed my life."

I was happy for her and I told her so. Michelle smiled and thanked me once again.

It was crowded as I made my way into the chapel of the church. I found a seat in the back and sat down. The funeral was hard and I cried my eyes out. There had been a sudden departure of the deceased. She drowned in her bathtub after taking an Ambien before she took her nightly bath. I thought about my experience with Ambien and felt lucky I wasn't a water person.

After that, I ran into Michelle three or four times and we always had great conversations. One of those times was at a sixtieth birthday party for a client, who was also Michelle's friend. Michelle kept her weight off, but by then she went back to her dark hair. She still looked so happy.

"Hi," I said cheerfully. "You're a brunette again!"

Michelle laughed. "The blonde was too much of an upkeep."

I agreed. "I have never gone blonde, but every brunette I know that has tried it, always goes back and fast."

Michelle nodded, and then added. "Hey, Carly I've been thinking. I need to come to you for my nails. Every time I see you and we talk, I just love your soul. Do you have a business card?"

I reached in my purse and handed her my card. "Please allow a couple of weeks for your appointment," I told her.

"I know how busy you are. I've heard." She looked at her nails adding, "I just had them done two days ago, but…I will call this week for the following week."

I was excited. "That will be great, thank you so much."

She did call with plenty of notice. Finally the day of her appointment was here. Michelle walked into the salon with lattes from Starbucks for both of us, nonfat of course. She handed me mine and I thanked her as I took the first sip. It tasted delicious.

"Have a seat, please." I told Michelle, as I motioned to my chair. I finished her nails in record time and they looked great. Michelle held up her hands and admired the sparkly teal blue color she chose.

"How much do I owe you?" she asked me as she continued to stare at her manicured hands and nails. "I don't even know what you charge."

I answered, "It's forty-three dollars, please."

"Forty-three dollars?" Michelle repeated as she raised her eyebrows. Obviously, this was more than she bargained for. "Is a check okay?"

"Of course." I always liked checks, although they had pretty much gone by the way side. Most clients use credit cards these days and if they write a check, they usually tell me they only use checks for their hairdresser and me! I reached in my drawer, pulled out an ink pen and handed it to Michelle.

She wrote her check and handed it to me. "There you go, Carly, I subtracted the latte off the total."

I was dumbfounded. *Well, that's a first. But she did save me a trip to Starbucks,* I thought, putting a positive spin on a weird and uncomfortable situation. Often times clients will call me and ask if I would like a coffee or latte, and other times they do what Michelle did, simply arriving with lattes. I usually offer to pay at some point during our time together, but Michelle took matters into her own hands before I had the chance. I might also add in all my years of doing nails, I have never had anyone accept my offer, even when they bring them in on their own. But there's a first time for everything, I guess.

"Okay, thank you Michelle," I said, trying not to act surprised. We both stood up at the same time and she gave me a hug goodbye.

"See you soon. "Michelle said as she walked out the door.

*Hopefully*, I thought.

I got ready for my next client by wiping my desk, which was covered in acrylic dust. I turned to toss the antibacterial wipe in my trash and knocked my latte off the desk and onto the wood floor. It landed with a huge splash, because of course, the lid popped off when it hit the floor. Coffee splashed everywhere. It was not only on the floor, but all over my desk, shoes and the full-length mirror next to the desk. I cleaned up the big mess and laughed to myself as I thought, *Thanks for the latte, Michelle! Grrrr.....*

# Green Come True

I never saw her as a client again. Our mutual friend told me that Michelle thought I was too expensive. I guess someone loving your soul only goes so far. At any rate, I still run into her from time to time and we are just as friendly as before. I still enjoy our conversations, and I enjoy her, even if her hands are tucked neatly under her folded arms when she sees me!

While I'm on the subject of money, let's talk about raising your prices. This is one of the hardest things to do, but you must step out of your comfort zone and do it! We are, by and large, self-employed. We do not automatically get raises, so we have to give ourselves a raise when the time comes.

Let's face it, we do not have just one boss, but several bosses, a.k.a. our entire clientele. I once waited over twelve years to raise my prices, and believe me it was tough. I was so scared to do it, but really had to think about my expenses. My rent, supplies and other fixed fees had certainly increased in the last year, let alone twelve!

In all fairness, I must say, there are those clients, and I do have quite a few, who automatically give me a raise every January. It is so nice and very much appreciated. But let's not forget to explore the best way to tackle those others who aren't so quick to step up. It is my belief that there is a right and a wrong way to do this. First of all, I research the competition in my area. I find out what they charge for the same services that I offer. For example, I contact the first salon and anonymously ask about an acrylic nail fill. Then I call a second salon and inquire the same about a manicure and pedicure. I make these inquiries under the radar, so it doesn't appear that I'm about to raise my prices. Instead, I pretend to be a curious consumer. It's kind of fun, actually; like I'm working under cover! I write all of my research down, and then I decide on a new price that is somewhere in the middle, usually rounding it off to a five-dollar increase.

The next step I take is to make up a new pricelist, beginning with an effective date, at least six weeks out. I then write down all of my services with the new price next to each one I offer. I end by thanking them for their patronage. I print it on the computer in a bigger font, so it is legible, and then add a fun color. I put it in a frame and hang it on the wall next to my desk. It must be visible to the client and within pointing distance from me. As each client comes in for services, during their appointment, I point to the sign and tell them I am raising my prices. I make sure I explain how long it's been since my last price increase. They look at the sign and honestly, I have never had anyone tell me they couldn't come in anymore. They usually just say, "Okay," or "It's about time."

This is not to say I haven't lost clients due to raising my prices. I'm sure I have, but they didn't state the reason, they just didn't re-book with me. Let's face it, we all hate to lose clients. But you have to think of it this way. If you lose one or two clients due to a price increase and you have increased by five dollars, you more than make it up in the long run. For example, if you do eight clients a day, that will be forty extra dollars, times that by a four-day work week, that is an extra one hundred sixty dollars a week, times the four weeks in a month, you will be adding six hundred forty dollars to your gross income per month.

Conversely, let's say you lost three pedicure clients at forty-five dollars each coming in once a month (pedicures are my highest service price-wise, so let's go with that). As a result, you lose one hundred thirty-five dollars. As you can see, you come out ahead by over five hundred dollars each month. You do the math and I think you will agree.

But as I said, you must do it the right way. It is not fair to the client to suddenly spring it on them as they are preparing to pay you. I have known people in this industry that have done just that. Trust me, you will lose more clients that way than if you are up front with them, as hard as it may be at the time. In the end, they will respect you for your consideration.

# 72

## Make Light of the Situation

eanwhile, back in Shangri-La, Stenmark and I were getting to know one another. Thankfully, Devin was out of the picture, Denny never contacted me again and I was very happy with how it all played out. I do have to admit, however, I felt bad at times when I would reflect on my voice message to Denny. It is not my nature to be bitchy, but I saw no other way to make it clear to him. I consoled myself by thinking of the Nick Lowe song, "Cruel to be Kind," and I felt better. I did hear that Devin was in a serious car accident and he was almost decapitated. It messed with his head so much, literally, that he became impotent. Okay, the impotent part really didn't happen but the laws of Karma say it should! I have always been somewhat of an empath. But the problem with being empathetic is that you feel sorry for the assholes, as well as good people, and Devin was definitely the former. I grieved for Devin, and it took me a long time to move through that grief, even when I was with Denny.

Then it seemed all of a sudden, I changed. I woke up one day as a completely different person with a new mindset, a new outlook on life almost as if I had a new soul. The girl who once cared way too much about Devin, no longer cared at all and I removed him from my life. I am confident that he just continued on his insane path, the one that got him to such an unhealthy spot in the first place, and I'm sure he never looked back.

Stenmark and I continued spending all of our free time together. We knew where we wanted to be and that was with each other. He moved into my condo in Park City and we were very happy just being together. However, we both realized that time was not on our side, as I was approaching fifty and Stenmark was barely past that. We were old enough to know better, that's for sure, but also we knew we didn't have a minute to waste. We began to discuss our future together, and that included getting married at some point.

Realizing this would be my fourth marriage, I thought about how I liked Elizabeth Taylor's response when she was asked about her multiple marriages. She married eight times and had one long-term domestic partnership. Her answer was always the same, *"I never dated, I just married them all."* That was my story and I stuck to it. When people found out my age at the time of my first marriage, they seemed shocked unless they were from Utah and knew the drill. Yes, I grew up in Utah, but at least I didn't marry my uncle at seventeen!

By the time Stenmark and I made the decision to marry, I'd become very involved in golf, thanks to him and more than half of my clientele. When we discussed our plans, I thought it would be fun to get married on the golf course, hole number four and after our vows, and we were pronounced husband and wife, all of the guests could yell, "Fore!" as Stenmark kissed the bride. I know my sense of humor is very dark! But honestly, I never felt bad about being married four times. I chalked it up to practice marriages, as I was a different person at age 20, 30, 40 and even 50 years old. *Thank the Lord.*

One day, as I golfed with my friend, Kacy, we were paired with a couple from Park City that neither of us knew, although Stenmark knew them both well from the golf course. They introduced themselves. "Hi, we're the Millers," they both said in unison as they shook our hands at the first tee.

*Oh, how cute!* I thought. I wondered if Stenmark and I would someday say, "Hi, we're the Stenmarks," when we met new people. I liked that. It had a nice ring to it and was fun to say.

"You are the golf pro's girlfriend, aren't you?" Mrs. Miller asked.

"Yes, I am," I said thinking the word *girlfriend* sounded so juvenile.

"So is this a serious relationship?" she asked me.

"I hope it is," I answered with a smile. I continued with a little bit of my history with men, just for fun. "So far, I have been with a famous musician, a ski instructor, a returned Mormon missionary, a doctor and now a golf pro. If this one doesn't work out, at this stage of the game, I am going for a plastic surgeon the next time around!"

They both cracked up. Fortunately, the Millers had a good sense of humor and I needed to add some humor to my fourth time around!

# 73

## Step Right Up!

Fortunately, I didn't have to look for a good plastic surgeon. Stenmark and I married the following year. Kacy, my closest friend in Park City, offered her beautiful home as the venue. Her talents at putting together an incredible wedding, including the delicious food were so impressive. Originally, she gave us two dates, a week apart, the twenty-third or the thirtieth of September. It didn't matter to Stenmark, and he left the choosing up to me. I thought about it and decided to rule out the twenty-third since Clark (ex-husband number three) had remarried on that date ten years prior. I already shared an anniversary with Clark. I didn't want to share another one with him.

We set the date for the thirtieth of September. It was fall in the mountains, which we know can be hit or miss for an outside wedding. We made the right date choice in more ways than one. It was a beautiful sunny day with temperatures around seventy degrees. The week before it snowed and covered the entire backyard and deck with a gorgeous white blanket. We were blessed with good luck! Our wedding was magical. We had close to 150 people in attendance, counting our children and my grandchildren, who have since become Stenmark's grandchildren!

Just when you think you know what love is, along come grandchildren. They have been the light in my life and being able to watch them grow up has been beyond comparison. I have truly loved every second of being a grandparent. I will never forget the look on Stenmark's face when my two-year old grandson called him Grandpa for the first time. I thought he was going to pass out. Marriage allowed us both to become stepparents and Stenmark a step-grandparent! All of these years later, he has grown used to it and I think secretly, he loves being a grandpa, as complicated as it can be sometimes. I know he loves and cares about my children and adores the grandchildren, just as I love and care about his son. After all, this is truly our life, a little bit messy and completely confusing at times, but it's real. Neither of us have tiptoed through any of it.

But this time I know, I put a wedding band on the left hand of the right man.

# 74
## Caught My Eye

**W**e lived in Salt Lake City and both of us commuted to Park City for work. I sold my condo in Park City when the real estate market took off about four years prior. My condo was the perfect size for me, but suddenly became small when both Stenmark and I lived there. We discussed the move in great detail, deciding on the Holladay area of Salt Lake City, so he could be closer to his son, McLane, who was growing up fast. Such a good dad! In the beginning, I didn't really mind the commute, but as time passed, I grew weary of it especially during the winter. Stenmark didn't mind it at all, but he was brave in the snow!

Time passed and summer drew to a close. One day, I noticed something very weird. Driving back from the market on a Sunday afternoon, we stopped behind a city bus. I noticed an advertisement for an exhibit at the new library. I turned to Stenmark and asked, "Are the letters on the back of that bus slanting down to the right?"

Stenmark looked at the bus, then at me and said, "No, they aren't."

I felt sick to my stomach. I began covering my eyes one at a time and looking at the back of the bus. The right eye seemed normal; the letters were straight. I covered the left eye; not normal. The letters were definitely slanted to the right. I knew the signs, and this was not good. I tried to remain calm. "There is something wrong with my left eye," I said in the calmest voice I could muster up.

Stenmark looked over at me. "What do you mean?" he asked with a worried tone.

I answered, "I don't know, but I need to call an eye doctor as soon as we get home."

It was a warm August night as we drove straight home in silence. After we pulled in the driveway, Stenmark put his hand on my leg and said in a reassuring voice, "It will be okay, Bennett."

I nodded my head and we went inside.

I called my Mother.

"Hi, honey," she answered cheerfully. "How are you guys doing?"

I began to cry, "Mom, there is something wrong with my left eye. There was a bus in front of us and the writing on it was slanting down."

"Oh oh," my mom said. She knew the signs far better than I did. My mother had been diagnosed at age fifty-four with an age related eye disease called macular degeneration and she lost her central vision in both eyes, but had a tiny bit of peripheral vision in each eye. We all joked that she could see better than all of us. She was that amazing.

"You better call Dr. Wilson right now," Mom said.

I knew that was her retina specialist. I heard his name enough times in the last twenty years to know exactly who he was. She gave me his phone number.

Of course when I called, I got the answering service, as it was Sunday night. I spoke with the doctor on call. He listened carefully as I told him what was going on.

"Are you experiencing any pain?" he asked.

"No, there is no pain," I answered as I thought about my mom's eyes. I was trying to be brave, but I was scared, having only my mom to compare with.

"Well, I can meet you at the office now or you can come over first thing in the morning and see Dr. Wilson at eight," the on-call doctor said.

"Thank you, I will come over first thing tomorrow," I told him.

"Very good, but if anything changes tonight, call me immediately," he said and gave me his cell phone number.

I thanked him and told Stenmark of my plans.

"I have to be at the golf course first thing tomorrow for junior camps," explained Stenmark.

"It's okay," I said. "I can go by myself. I'm sure it will be fine." I was trying so hard to be optimistic.

Stenmark kissed me on top of the head.

I went to bed, but hardly slept. I tossed and turned most of the night. *Maybe when I wake up, it will be better. Maybe my eyes were just strained. I do suffer from very dry eyes, maybe that's it.*

The next morning I got up before the alarm went off. I said a prayer as I jumped in the shower. My eyes both felt fine, no pain whatsoever. *That's a good thing!* I dressed quickly and brushed my teeth. Then I did my own little eye test once again with a *Cosmopolitan* magazine. The letters were still slanted in my left eye. *Stay positive, Carly. It could still be eyestrain.*

I heard Stenmark in the shower, as I made my coffee. I put his raisin bread in the toaster and threw some bacon in the microwave. Then I noticed the door frame of the pantry. It was blurry and wavy. In fact, anything that was supposed to be straight was wavy. I jumped as the toaster popped up the raisin bread.

Stenmark walked into the kitchen. "Are you okay?" he asked.

I lied and answered, "Yes."

He sat down and ate his toast and bacon.

I grabbed an apple out of the fridge and kissed him goodbye. "I better go. I want to be sitting there when they open." I told him.

"Okay, call me and let me know what is going on as soon as you know." Stenmark said.

"I will, I promise," I told him as I walked out the door.

On the short drive to the doctor's office I turned on the car stereo, hoping for a good song, one I could sing along with to take my mind off my eyes.

"You Light Up My Life" by Debby Boone was playing. I quickly turned off the radio. *I hate that song!*

I continued to drive in silence to the hospital and found the Physician's Center. As I pulled into the parking lot I saw an elderly couple walking towards the door. I parked my car and watched the two as they approached the door. The man was helping the woman to the door. She was wearing very dark glasses and she looked as if she was impaired visually. I started to cry. I felt sorry for myself and I didn't even know if anything was wrong yet.

*Snap out of it, Carly.* I walked to the front door and into the building.

I saw that Dr. Wilson was on the sixth floor. I walked to the elevator just as the door opened. I went inside and pressed the number six. It was a long ride up and seemed to take forever, but finally the doors opened and I walked down the long hall and up to the receptionist, who greeted me with a friendly smile.

"Hi, how can I help you?" the pretty redhead asked.

"Hi, I need to see Dr. Wilson. I spoke to the doctor on call last night. There's something wrong with my left eye." I told her.

She answered quickly, "Oh, I am sorry, but Dr. Wilson is in surgery today."

My heart sank. I looked up at all the doctor's nameplates on the wall behind the receptionist. I recognized one of the names. "What about Dr. Kim?" I asked anxiously.

"Yes, he is here but he is completely booked today," she told me.

"My husband knows him from the golf course in Park City," I said on the verge of tears.

She sensed my desperation. "Um, hold on just for a second. I will be right back," she instructed me. I nodded my head, holding my breath.

The receptionist came back fairly quickly and she had a smile on her face. "Carly, if you have a seat, Dr. Kim will work you in. It might be about twenty or thirty minutes, though."

I answered fast, "It's okay. It is my day off." I walked to the waiting area, desperately trying to hold it together, but I must admit I was on the verge of completely falling apart. I was terrified. My mom was the only person I had to compare my eyesight with and she was blind. Over the years I told myself I would escape her fate, as this eye disease is more common in light-eyed people like my mom with her green eyes. I was more like the Cherokee side of my father, dark skin and dark eyes. My mom was also a heavy smoker and that can be a contributing factor as well. I know she did not take the vitamins to help slow down the progression either. But I was so much healthier than my mom. I never smoked, I eat healthy, I am a runner and I work out.

What the hell happened here?

Genetics, that's what happened. My maternal grandfather had it, my mother and now possibly me.

# 75
## Come Up for Air

I tried to calm myself by thinking it could be a mistake, something else. However, deep down I freaked out, my heart raced, and I felt sick to my stomach.

The door from the office into the waiting area opened and there stood a tall, slim, and pretty woman, very elegant-looking, with a clipboard. "Carly?" she asked.

I stood up and walked towards her.

"Hi, I'm Maya," she said with a smile as she extended her hand. We are going to check your vision with a routine eye exam."

I nodded.

"First, we will dilate your eyes."

*Oh, I hate this part.*

Maya dropped a couple of drops in each eye and then puffed some air at my eyes. "Pressure looks great," she told me with a smile.

I breathed a somewhat sigh of relief.

"Now, let's check your vision." It was a pretty extensive vision test, but I assumed it needed to be thorough. "Your vision isn't bad," Maya informed me, right eye is twenty-thirty, and your left eye is twenty-forty."

*That's legal to drive.* I thought.

Maya opened the door and led me back into a long hallway with several gray haired men and women sitting in chairs. *Waiting their turn.*

I sighed as I took a seat next to one of the women. *I don't belong in here with these people that are so much older than I am. What the hell? Nothing against the elderly, I love them, but I still think of myself as a twenty-year-old!*

I picked up a golf magazine left on the chair next to me and flipped through the pages until a woman in a white lab coat appeared from the back of the long hallway. "Carly?" she asked. She had a clipboard, as well. She took me to a back room with three or four large machines. "Have a seat," she instructed. "We are going to scan your retina."

I sat in the tall chair as instructed and she scanned both eyes one at a time.

"Okay, have a seat back in the hall and Dr. Kim will be right with you."

"Thank you," I said, as I obeyed and sat down. The golf magazine was still there, and I picked it up. I opened the magazine and as I glanced at the page, I realized my dilated eyes had a different idea. I decided to pretend I was reading. I needed a diversion.

A few minutes passed and I saw Maya open the door to one of the private rooms. She smiled at me as she led an elderly man and younger woman out of the office.

The younger woman handed him a pair of dark glasses. "Here you go, Dad." I watched her lead her father by the arm as they walked out of the door to the end of the hallway. *Is this what I have to look forward to? One of my kids leading me around when my sight goes? Think positive, think positive, and don't you dare cry, Carly!*

Maya reappeared and motioned for me to come into the room with her. She pointed to another large chair, "Sit here, Carly. Dr. Kim will be right in."

"Thank you, Maya."

She smiled, walked out and quietly closed the door.

I looked down. I still had the golf magazine in my hand.

The door opened rather quickly and in walked Maya with a tall, handsome and well-dressed man. "Hi, Carly, I'm Dr. Kim. Let's see what's going on with your eyes."

I smiled and nodded as Dr. Kim looked at a computer screen with some gray, fuzzy thick lines on it. He didn't break his gaze from the screen. "So, Ken Stenmark is your husband?"

"Yes." I answered.

"He is such a great guy. I really like him," he said as he turned to me. "We pulled your mother's records and I read them over," Dr. Kim said.

"Thank you and thank you for squeezing me in today." I said nervously awaiting the news.

Dr. Kim smiled as he said, "It's my pleasure, Carly." He pulled his chair next to mine, and my heart sank. *Be brave Carly.*

Dr. Kim continued, but his smile had vanished and he had a look of seriousness combined with concern on his face, "I need to let you know you have both types of macular degeneration, the wet type in your left eye and the dry type in both of your eyes. Now we need to treat your left eye for the wet macular degeneration and we need to do it today."

*Boom! There it was. My worst fear confirmed What will happen now? Will I be blind soon? How will I manage work without my eyesight?* Questions and more questions flooded my brain at rapid speed. I was scared to death. My stomach turned and my hands began to shake. My heart raced at Mach 2. I could barely breathe and I thought I was going to pass out from fear. I have never experienced a full on anxiety attack, but it felt like I was having one right now! *Oh, dear God, please help me get through this!*

I thought about my mom once again. She never expressed this kind of emotion, fear or anxiety about her eye disease. Never! I knew she had both wet and dry macular degeneration in both of her eyes and I knew the difference between the two. They were both scary and both bad. I really can't say one is worse than the other, but the difference between the two is with the dry or atrophic type version there is no leakage of blood as this occurs in only the wet type, but you can experience central vision loss with the dry type.

Dry macular degeneration is more common than the wet type, but it tends to progress more slowly, and they have vitamins to slow down the progression even more, at least that's the hope, as there is no cure for the dry version. From what I have studied the central vision appears blurry, leaving blank spots in vision, although peripheral or side vision is rarely affected. People with it also need more light to see as the disease progresses, and driving at night becomes very difficult, and at some point nearly impossible for some. But with the wet type of the disease, abnormal blood vessels form under the retina and begin to grow towards the macula. These new blood vessels tend to break, bleed and leak fluid. This causes damage to the macula and it begins to pull away from the base. I do remember that this action can cause rapid and severe loss of vision. As with the dry type, there is also no cure, but there is a treatment for the wet type.

As I sat there trying to digest the news, Dr. Kim's calm voice snapped me back into my new reality. "Carly?"

*Oh, yes the treatment for my left eye.*

"Yes," I said with some hesitation. Then I asked, "How do you treat it?"

"We give you an injection of Lucentis in your left eye, which is an eye medicine we use to treat wet macular degeneration."

*Wait! Hold everything! I am getting a shot in my eye??? I knew there was some sort of treatment for wet macular degeneration, but I didn't realize it was a shot in the eyeball! This is unreal! I was so scared at the mere thought of it! I think I was in somewhat of a trance. What happened here? My heart was racing and it felt like I couldn't breathe. Had I left my body momentarily? Focus, Carly, focus! I have to return to Planet Earth and accept this new reality.*

They both sensed my fear. Maya picked up a small bottle of eye drops and she walked over to me. Dr. Kim put his hand on my arm and reassuringly said, "It will be okay, Carly, we numb your eye first. Just hold very still for me," he said calmly as he leaned back the tall chair and motioned for me to sit down. I walked over and complied. Thoughts flooded my brain and once again I felt afraid, worried and unaware of what to expect, but I had to calm myself. I had to hold still, but dammit I couldn't even close my eyes as one usually does when frightened out of their mind!

*Are you freakin' kidding me right now? Is this really happening? Holy shit!*

## 76

## I Blanked Out

I don't remember that first shot. I guess my mind went to my happy place. *But really is there a happy place when there is a needle being put into your eyeball?* I knew I received the shot, but even to this day six years later, I have absolutely no memory of it.

"You did great, Carly," Dr. Kim said, as he rubbed my shoulder. "Maya will go to the desk with you. I need to see you in three to four weeks. I want you take these vitamins twice a day to slow down the progression of the dry macular degeneration."

"Okay, thank you," I said, as Maya handed me the vitamins. *Oh, and P.S., I was thanking him for putting a needle in my eye!*

Dr. Kim stopped me in the hall, "Is Ken here with you?"

"No, he has junior camps today at the golf course," I said, still in a state of shock.

"Is anybody here to drive you home?" Dr. Kim asked with a look of concern.

"I drove myself, but I only live five minutes away," I answered.

"Carly, promise me you will sit in the lobby for at least one hour before you leave."

"I promise."

"Oh, and can I please have Ken's cell phone number?" Dr. Kim asked still looking a bit concerned. I rattled off the cell phone number. Then he thanked me and walked away with Maya.

The receptionist handed me a card with my next appointment on it. "We will see you then, Carly."

I nodded for the hundredth time that day, "Thank you. See you then." I started to open the door, but stopped when I heard my name.

"Carly." Maya walked towards me with her arms stretched out. She threw her arms around me and hugged me tight, "I am so sorry, Carly."

*Oh, no not sympathy! That's the last thing I need right now. I know you mean well, Maya, but I am barely holding on here!*

I managed to nod my head again and tried to say thank you, but I was so choked up, the words wouldn't come out. I just shook my head back and forth as I opened the door. I looked out at the waiting room filled with more elderly people. God bless them but I couldn't sit there amongst them as I promised Dr. Kim. I made a run for the elevator sobbing all the way. I pressed the "up" button on the wall over and over again. It seemed like an eternity for that elevator to get there as I braced myself against the wall, sobbing uncontrollably. The door finally opened. I ran inside and searched for the button to the lobby. Everything was so blurry, but I managed to find it and gave it a quick push.

In the parking lot I found my car by continually beeping the automatic lock. Fortunately, my hearing was still good. Once inside, I locked the door, turned on the stereo and put my seat all the way back. I had no idea what time it was and I couldn't see the clock on the dashboard. *Why do they make everything so damn small these days? It is so annoying! It has to be after eleven, so I will sit here in my car for at least fifteen songs, four minutes per song should be an hour, give or take a couple of minutes. I know it is not safe for me to drive and I did promise Dr. Kim.*

I closed my eyes and fell asleep. Yes, I think the stress definitely got to me, no doubt about it. I only remember three songs: "Mr. Tambourine Man" by The Byrds, "You're So Vain," by Carly Simon and "Light My Fire" by Jim Morrison, my celebrity crush boyfriend, the lead singer of the Doors. That's all I remember. I was out.

Suddenly, I sat up and reached in my purse for my eye drops. I put them in my eyes, blinked a couple of times and started my car. The DJ's voice on the radio announced the time. It was two o'clock! My vision was not quite perfect, but was certainly an improvement compared to when I got into my car. I drove slowly and carefully and arrived safely at the house.

I went in and took a couple of Advil, as my eye was aching a bit, jumped in the shower, still in disbelief about my morning. I took a long hot shower trying to wash it all away. I dried my hair with a towel and looked closely at myself in the mirror. Although my eyes were puffy and red from my crying jag, they looked normal, no evidence of the shot.

As I slipped into my pajamas and robe, I thought about my children. I needed to let them know. They all needed to be on the vitamins. I put on my strongest pair of reading glasses and sent them a group text. "Hey kids, I went to the eye doctor this morning and I now have the wet and dry versions of macular degeneration, like Granny has. Please do not call me back, I will need today to digest all of this and then I will speak to each of you. In the meantime you all must go to the store and get some eye drops that are specifically for AREDS, Age Related Eye Disease Syndrome, to prevent this in your future. I love you all so much."

I hoped they could read my text, as my vision was not back one hundred percent. But felt if I could drive safely, I could surely text. I knew emotionally I couldn't handle a phone call to my children right then. I had to get the text messages out of the way and off of my mind. I reluctantly picked up the phone, but before I could dial the number for "Loverboy," (my contact name for Stenmark) my phone rang…and it was Loverboy. "Are you okay, Bennett?" His voice was soft, low and, I sensed, full of concern.

I held back tears and said, "Yes, I think so."

"Dr. Kim called and spoke to me for about twenty minutes. He told me what is going on. It will be okay, babe, I promise you. I am so sorry I am not with you. I have been trying to get off work, but it is just so busy with all of these junior camps." His voice sounded worried.

"Honey, I'm okay. I'm home and I will stay here and rest my eye. Don't worry about me, you just work and I will see you when you get here," I said trying to sound upbeat and calm.

Stenmark's voice broke up, as he said, "I will see you soon. I love you, babe."

I blinked back tears, "I love you, too."

Then I called Mom and gave her the news. She held back tears, trying to be strong, as always, but I could tell she felt bad for me.

After we hung up, I sat down the phone and laid my head back, closing my tired eyes. I couldn't sleep as thoughts of my life flooded my brain. *How will I continue to work? My job requires extreme focus. I need to see every little thing while I do fingernails. What if I am forced to leave my job, my career, and my clientele that I have worked so hard to build and maintain?*

*I LOVE THEM AND I LOVE MY JOB! I don't want to stop working, plus we need my income. It takes two of us steadily working, particularly in this day and age. This really sucks, but I must remain positive. You attract what you put out to the universe, Carly. Stay focused on that. You become what you think! I must remember that…and it won't hurt to throw in a prayer or two or three or four!*

I fell asleep on the couch, listening to Judge Judy on TV. I always loved Judge Judy.

Suddenly, I heard the garage door open. I looked at the time on my cell phone, seven o'clock. The door from the garage into the house opened and Stenmark walked in. I sat upright on the couch as he walked over to me. He reached down and scooped me up in his arms. He sat down on the couch with me on his lap. I buried my face against his broad shoulders. "I better write a fuckin' hit song quick," he said.

We held each other and cried together.

# To the Finish Lime

I went to work the next day and was pleasantly surprised at the clarity in my vision. I didn't know what to expect. I thought about what to say to my clients. Yesterday, I had decided to keep it to myself, but this morning on my way to work, I knew that I couldn't do that. I also knew I desperately needed the support of my clients more than anything. I made the decision to tell a few close clients who had become friends over the years. They would be supportive. The last thing I wanted was to tell everyone and have to deal with them being critical of my work and worrying I could no longer do my job as well as before my dreaded diagnosis. I knew I needed a lot of support from my clients. Let's face it, I have grown to love and trust these people over the years. I would tell them in my own time, as I had to be able to handle the sympathy part of the conversation! I must say I was pleasantly surprised and happy when I confided in my clients. They couldn't have been more kind, understanding and supportive, and I couldn't have been more grateful. This journey was going to require all of that from both sides.

My first client of the day was Zena. She arrived promptly on time with lattes in hand. She was bright and cheery this early morning in her lime green pantsuit.

"Hey, Car," she said with a big smile.

"You look great in that color, I love it!"

"Thanks Car, I know it's one of your favorites."

I thought about how perceptive Zena was. "How are you today?" I asked trying to sound cheerful.

"I am doing great," she answered as she handed me my latte, "How are you?"

"Doing good, except I have something important to tell you." I took a deep breath and looked her in the eye. "You know about my mom's eye disease?" I asked.

"Yes, I do. Is it worse?" Zena asked with concern.

"No, it's not that. I found out yesterday that I now have the same thing," I told her.

Zena's expression turned to a worried look as her eyes welled up with tears and she put her hands on mine. "Oh, honey, I am so sorry," she said softly.

"Zena, thank you, but please don't give me sympathy. I can't start the day off like that. It's too fresh."

*Maybe I should have waited for the digestion part of this journey before I told my story. Too late now, Carly!*

Zena smiled and rubbed my arm as I told her all about the eye-shot, she squirmed and looked uncomfortable. "Eww...how often will that have to happen?" she asked.

"I will go back in four weeks and I guess he will tell me then. I don't know yet. Maybe I will get another shot," I said as I shrugged my shoulders.

"Oh, Car, I am so sorry."

"Thank You, Zena."

She had tears in her eyes as she told me, "I couldn't do it. I couldn't get a shot in my eyeball!"

"If it was saving your vision, you could, trust me. You could do it."

Zena smiled sympathetically as I finished her manicure. She stood up to leave. "Let me give you some good energy, girl," she said as she hugged me. "It will be okay, Car, I have a strong, good feeling about this," Zena said as she turned to leave.

I watched my friend, Zena, the eternal optimist as she left the salon and I felt so much love from her in that moment.

*It has to be okay. It just has to be okay. Hope springs eternal.*

The rest of the day, I told another portion of my clients and I was able to stay calm, hopeful and strong. I only confided in the ones I trusted and considered friends. I decided to keep it to myself with the clients who were strictly clients. That's all I needed, a mass exodus. The last thing I wanted people to think was that I was going blind. I wouldn't be able to handle losing my clientele along with my eyesight. Poor and visually handicapped is not a good combination. I was so touched by the support I received from virtually everyone in which I confided. Slowly, I began to tell the rest of my clientele and once again, I was pleasantly surprised at the out-pouring of love, care and genuine concern.

Although, during the first few months, my nail files looked almost snake like, yes it appeared to be moving and that was freaky. I kept that little tidbit to myself and just dealt with it. The same with the golf clubs, not to mention the golf ball looked egg shaped instead of circular, which made the game even more difficult to play than it already was. However, after a while, the eye injections began to help and I literally saw a huge change for the better. The eyes really do work together to help each other and that has made a difference, as well.

*I may be able to finish this race after all.*

With that thought in mind, I continued working, doing what I still loved after thirty-plus years, as I reminded myself. *You always said you could do this in the dark, Carly!* I just didn't realize I would be put to the test one day.

# The J's Have It!

t has been close to seven years and I now get shots in both of my eyes, as the disease has progressed. The right eye, which I considered and called my "good eye"' now has the wet type of macular degeneration, as well. I found this out last December at my monthly eye appointment and Dr. Kim began the treatment in both eyes. *Goodbye "good eye" and Merry Christmas to me!*

This is an age-related eye disease, and unless they come up with a cure, my vision will slowly become worse over time. Right now, my vision is stable thanks to the injections and for that I am extremely thankful, as I am still able to work full time. My mom was unable to receive the benefits of the shots because by the time they were approved and found to be helpful her eyesight was too far gone. She accepted her fate without complaining, blaming or feeling sorry for herself.

My mom was a very brave soul who was able to see better than any of us!

Still, I don't drive at night except to and from work and around Park City, as it is such a short distance, plus familiarity helps!

You know, I was always complimented on my "big, beautiful, brown eyes" so I was worried it would change their appearance with the treatments. My eyes would be fine, unless the doctor accidently hits a blood vessel, which in the six years has only happened three times. Truly how can he not once in a while? After all, he is only human and there are numerous blood vessels in the eye, so I'm told. As for the appearance of my eyes, they look pretty much the same to me. My eldest grandson, Brayeden, tells me it looks like I am crying and my eyes sparkle a bit to him since I've been getting the shots, but that's hard for me to tell by looking in a mirror. I'm always asked by everyone if it hurts. At the time of the shot, I only feel pressure from the needle. As soon as I get home, I take a couple of Tylenol, as when the numbing drops begin to wear off, my eyes are sore and they do hurt and of course, I can't see until the next morning, so I always need to lay down and sleep for two or three hours afterwards. I prefer my shots later in the day because it really makes the rest of the day unproductive.

I must say, I have the most wonderful, caring and sensitive doctor. I lucked out when I found Dr. Kim and his staff, as well. It takes a whole lot of trust and confidence to let someone stick a needle in your eye. Dr. Kim always makes me feel as if he is doing everything in his power to help my eyesight and I believe he is. Over the years he has tried various things to improve my vision including cold laser treatments on three different occasions. Those are fun, as you can't be in the light for four days (yes, I am a vampire during that time) and when you leave his office, no skin at all can be showing. These treatments have been done during the winter months to make bundling up somewhat easier and maybe to prevent a heat stroke! I really have had to tackle this part of my life with an enormous amount of humor.

They say that in life, we all have to play the hands we are dealt and I've always agreed. I just won't be able to see mine!

Stenmark is consistently, constantly and lovingly reminding me that the experts are always working on a cure for this. After all, the percentage of people with macular degeneration has dropped quite significantly in the last fifteen years. They say that perhaps this decrease has happened due to the awareness of smoking cigarettes, which is a known cause of the disease. My mom smoked her entire life, but I've never smoked cigarettes so go figure! Also, I am on the young side of this disease, usually occurring in people over seventy years of age, but then again, family history is to blame. My mom was diagnosed at age fifty-four and I was fifty-six when I received the news.

Last month I had a "pellet" inserted into my left eye to work in conjunction with the Lucentis, my eye medicine. I was told that the injection would be done with a larger needle. *Oh, great! I look forward to that!*

This injection required me to hold very, very still, hence the info about the needle. I was also informed that it is time released. The "pellet" has been strange, as I can see it and I can also feel it. I keep pushing my bangs away from that eye! I know it's there because it feels like I have something in my eye.

*Oh, wait! I do have something in my eye, a freaking pellet!*

This was supposed to help stop the "leaking" from the abnormal blood cells, but so far we have not seen an improvement. Even though I joke about it all, Dr. Kim keeps trying and sometimes I sense frustration on his part. To date, my vision has remained status quo and we are all happy about that. I am so appreciative and thankful for Dr. Kim's expertise, professionalism and his huge sense of care and concern. He has absolutely dotted all of the i's and crossed all of the t's! He makes it so much easier to remain positive and carry on.

I thought this journey would be the most difficult thing in my life until I experienced the death of my parents, a year and five months apart.

I've lost both of my parents in the last five years and that truly has been the worst experience for me to endure. I know it is the circle of life, as they say, and that everyone loses their parents. But it hit me so much harder than I ever would've imagined. I have known clients and friends who have lost their parents, and I sent cards and flowers, and in some cases even attended the services for their parents. But I never envisioned the impact of losing my own mom and dad until it happened. The grief was almost unbearable. But then I thought of friends who have lost children and I am sure the pain I felt paled in comparison to the pain of a bereaved parent. *Dear God, give me anything but that, I pray.*

# Bastille My Heart

*A*ll in all, I have so much to be thankful for. I really do. I have such a wonderful husband, who has loved and supported me during hard times and still continues to do so ten years later. He is so amazing and he loves me even when I am crazy and God knows I can definitely go there as we all can at times! It really is true that love is just another word until someone comes along and gives it meaning. Stenmark has done just that for me. He stole my heart and I will definitely let him keep it!

I have four exceptional children, thirteen (even more) exceptional grandchildren, and to date, four awesome great grandchildren, all of whom I dearly love. They have all captured my heart. When I was single and going through all of my tough times, my children never stopped believing in me. I was young and didn't have a clue when I became a mother. We all grew up together and learned the hard lessons as we went along. My grandchildren filled the void inside of my heart when my children went off to live their lives, working their own jobs, raising a family and trying to make ends meet. I had weekends to look forward to with my grandchildren. My life was less lonely and full as I skied, golfed and hung out with grandchildren. I still, to this day, miss those fun times. I would need to write another book filled with those stories alone.

I have a more-than-full clientele whom I appreciate daily. They have stayed loyal and true, and have been with me every step of the way. I know there were times when I was stressed, worried and pre-occupied. It probably affected my work to some extent, but they were always there for me. They hung in there with me through husbands, kids, grandkids, health problems, and losing my parents. In fact my best buddy in Park City, Kacy helped me achieve a life-long dream of someday visiting Paris. I always joked about seeing my boyfriend, Jim Morrison's grave. Jim Morrison was the lead singer of the famous rock band, The Doors, who died in Paris and was buried at Pere Lachaise Cemetery.

After my father's death, unbeknownst to me, Kacy sent out an email to all of my closest clients and friends asking them in lieu of flowers, gifts, etc. if they would be willing to contribute to a fund to send me on a trip with her to see Paris, France. (Kacy was familiar with Paris, more than familiar, not to mention she was fluent in French.)

So these wonderful clients and friends of mine either sent the checks to Kacy or myself, or delivered their contribution directly to me at the salon. I was so overwhelmed by this, but have to admit, I was also a little embarrassed. I am not the type of person who accepts gifts in the form of money very well. I tried to refuse a large check from a close friend, but she demanded I take it saying, "I thought it was a brilliant idea and was so happy Kacy thought of it. We all knew what you went through with your dad and we wanted to do something extra special for you. You deserve this, Carly."

I fought back tears but managed to say," I am so touched and so very grateful, thank you."

Then she added, "We decided if you put up a fuss about it, we would all go to Zion's Bank and give our checks to Denise to deposit into your account!" (Denise is the Financial Center Manager and the Executive Banking Officer for Zion's Bank and also a close friend of mine and apparently theirs.)

I was amazed at the out-pouring of generosity. I ended up with close to three thousand dollars, and it didn't stop there. Kacy and her husband offered to donate miles for my round trip ticket to Paris and the cost was under one hundred dollars. But it didn't end there either. My flight attendant friend and client unexpectedly moved Kacy and I into first class seating once the plane was in the air. We had champagne with our dinner, watched a movie and fell asleep in their "flat bed seats" which resembled twin beds! This was perfect because our flight was at five p.m. and was a little over ten hours. We woke up in France refreshed and ready to go. I remember when Kacy picked me up for the trip to the airport that afternoon. She could tell how happy and excited I was. She turned around from the front seat and asked, "Are you ready?"

I answered back, "*Je suis prête!*" My lifelong dream is about to come true.

# 80

## Let Life Unfold

nfortunately, and sadly I also lost the love of a sister, Anna, who was angry with me, accusing me of stealing money from my father while he was dying and using it to fund my Paris trip. I documented everything I did, it was all there in black and white, I even sent Anna and my other siblings copies of everything, but it made no difference in her feelings. She did not believe me.

As a result, Anna has not spoken to me in almost four years and has continued to believe I am guilty of embezzling from my father on his deathbed, calling my inheritance of $547.00, "blood money" and flitting off to Paris! Anna wrote negatively about me on Facebook and eventually "unfriended" and blocked me. That is said to be the ultimate "diss" these days in the ever growing popularity of social media. (Ahhhh…the age of technology.)

But not before she put a "curse" on me to be hit and killed by a bus while I was visiting Paris! Well, guess what, sister wing nut? I'm still very much alive.

But I forgave Anna, because it was good for *my health*. Believe me it was one of the hardest things I ever had to do. To try and forgive someone who you still love and care about, particularly someone who wasn't even sorry…now that's strength right there!

Fortunately, I have four other wonderful siblings who are sane, two sisters and two brothers. We all have mutual love and respect for one another, and have certainly had our ups and downs, disagreements and difference of opinions. But that is a whole other story! We pulled together during our mother's unexpected death and our father's lingering death as well. It was tough on all of us, but we all did our part, in spite of those differences.

After you lose your parents, you do need and appreciate the love and support from your brothers and sisters, and I am extremely thankful for them. The siblings who appreciated the work I put in while dealing with my father's *"large"* estate will always have a special place in my heart.

A few years after my parents passed and my grief was beginning to subside somewhat, I made some life decisions. I always felt bad about having what I call the "loose ends" in my life. It was time for me to start tying those up. (I'm sure that doesn't surprise any of you!) The worry of losing my eyesight as I age is always in the forefront of my mind. After all, how could it not be there? I started to make plans, finishing this book was at the top of my list. I've been compiling information since the beginning of my nail career and would write every so often. How I ever possessed, at the age of twenty-six, the wherewithal to jot these interesting, funny and sometimes distressing stories down in a notebook accompanied with the dates of occurrences, month, day and year, I'll never know! Go figure!

Another thing I decided to do at the beginning of last year was to go back to high school and get my diploma. As some of you know, I decided to pretend I was an adult and get married at the ripe old age of seventeen and I never graduated from high school. I think I'm smart enough to take the GED test, but I really wanted a high school diploma. My youngest brother Jeff was the only family member at the time to graduate from high school, including my parents! I wasn't sure my children even knew I was a high school dropout. I know for sure my grandchildren did not know. I insisted my children graduate from high school and desperately wanted my grandchildren to achieve that, as well. The last thing I wanted to hear from those young, impressionable, intelligent kids was that Grandma didn't graduate, and she owned her own business! I stressed the importance of being a high school graduate to them as often as I could and it has paid off in my eyes. My first and eldest grandson, Brayeden just told me he was going to go back and get his high school diploma and I couldn't be more proud of him. Now this will make four of my grandchildren high school graduates, so far.

I am happy to say I have now become a graduate of Park City High School! I have to admit, it's really hard to go back to school as an adult. I should have stayed in school when that was my only job. Working full time, trying to study and complete assignments along with running a business and just life in general is definitely difficult, but well worth it. I only told my husband and a couple of close friends what I was doing. I was going to keep it to myself, but worried if I disappeared three nights a week for three hours, my husband might hire a private investigator to see what I was up to! Everyone has been so supportive and I am confident that support will help me through the tough times! You have to know that you can start late in life, be uncertain and still manage to succeed!

I think it is important to remember to never get so busy making a living that you forget to make a life. I believe that one was hard for me. I can't help but think it affected my relationships and some of them failed as a result of me not being able to focus on making a life. I am older and wiser, and now I know better, my priorities have shifted. I understand the importance of being present in your life, especially when you have a loving, caring and considerate mate (and I have had a few), and of course, a loving, caring family.

Stenmark and I have discussed our future in great length, especially considering my eyesight problem. I definitely do not want to wait until I cut off a toe before I retire, but I do love my clients and my life as a nail technician. However, I do want to enjoy life outside of the nail room. When I finally do retire, I know I will miss certain things about my work, but I also know I am not getting any younger, dang it! I know that as we get older we have to expect change and try to embrace it. Stenmark has always teased me about the *fun* process of aging by saying, "You're just not going to handle it well. I'm going to have to drag you through middle age, kicking and screaming. There will be heel marks all over Park City!" *And he is right.*

I really don't know what the next chapter will bring on my journey of life, but one thing I do know for sure...*Je suis prête!*

## The End

# Acknowledgements

Over the years I've met so many wonderful people who have enriched my life. It would take another book to personally thank all of you, but you know who you are.

Thank you to my clients and friends for sharing your lives and stories with me over the years and trusting me enough to write about some of them in a humorous way, while keeping the really juicy parts private! Without all of you, there would be no *Nail Files*.

Thanks to my brother, Gary Gautney, for the exceptional artwork on the cover of this book. Your talents are beyond amazing and I love you dearly.

Thanks to my editor and friend, Stacy Dymalski. You taught me how to write and how to make it mean something. Thank you for your kindness and sympathy when I accidently didn't "save" a huge portion of my writing, and for not making me feel like a complete idiot! Thank you for your understanding when I took too long to get something back to you. Your constant hand holding, and pushing me to expand my mind and dive head first into my emotions (especially on the tough parts of my personal life) was not only appreciated, but first rate. You are a gem!

Thank you to Katie Mullaly for her expertise in formatting this book and her publishing skills. Thank you for guiding me through the proof-reading. You are talented and knowledgable. I'm happy to have made a new friend.

Thank you to Linda Galindo, the "Accountability Queen" for giving me the "not so little push" I desperately needed to move forward with this book.

I'd also like to personally thank the salon owners I've worked for over the years in Park City.

Lori Smith from Lori's Nail Parlor was truly the first person to really give me a chance and helped me immensely perfect the art of doing nails. You are a friend and a teacher extraordinaire!

Dan and Nancy Dexter from Dexter and Company. You guys rock! Your friendship for the past thirty-plus years has meant the world to me, even during the rough times! You two are not only fab hairdressers, but are still two of the coolest cats I've ever known!

Ann MacQuoid and Debra McFarlane from Vie Retreat; these ladies guided me and each in their own way shaped me into a true professional. I've had the pleasure of not only their friendship over the years but their continued patronage as well. They are both amazing women!

Nancy Sim from Silver Shears. You are a true friend and compassionate soul. I've loved working with you and you have my favorite sense of humor. Dry! I love the way you can tell a joke and I am envious of your innate ability to always remember them!

Thanks to my family, especially my sister, salon owner, and often times partner in crime, Rebecka Gautney, for adding to this book with her unbelievable but true stories, which by the way, I barely touched on!

Thank you to the nail polish companies, OPI, Essie, CND, Caption, Creative Play, Morgan Taylor, Gelish, and Sparitual for the inspiration for my chapter names. I wish I were that creative! Maybe in my next life…

Thanks to my awesome children, Sean, Chantele, Ricky and Megan, and my stepson, McLane. You've all made a huge impact on my life and I love you all. My even more awesome grandchildren, April, Brayeden, Autumn, Cassidy, Alaska, Celica, Avery, Trinity, Colton, Tristin, Landon, Easton and Tyson and my great grandchildren, Chance, Kinley, baby Ezra and the "tiny human."

You've all touched my heart and my life became real once you entered it.

It's a mouthful sometimes but I wouldn't have it any other way!

A huge thanks to my wonderful husband, Ken Stenmark. Thank you for listening without judgment (again, my personal life stories) when I would hesitantly read a chapter and ask for his input while I quietly questioned my own writing ability. Being an accomplished songwriter himself, his advice was invaluable.

Thanks for the suggestion of adding the "Nail Files" to complete my book title. It was the perfect exclamation point it needed! Thanks for understanding when I was locked in the room, chained to my computer for whole weekends at a time, and for telling me when to take a break from it all, letting it sit and instructing me to look at it with fresh eyes in the morning. Thank you for knowing when enough was enough and suggesting I stop rewriting it over and over and over again! Your wisdom, encouragement and experience helped me more than I can say.

Your love and support has been incredible through this long awaited and sometimes painstaking venture and I really can't thank you enough. I love you, babe!

Lastly, thank you to the people, places, restaurants and parts I referenced in this book located in Park City, Utah. When I took that exit over thirty years ago, I never dreamed of the life I would be able to create here in this beautiful place I call home.

# About the Author

High school drop out and self-taught nail technician, Carly Bennett, a 28-year-old divorced mother of four, hoping to escape an abusive relationship jumped into her $100 car, a tan rusted out 1962 Chevy Impala. She headed east into the mountains and began her uphill battle, armed with nothing but a nail file and an old tube of red Avon lipstick, and found herself in Park City, Utah.

Carly grabbed a newspaper and settled in a booth at the Mt. Air Café where the search began for a place to rent, a place to work and a fresh start for her and her family, including the cat. She handed her new landlords a post-dated check, drove back to the city and told her children they were all moving to the mountains!

Fast forward a few years and a handful of salons later, she documents her clients' stories, peppered with humorous anecdotes from a somewhat checkered past. Carly takes us by the hand and pulls us into her world, as it became an exciting adventure with her clientele. They laughed and cried together as their stories unfolded. It didn't take long for her to realize that caring for their souls was equally as important as caring for their nails.